THE PULSE

IN OCCIDENT AND ORIENT

**ITS PHILOSOPHY AND PRACTICE
IN HOLISTIC DIAGNOSIS AND TREATMENT**

GW00597315

Reuben Amber
&
A.M. Babey-Brooke

AURORA PRESS

205 Third Ave. 2A   New York, N.Y. 10003

With Love

To

Mary and Joseph Babey

Our Closest Collaborators

First paperback edition published in 1986 by:
Aurora Press
205 Third Ave, Suite 2A
New York, NY 10003

ISBN 0-943358-29-9
Library of Congress Catalog Card No.: 86-070605

FOREWORD
Stuart Watts

Medicine, along with philosophy, religion and art has always been at the zenith of cultural achievements. The traditional medical thought of China, India and the Middle East has when acknowledged been regarded as primitive, unscientific and impractical by the contemporary western mind. It is due to its continued clinical effectiveness that we are now being forced to re-evaluate, with a less prejudicial perspective its current value.

Operating primarily within the conceptual framework of nineteenth century materialism and dependent on a vast array of technological diagnostic methodology, the western doctor has lost contact with the subtle functioning of inner life currents. Hence, modern medicine though refined in some areas, has become increasingly invasive, often to the detriment of the dynamic processes which in their functional totality constitute our lives. For example, only recently has Chinese medicine begun to emerge from the contempt with which our technological worldview has regarded it. While apparently incomprehensible and therefore "primitive", it is in fact a tremendous resource awaiting our discovery. Time and a refined sensitivity are required to learn how to feel the pulse, understand what it means, and apply the significance of the pulse in relation to the external manifestation of an energetic configuration.

The underlying and understated importance of pulse diagnosis, is that it is fast, non-invasive and an extremely effective method to be used in monitoring and assessing the patient's condition. Not by reading alone can a practitioner gain a useful level of competence in pulse diagnosis. The material must be studied, applied and re-examined in the light of clinical experience. An in depth study of *The Pulse* should be mandatory reading for all health professionals, trained in Eastern or Western disciplines. As an advanced practitioner of Chinese Medicine, I am in constant awe of the unfolding diagnostic information, the pulse can reveal. It has been a consistently helpful guide into the inner energetic functions of the patient as well as a subtle dectector of the progress of any illness caused by an imbalance of the life force.

The Pulse long out of print, contributes to a synthesis of various medical modalities. By comprehensively delineating the major systems of pulse diagnosis, it helps bridge the gap between contemporary scientific models and the wholistic viewpoint of traditional medicine.

I am proud to introduce this new edition of *The Pulse,* and encourage you to rediscover the new dimension in healing, this information can release for you.

Stuart Watts
Director, Southwest Acupuncture College
Santa Fe, New Mexico

Table of Contents

Chapter

Rodin knew that, first of all, sculpture depended upon an infallible knowledge of the human body. Slowly, searchingly, he had approached the surface of this body from which now a hand stretched out toward him, and the form, the gesture of this hand contained the semblance of the force within the body. The farther he progressed on this remote road, the more chance remained behind, and one law led him on to another. And ultimately it was this surface toward which his search was directed. It consisted of infinitely many movements. The play of light upon these surfaces made manifest that each of these movements was different and each significant. At this point they seemed to flow into one another; at that, to greet each other hesitatingly; at a third, to pass by each other without recognition, like strangers. There were undulations without end. There was no point at which there was not life and movement.

Rodin had now discovered the fundamental element of his art; as it were, the germ of his world. It was the surface,—this differently great surface, variedly accentuated, accurately measured, out of which every thing must rise,—which was from this moment the subject matter of his art, the thing for which he laboured, for which he suffered and for which he was awake.

Rainer Maria Rilke, **Auguste Rodin,**
translated by Jessie Lemont and Hans Transil,
New York, Sunwise Turn Inc., 1919, pp. 23-24.

Introduction

Recounting the story of the pulse, which has led the authors to explore many paths of cultural history, may stimulate the reader by its cross-fertilization of ideas. The lore recited by the Ayurvedist, the Chinese, the Unani, the Greek, the Arab, and the modern Westerner recounts the age-old quest: man's search to heal and to regenerate. Each culture devised a methodology out of its philosophical religious ideational matrix, wherein the doctor could not detach himself from his medical training since his knowledge and skills were products of the sociological surroundings of the time; his interpretations in aiding the ill were reflections of the lights and shadows cast by the beliefs of his society — be his teachers conservative or radical. As the reader assesses what each country taught and traces the interchange of ideas, he will weigh the evidence and inevitably glimpse relationships which will guide him in rephrasing the old medical generalizations and cliches into more meaningful relations.

Bertrand Russell once remarked, "We shall have to admit Asia to equality in our thought not only politically but also culturally. . . . What changes this will bring about I do not know, but I am convinced that they will be profound and of the greatest importance." With regard to this study of the pulse his statement is directly pertinent. Perhaps the methods used in the past for explanations of how other civilizations diagnosed the ills of man will eventuate in a sound medical philosophy and will advance medical knowledge so that the twentieth century practitioner, aware of time-binding factors, will gain new insights to launch him into a different reassessment. But even without such utilitarian purposes, it is hoped that this narrative will advance the cultural-historical-medical knowledge of the family of man as he holds his brother's hand.

Of the two diagnostic methods used by all peoples — Egyptian, Greek, Arab, Indian, Chinese and Westerner — sphygmology is much older than urology and more universal as a practice. Both methods were used by the ancients, but a review of the early history of the pulse will reflect the different roads that the various peoples followed — some leading to broad highways and others to dark, blind alleys.

The early Egyptians were aware of the importance of the pulse as early as the thirtieth to the twenty-sixth centuries (dating from the Old Kingdom or the Pyramid Age) as the Smith and Ebers Papyri reveal

i

even though they come from the seventeenth and sixteenth centuries. The Edwin Smith Surgical Papyrus remarks,

> Now if the priest of Sekhmet or any physician puts his hands (or) his fingers (upon the head, upon the back of the) head; upon the two hands, upon the pulse, upon the two feet (he) measures (to) the heart because its vessels are in the back of the head and in the pulse: and because its (pulsation) is in every vessel of every member.

Similarly, the Ebers Papyrus in its anatomical-physiological section which is said to date from 1550 B.C. reports the following secrets:

> The beginning of the physician's secret knowledge of the heart's movement and knowledge of the heart. . . . There are vessels from it to every limb. As to this when any physician, any surgeon (literally, Sachmet or priest) or any exorcist applies the hand or his fingers to the head, to the back of the head, to the hands, to the place of the stomach, to the arms or to the feet, then he examines the heart, because all his limbs possess its vessels, that is: it (the heart) speaks out of every limb.

In view of the lengthy Egyptian experience with sphygmology, it is to be noted that the Greeks made no reference to the pulse until the time of Democritos (460-370 B.C.) and his contemporary Hippocrates, the father of modern medicine. The Greeks were considerably later than the Chinese and the Indians in utilization of pulse diagnosis. Praxagoras (340-320) was the first of the Greeks clearly to distinguish between veins and arteries; stating that the veins carried blood and that the arteries were filled with air, he made a deep study of the pulse which was then continued by Herophilos who taught the Greeks that the pulse had four important characteristics: size, frequency, strength, and rhythm. Thus one may observe that sphygmology was established on a firm basis among the Greeks with Praxagoras and that the most significant Greek treatise on the pulse was not written until the time of Trajan (98-117) when Rufus the Red Haired, as his name betokens, explained the pulse, defined it superbly, and showed that the pulse and heart correspond to the systole and not to the diastole. (This fact was forgotten in the West and had to be rediscovered by Harvey in the seventeenth century.) He may also have described the carotid sinus reflex. Rufus's contemporary—Archiogenes of Apames, as a member of the Eclectic School — also elaborated a theory of the pulse. Whether or not Galen (129-195), the outstanding Greek physician who influenced Western medicine up until the seventeenth century, was familiar with the works of these two men is a moot question. Galen himself wrote eighteen separate essays concerning the pulse, but listing the translations and commentaries would fill a volume. Most Greek knowledge of the pulse was then summed up in the seventh century by Theophilos Protospartharios, and his account was translated into Latin and Hebrew. Greek sphygmology thus became available to the Arabic, Latin, and Hebrew reader by the ninth century, a fact which would lead to the conclusion that the flow of medical information was from East to West, but here various phases of pulse history must be clarified.

The Chinese and Indian studies of the pulse need to be briefly contrasted with the Greeks'; for the ancient traditions set up in the Orient continued alertly to be practiced and improved upon so that the East is ahead of the West in the twentieth century with accommodating the readings of the pulse to the principles of automation.

The Chinese accounts dealing with the pulse date from the time of the legendary emperor, variously interpreted as extending from 500 B.C. back to 2500 B.C., and continue into the sixteenth century A.D. The writings by five authorities are used to this day in the practice of Acupuncture, one of the oldest systems of medicine. Briefly their accounts of the pulse are found in the **Nei Ching**, by the legendary Yellow Emperor (some authorities claim that Harvey's* epoch-making discovery was anticipated in the **Nei Ching** by at least two thousand years), the **Nan Ching** by Pien Ch'iao of the fifth century B.C., the **Synopsis of the Golden Chamber** by Chang Chung Ching of the second century A.D., **the Classic of the Pulse** by Wang Shu Ho (265-317 A.D.), and the **Pen Tshar Kang Mu** by Li Shih-chen (1518-1593). By analogy, their current canons date from before the time of Plato to the days of Shakespeare. Imagine a text by a predecessor of Plato and a volume by Shakespeare used in the Western medical schools today because they are valid for their observations about the body! This is what prevails in the schools of Acupuncture in the Orient today.

The Ayurvedic versions of their history date from the sixth century B.C. according to modern scholarship and, as with the Chinese, are used to train the medical students of India to this day in indigenous medicine. Most of the classics of the two major schools of ancient Indian medicine appear to be lost except for the accounts left by Susruta and Caraka that are explained in the section on Ayurvedic bibliography in this study. The Ayurvedists, however, date and explain their own medical history with a different chronology: they claim that the sages who wrote on medicine, including the pulse, were Kanada, Agnivesha or Agnivesta, Bhela, Gautama, Harita, Kapila, Jatukarna, and Parashara who existed long before the sixth century B.C. date of modern scholarship and though their writings were lost, they were mentioned in the age of Tantric culture. Later writers — like Caraka, Dridhabala, Nagarjuna, Susruta and Vagbhata—elaborated on the works of the predecessors, especially of Kanada, who is said to have flourished in 2358 B.C. long before the time of Agnivesha. Kanada was their medical and philosophical authority and his treatise on the pulse, the **Nadi Vignanai,** together with Ravana's **NADI PARIKSHA** are the classics of Indian pulse lore. Other medical treatises on the pulse which were done by the elder and younger Vagbhata came into existence perhaps about the seventh century when the country had been exposed to Buddhistic teachings or, according to Indian chronology, about 81 B.C., the time roughly of Virgil. (The authors do not

---

*The **Nei Ching** reads, "All blood is under control of the heart. The heart regulates all blood of the body."

attempt to disentangle these contradictions of chronology.) No matter what date is assigned to these classics, they became a part of the pulse medical traditions which could be seen continued in the analysis written by Sarngadhara some time before the thirteenth century. No one can deny that the Ayurvedists elaborated and devised their own system of sphygmology which is deserving of study.

The schools of indigenous medicine both in India and China are aware of the works of Bordeu and Nihell, published in the Occident in the eighteenth century, and of Broadbent, physician to Queen Victoria, all concerned with the pulse: a spectacle of continuing interest in medical study. In the East, this stress is part of the curriculum training and the armatorium of the physician whereas in the West, it is the output of what may be termed medical mavericks; notwithstanding the labels placed upon them, the efforts bespeak the story of the quest.

The Arabs continued the traditions established by the Greeks, the Ayurvedists, and the Chinese; they borrowed from all but fused these concepts and techniques with their own remarkable observations, a spectacle of historical interchange of ideas which is now on its way to being repeated in the twentieth century under the impact of the cybercultural revolution. In 1313 Rashid al Din al Hamdan, a Persian physician and patron of learning, had an encyclopedia of Chinese medicine prepared and among its subjects was included sphygmology. The Chinese manual of the pulse by Wang Shu-Ho was translated and the great Arabian physicians—like Razes, Al Majusi, Avicenna's teacher and Avicenna himself—all were experts who wrote on pulse diagnosis. Indeed Avicenna even used the pulse as a lie-detector test. The Arabs were also familiar through translations with the Ayurvedic technique and the basic Indian writings by the theoretician-physicians Caraka, Susruta, and Vagbhata elder and younger. In their access to the thoughts of three different cultures, the Arabs indicated through their practices, that they chose more frequently from the Ayurvedic than from the Chinese texts.

As one recounts the history of pulse lore in Greece, India, China, and the Arab world, one inevitably asks if the Greeks borrowed from the Indians or from the Chinese. Then one must comprehend the differences characterizing each culture. The Indians and the Chinese went their separate ways: they devised different techniques for taking the pulse and different interpretations. Though both cultures stressed the energy concept — with the primary energy as the life force and the secondary energy as the chemical, the electrical, or the thermal — they differed here in interpretation because their concentration was and is on different aspects of the same problem. This important concept of the energy flow is, however, unknown in Western medicine.

The Indian interpretation of medicine reached Europe via the translations of the Arab world and in time became allopathic medicine as it is known today. The Chinese view filtered through the Orient by way of Korea, Hong Kong and Japan where the spectacle is present today of a culture's accepting the challenge that is a counterpart of the Arab's cultural accretions and enrichments of the translations from East and

iv

West. Japan today is fusing the Chinese interpretation of the pulse with the input-feed-back devices of the cybernetic machine and is gearing sphygmology to the twentieth century needs of automation.

The Oriental physician affirms that the weakness of Western medicine is its failure adequately to use the pulse, which is the symphony of the entire body. Further, he states that Western medicine measures single factors which are discordant notes in the harmonic whole; then the Japanese indigenously trained doctor proves this statement by assessing body ills on the Kazmac machine, based on cybernetic principles. To such criticism, the Western physician replies that reading the pulse is an art, not a science, and that art cannot be taught. Further, the Westerner makes disparaging comments about the practices of the Eastern schools of indigenous medicine: he likens Chinese Acupuncture to astrology and he labels its practices as irrational since it has over three hundred points guided by regulations that are "superstitious mumbo-jumbo"; he condemns the Ayurvedist's applications of the Tridoshas as "pseudo-scientific."

This is not the time nor the place to treat the subject of Acupuncture or the Tridoshas since that will be done in the text. But an answer to the Westerner's criticism of Acupuncture when he likens it to astrology would be to cite the instance of neurology concerning the dermatones and visceral reflexes. Would the Westerner equate this phase of medicine with astrology because it has more than three hundred tests? It is difficult for the layman, even if he has a Ph.D., or for a professor to associate a pain in the wrist with the brachial plexus situated in the neck. As there is a relationship with the nerves to their dermatones so there is a relationship of the points in Acupuncture to their respective tissues and organs. For the scientific minded, these points can be measured and demonstrated with electrical instruments.

The modern physician prides himself on the fact that medicine today is a science, not an art. His rationale goes something like this:

Up until the nineteenth century, medicine was an art. The medieval physician had no instruments to check his intuition; today, however, the modern physician relies on the body of scientific knowledge which is steadily increasing and on the battery of tests and medical gadgets. Scientific knowledge is objective and susceptible of being added to and being improved upon, capable of being transmitted. Art, on the other hand, is highly personal and as such cannot be transmitted. One can teach the medical science, but the art itself, medical intuition, is unteachable. In other words, the doctor is made, not born.

The answer to this rationale may or may not convince the sceptic Westerner who believes he is right and every one else is wrong. But scientific facts by themselves are useless unless they are integrated and properly interpreted. Most diseases are dynamic chain reactions which affect the whole organism, not just a part. Treating the part may and usually does throw the whole system out of harmony. If one of the very specific cog wheels in the chain is changed, then the whole system is involved. The random treating of one wheel is like improving a watch by dropping it. To improve the watch or repair it, one must change it so that all wheels work simultaneously. To get the patient well, one must treat the whole person. That is why the Oriental physician does not treat symptoms or diseases, but the total person. Just because the Western physician knows more and more about less and less does not make him a good healer. The technician is made, but the doctor is born.

The taking of the pulse may call for some mechanical skill, but the interpretation of its story is an art. The fundamentals can be learned up to a certain point so that most individuals can become very proficient as experiences in teaching the arts have demonstrated. How proficient the person may be is another story. In the treatment of disease, there are so many unknown quantities — heredity, environment, psychology, etc.— that the practice of any one of the healing disciplines can by no means be termed an exact science. The editor of the medico-legal journal **Trauma** (in February, 1960) advised lawyers dealing with medical cases to engage in thorough research because of the apparently conflicting nature of medical opinion. "It is frequently said that medicine is not an exact science. Most areas are gray, not black or white. It is therefore possible to find written authority for almost any premise the researcher seeks to establish." Then he cited an example. "It is possible to find an impressive array of articles advocating the use of the myelogram in the diagnosis of intervertebral disc injuries. It is just as easy to find a similar group of articles which say that the myelogram should not be used for routine disc diagnosis." The editor continued and warned against the changing nature of medical knowledge. "Be certain to use the latest edition of the text." By way of illustration to help lawyers plan their arguments, he cited the opinion by Dr. Paul Dudley White, heart specialist, expressed in the fourth edition of his book **Heart Disease** as completely different from his opinion expressed in the third edition of the same book.

A review of the principles of the feed-back technique of the cybernetic appliances will further illustrate that reading the pulse is an art as well as a science. Certainly the Oriental physician is not averse to using an instrument, but he does not substitute the machine for his personal skills. In Japan, a cybernetic machine is being used for diagnosis and for treatment.* In its trial run so far (1965), it has shown itself to be superior to the allopathic methods of diagnosis. This answer may be found in how the physician relates his facts to be programmed into the computer, and here it rests on the philosophic framework of the pulse-organ relationship bred into their medical training by centuries of work on the pulse, factors alien to the Western allopathic philosophy.

---

*The Kazmac, a Cybernetic Medicine Data Processing Apparatus, was built completely to retain the logic of physical therapies of Oriental medicine in its memory. It was planned under the supervision of an associated research group (The Fundamental Associated Research on the Chinese Religious Civilization and the Oriental Medicine, University of Tokyo, Tokyo University of Education, Wasedo University and Yokohama City University). The Kazmac is applicable to all schools since it can follow every school's method. Oriental medicine has many schools.

Japanese Oriental medicine is divided into three systems: (1) Wuhang (Shikitai); (2) Mochén (Myakushin); and (3) Ping Chêng (Byosho). The Wuhang (1) is composed of four subdivisions:

A. Wang (Bou) is information based on the physician's vision.

B. T'ing (Bun) is information based on the physician's audition and his auditory sensitivity.

C. Wên (Mon) is information based on the patient's own description.

D. Ch'ien (Setsu) is information based on the physician's sense of touch.

The Mochên (2) is information concerning the pulse nature which is found by palpation of the physician's three fingers on both radial arteries of the patient's wrist. The palpation pressures are given at three grades of Fu (Fu), Chung (chu), and Ch'ên (Chin). Here the doctor takes the pulse and feeds the information into the machine. At present the machine cannot differentiate the various pulses (a machine can play the notes of a symphony, but cannot express the various shadings and nuances of the concert performer). The Ping Chêng (3) is composed of various findings determined by medical examination, but it excludes subjective symptoms and the Wuhang (1).

The workings of the machine will be defined in the language of the cybernetic directives. The details may be overlooked for the basic generalizations about input and patternings. The categories of the diagnosis defined by the information belong to the twelve Chinglos (Keiraku) — Chinglo which is a system of vertical contacts of therapeutic points. It is modified by Hsü (Kyo, depression) and Shin (Jitsu, acceleration). In this way the ouput comes in twenty-four sorts of patterns, which are directly linked to the selection of treatments.

The Kazmac adopts the four systems of Pingchêng, Wuhang, Fouchituchen, (Kohaifukushin) and Mochên as inputs. The Fouchituchên is arranged as an independent system because of its important diagnostic contents although essentially it belongs to the Chi'en subsystem under the Wuhang. In short, the Pingchên is a collection of symptoms, the Wuhang of objective findings, the Fouchituchen of decisions of Yümuhsüeh's (Yuboketsu, examining points) on body surface, and the Mochên of natures of the pulses of the radial arteries. These are used in the input information of the Kazmac.

After the inputs, there are computation circuits of which operations are based on the diagnostic logical processes, weight setters which can be set following the weight of each system, an adding circuit which unites all the systems, scanning and controlling circuits, an a-d converting circuit, an indicating circuit, and indication tubes which display the last solutions. However, the inputs of the Mochên (Myakushin) are linked through the indicating circuit to the display of Chinghsueh's (Keiketsu, treatment points) which are distinguished by correlation of Hsiangshenghsiangk'ês (Soshosokoku, correlated internal organs requiring treatments) and by pulse natures of the Hsu (Kyo) and Shin (Jitsu).

As the Kazmac is built by these components, the internal analog computer acts when the inputs are set by the toggle or the rotary switches and are given to the Kazmac as the digital values, and the outputs are digitally displayed by the twelve Chinglo's (Keiraku) after the A-D conversion.

Though the Kazmac is a superbly devised cybernetic machine, it must rely upon the skill of the doctor to take the pulse!

The challenge facing the twentieth century physician is still "Know Thyself", but not as Socrates phrased it to apply to man the political animal but rather as the Oriental interprets it to signify know thyself as a total being. Man today may cite Don Juan's expression of Shavin philosophy to apply to the study of the pulse and to the challenge posed by Eastern medicine for Western: "I tell you that as long as I can conceive something better than myself I cannot be easy unless I am striving to bring it into existence or clearing the way for it. This is the law of my life. That is the working within my way of life's incessant aspiration to higher organization, wider, deeper, intenser self-consciousness, and clear self-understanding."

Chapter I

THE PULSE

AN APPRAISAL OF EASTERN AND WESTERN VIEWS

Before one can discuss the methods of taking and reading the pulse in four different cultures of Occident and Orient, it is necessary to explain the complex of their philosophic framework and clarify their fundamental precepts. Pragmatically, one can have the right method and the wrong theory or the right theory and the wrong method. Important is the realization that the Hindus, the Iranians, and the Chinese developed a methodology for the palpation of the pulse which made them experts in the diagnosis of disease — a fact in existence not for a decade, but for centuries. The techniques were mastered by specialist and practitioner, by inferior or superior physician, for so were they classified in the Orient. In these indigenous systems — Ayurvedic, Unani, and Chinese — great proficiency exists to this day. Sir William Henry Broadbent (1835-1907), physician to Queen Victoria, attested to the diagnostic pulse skill of the Ayurvedic and Unani physicians. Dr. B. Hume, a twentieth century professor at Johns Hopkins who wrote on Chinese medicine, was "flabbergasted" to see a Chinese physician read the pulse and make a diagnosis more accurate than that reported by a Western physician with all his laboratory facilities. When the scholar Joseph Needham in 1938 began writing a systematic history of the science, scientific thought and technology of the Chinese, he thought that the essential problem was why modern science as the West knew it since the seventeenth century had not developed in Chinese or in Indian civilization but only in Europe. By the fall of 1964 after the publication of four of his planned seven volumes, he observed that a second problem was equally as important: why between the first century B.C. and the fifteenth century A.D. Chinese civilization was much more efficient than the Occidental in applying human knowledge to practical human needs? This study will show how the Easterners' reading of the pulse provided invaluable insights and techniques by which all cultures could profit.

To the Western physician, the pulse in its relation to health and disease is relatively unimportant. The average doctor uses the pulse as nothing more than a diagnostic aid to the diseases of the heart and circulation, and a minor one at that-just another in a series of laboratory tests to be fitted into the jigsaw puzzle of health. But to the Ayurvedic, Unani, and Chinese doctors of yesterday and today, the pulse was and is a subject of primary importance; all other diagnostic techniques are ancillary to the pulse readings. As the dynamo of human life telling the condition of the body at all times, the pulse is the most important element in preventive medicine as well as in the diagnosis of disease. According to Ayurvedic and Unani[1] medicine, there are as many as six hundred different varieties of pulse, and each one tells its own particular story.

In the literature of these countries, one finds the same theme: the extreme proficiency of the practitioners in taking the pulse and their great expertness in the art of diagnosis. Illustrative is the story of the Unani physician who was called upon to treat the Sultan's wife. As it was then forbidden for a Muslim woman to show either her face or her body to a strange man, the physician had to make his diagnosis by feeling the wrist which was extended through a slit in a curtain. So expert was the doctor that he had no trouble in diagnosing and treating his patient. The Sultan impressed, complimented the physician upon his skill. The doctor then replied that this examination was no test of his skill. "My fingers are so sensitive that by tying a string around the pulse of a patient and by the vibrations, I can always make the right diagnosis."

The Sultan then decided to test the doctor and at the same time teach him a lesson. He told the doctor, "A string will be tied around the pulse of an individual hidden behind a curtain. If you diagnose the disease, you will receive a magnificent reward. But if you fail, you will be banished from our kingdom and all your wordly goods confiscated."

When the time arrived for the trial, a string was tied in such a way that the tibial pulse of a cow could be felt and the cord which was thrust through the curtain slit was then given to the physician. He held the string for a minute and replied. "All this creature needs is grass."

What can one learn from this account about the Oriental's techniques of reading the pulse? There is more to it than the doctor's discovering by way of a vibration that the subject was a cow. Their art of diagnosis is effectively linked with the taking of the pulse—wherein the East is markedly different from the West. The differences and the way all cultures can learn from one another will be the purpose of this study.

The Westerner is inclined to write off Chinese and Ayurvedic medicine as a mass of superstitious ignorance which should be scuttled or excised from the cultural matrix of healing as though it were a vermiform appendix—no longer serving a purpose. The Oriental physician regards Western medicine[2] as an offshoot of its own system, and a bad one at that, without any theory and with a reliance on gadgets[3] and instruments to cover up its lack of competence in diagnosis and prevention of disease. To the indigenous physician, Western medicine is wrong both in theory and practice: In theory because it is based on morbid anatomy, the

---

[1] The Unani physician was required to study music so that he could distinguish the different sounds and tones of the pulse.

[2] Royle says that Hippocrates, the father of Western medicine, borrowed his **Materia Medica** from India. Garrison reports that Aristotle is believed to be indebted to Hindu physicians and surgeons.

[3] The term gadgets is not used in a derogatory sense. Oriental medicine in Japan and elsewhere is using cybernetic machines in diagnosis. The input of these machines is based on a theory of medicine, not on trial and error nor on symptoms, as they claim is being done in the West. In short, Oriental healing states that the Occident does not have a theory of medicine; therefore the result, to use the cybernetic vernacular, is "garbage-in and garbage-out."

science of death, and on the laboratory instead of on the science of living. Man does not live in a laboratory nor in a vacuum, but in the world of society which molds his mental and physicial state either in health or in disease. In practice because the emphasis is on the treatment of symptoms, **static medicine,** and parts, not on the causes and prevention, not on dynamic medicine, and not on the treatment of the individual instead of the disease. The Chinese would say that the Western doctor is an inferior physician because he cannot keep the patient well so he must treat the illness whereas the Eastern physician is the superior doctor because he keeps the patient well.

Whether the Occidental is right and the Oriental wrong, or whether the Westerner is wrong and the Easterner right, whether both are wrong or both are right, or both right and wrong—all these are of no concern to this study at present. What is of importance is the contributions, if any, each culture made towards the theory, diagnosis, and actual art of healing.

Two of the oldest systems of healing that are still practiced today are Chinese Acupuncture and Ayurvedic medicine. Both were in flower before Western medicine was born. Whether each developed separately or one or both influenced the other are subjects of great importance to the historian and to the sociologist, but not to this study. Some of the similarities and differences will be briefly discussed. Both were attacked in the intellectual, economic, and political arenas by the rise of Allopathic medicine in the 1890's and in the thirties and forties of the twentieth century.[4] The pressure is greater today in the sixties; yet both systems are stronger now than at any time. Why? Because they get results. If they did not, they would have gone the way of the dodo a long time ago. While it is true that correlation and relationships were sometimes stretched to an absurd degree by the Chinese, this practice and misapplication[5] of theory do not negate the remark that the original conclusions were based on expert, accurate, and careful study of the body in its surround. In fact, the laboratory of their experience tested the human being, not the animal where species differences play a large part; and these resulting observations and principles were found good over the centuries. Because a technique is new does not make it better than the old unless it can do what the old could not do and is more rational or more practical. The corollary to this statement is also true.

Both systems of healing treat the man, not the disease, and are concerned with the total organism, with his inner and outer environment.

---

[4] The authors are of the opinion that the type of society determines its cultural and healing patterns. With the coming of the industrial revolution, the oil and drug interests pushed Allopathic medicine so that there would be a market for their products. See U.S. Senator Estes Kefauver Investigation of the 1960's.
    The rise of the industrial revolution required mass medicine or Allopathic, not individual, medicine like Ayurvedic and Acupuncture; this stress led to the legal and economic suppression of Ayurvedic and Acupuncture teachings. With the advent of the cybercultural revolution and the shortening of the work week, Oriental or individual medicine will flourish again.
    In the West Acupuncture is recognized as a specialty of medicine in the USSR and France. Two additional years are required after the medical degree. On the mainland of China, all doctors must know Acupuncture. Books on Acupuncture are becoming available in most languages of the world.
[5] Sir William Ostler stretched and misapplied the germ theory when he was of the opinion that scurvy and beri-beri were caused by a virus. Today we know that it is a deficiency disease.

Psychosomatic medicine, which is the new vogue in the West and which became popular in the early thirties, was accepted and taken for granted thousands of years ago. There never was any dichotomy between the soma and the psyche. The two systems of healing recognized that all imbalances or disease could not be classified as only physical or emotional, but contained elements of both. The treatment for emotional diseases differed in Ayurvedic and Chinese medicine because of their philosophical and sociological approaches. The Indians accepted sex as a necessary evil but liberation could come principally through asceticism. To the Chinese, sex was healthful if practiced in the right way and in moderation. To the Hindu, the gods punished, rewarded, and were responsible for creation, preservation, and destruction. The Chinese, on the other hand, relied on themselves, not on a supreme being, and were therefore free of guilt, fear and punishment. Because the Indians believed in Karma-Reincarnation[6] (punishment for mistakes in the previous lives and interest in the development of the soul), it became a fact which had a bearing on health and disease, and in diagnosis and treatment, the Ayurvedist took this belief into account. To the Chinese, there is no Karma and if belief in **Hsienship** is interpreted as reincarnation, it can be said to be material immortality in this world. One builds his happy life right here on this earth.

The Hindus attributed emotional disturbances to demons and evil spirits[7] who possess the individual. The West is familiar with this belief too. The Chinese, on the other hand, took the terror and calamity out of disease, as can be concluded from their classification of phenomena in the **I Ching** hexagrams which in theory and practice were the field force in physics and medicine. Fear has been and is responsible for more physical and emotional ailments and deaths than the actual disease itself. Today in the United States, the fear propaganda of cancer causes more harm than the so-called cures. From a psychological point of view, the Chinese were as modern as a space ship. Ayurvedic and Acupuncture anticipated Selye and Freud hundreds of years ago; in fact the Chinese make Freud sound like an ancient; in Acupuncture, there are definite points for treating emotional ailments.

Both Ayurvedic and Acupuncture describe and treat disease as a dynamic process, not as a symptom. Disease is an imbalance in the life force whether it be the Chi Hua as manifested in Yin and Yang of the Chinese or Prana as manifested in the Tridoshas Vayu, Pitha, and Kapha of the Hindus. This life force concept is unknown in the West where the concentration is on chemical and electrical energies but in the East[8] is emphasized as an influence on the other energies. If nervous, chemical or electrical energy is dammed or shut off from a part, life still goes on; but if Chi Hua or Prana leaves the body, death ensues: e.g., if nerves are

6 In this case. the nearest Western equivalent would be the inherited characteristics with this main difference: the Westerner views the individual as having no control over his heredity; in Karma, the individual is responsible for his inherited characteristics and he chooses these characteristics willfully to pay back wrongs done in previous lives and to advance soulward to Samadhi, Nirvana, and Moksha, their term for liberation.

7 Buddhist influence crept into Chinese medicine so that evil spirits and demons were taken over by the Chinese, but not to the extent prevailing among the Hindus.

8 The Chinese, in addition to the life force, dealt with signals and with systems of controls instead of with the chemical, neural, and electrical energies of the body.

damaged or severed, paralysis results, but the part does not die, for it is fed by the circulation of the blood. If the circulation of the blood is cut off, the organism does not die although gangrene may set in and amputation may be necessary. However, if Chi Hua or Prana is cut off from any part of the organism, it dies.

The Chinese state that the meridians are the vessels which carry the life force throughout the body. Their concepts of the meridians combined with the Chi Hua were elaborated upon by various scholar-observers until the cutaneous points established by tradition were incorporated with other doctrines. Relevant to the study of the pulse is the explanation of how their theory related the flow of Yin or Yang through the meridians. The Yang organs are the large intestines, stomach, small intestine, bladder, tri-heater, and gall bladder; the Yin organs are the lungs, spleen, heart, kidney, heart constrictor, and liver. Ancient or modern, all their medical writings stress the relationship of pulse, meridian, and organ. Here the comparison will be made of what was reported in the long distant past in their texts with what a modern authority affirms on Chinese Acupuncture. Dr. Wu Wei-Ping is a master Acupuncteur who is at present chief of the Chinese Hospital of Acupuncture and Moxibustion in Tai Pei; he said this about the meridians in his text which has been translated into French and then by Dr. P. Chancellor into English:

> According to the concepts of the ancient masters, the Ching, or the Meridians, which are in direct correspondence with the energy mutations of the Tsang Fu, or organs, are in reality nothing other than "supports" for Ch'i Hua. If Occidental medicine has its fundamental basis in the science of anatomy and dissection (the science of death), Chinese medicine rests primarily and solely upon the law of Ch'i Hua (the science of life) the source from which the concept of the Meridians stemmed.

The **Ling Ch'u Ching** reports the same kind of affirmation:

> It is thanks to the Meridians that the interior of the body can communicate with the exterior milieu. Not only are the organs interrelated, but they may also enter into harmony with the exterior parts of the body and prevail upon the Liu Ch'i, the sex energy thus linking man with the cosmos.

To the Ayurvedists, the life force[9] flows through the chakras instead of the meridians. The nearest Western equivalent would be endocrinology although the chakras are much more inclusive than the endocrine system. The Ayurvedist does not have the horary cycles or the flow of energy to the organ, as does his counterpart, the Acupuncturist, nor does he have the pulse organ reflections or relationships. Ayurvedic, Chinese and Unani physicians are acquainted with the Marmars[10] or death points

---

9 The life force takes multiple pathways, primary and secondary.
See Amber's law of redundancy in **Color Therapy** or **Nu Reflex Therapy.**
Did the Chinese anticipate the works of the twentieth century neurologists such as Von Economo, Broadman, Brocca, Pottenger, Erb, Head, Sherrington and others? At any rate, it is known that the visceral organs do reflex to the skin.
10 The Ayurvedic and Unani physicians noted over hundreds of years that in war times certain types of battle wounds, no matter how slight, always led to death. They charted these spots and called them Marmars or death points. The Chinese also were acquainted with these points. See "Fatal Spots", in Hsi Yuan Lu Chi Tsing, **A Standard Work on Forensic Medicine** (1241-1253).

(of vital concern to the surgeon), an approach which is relatively unknown to the Westerner.

The Acupuncturist plumbs the life force Chi Hua through the twelve classical pulses,[11] as will be explained in this study; the Ayurvedist and Unani gauge Prana by the pulses of the Tridoshas. All agree that the pulse is the measure of life.

To the Ayurvedic physician, the pulse below the thumb is the principal artery which correctly tells the condition of the patient. This pulse, situated just below the root of the thumb, is one of the most sensitive spots of the body; according to Indian legend, Jivatman, the microcosmic soul, is the size of the thumb. The Sanskrit rule observes, "The learned physician should read the happiness and misery of the body by feeling the pulse at the root of the thumb which stands as the witness of the soul." To both Unani and Ayurvedic doctors, certain signs become extremely meaningful: If the patient just before death or when he is in extreme danger inserts his own thumb into his palm and clenches his hand into a fist, the physician considers the action a symptom of grave seriousness. (Is it possible that by this gesture, the dying man seeks to grasp his soul, to search for his soul, or to protect it?) The pulse indicates whether the body is healthy or diseased. If it is diseased, the pulse reveals the condition as fatal or not. Later on, it will be shown that even the time of death can be predicted by the death pulse in both Indian and Chinese cultures.

The Ayurvedist, theorizing like the Westerner, has as his basic philosophy, atomistic cause and effect. The Hindu concentration was determined by physiology and philology where the Greek concentration was determined by the concept of geometry and methodology. The Chinese Yin-Yang philosophy, on the other hand, was based on waves, not atoms; algebra, not geometry; dialectic relationship, not cause and effect; the gestalt, not the part; dynamic change, not static condition. Chinese beliefs can best be stated by one of its own philosophers, Liu Tzu of Liu Chou, who remarked about 550 A.D.:

> When the Yang has reached its highest point, the Yin begins to rise, and when the Yin has reached its highest point, the Yang begins to rise. Just as when the sun has reached its greatest altitude, it begins to decline and when the moon has waxed to its full, it begins to wane. This is the changeless Tao of Heaven. When forces have reached their climax, they begin to weaken, and when natural things have become fully agglomerated, they begin to disperse. After the year fullness follows decay and the keenest joy is followed by sadness. This too is the changeless condition of man.

Einstein's theory of a contracting and expanding universe is the Yin-Yang principle. Chinese physics was based on the prototypal wave

---

[11] "The knowledge of pathology depends upon a thorough acquaintance with the pulse, a science which occupies all the attention of the Chinese physician. . . . With the greatest confidence he predicts the course which the disorder is to take, and in how many days the patient will be relieved from his complaint."

See Rev. C. Gutzlaff, "The Medical Art among the Chinese," **Journal of the Royal Asiatic Society of Great Britain and Ireland**, London, John W. Parker, West Strand, MDCCCXXXVII, Vol. 4, p. 168.

theory and Chinese philosophy tended to find reality in relationships; European philosophy explained reality in substance, and the Hindus, in religion.

Philologically striking is the fact that the languages of all civilizations which developed atomic theories had alphabets, but that the Chinese who devised the wave and field theories had written characters, ideographs, which probably influenced their thinking along gestalt or organismic lines. Another important fact is the continuity of information by means of the written word. Here India and the Western world were in reality little villages, each with its own language making communication difficult and, in some instances, almost impossible. Even among the villages (or nations) time and usage often change the meaning and intent of the language. A dead language, like morbid anatomy, gives very little information about the living civilization. The Chinese ideograph is their universal language and has the same meaning for the modern as for the ancient, a great advantage to the scholar and for the continuity of thought. Contrast this aspect with the practice in the West, where the language of the scholar was Greek, Latin, Hebrew, then Arabic, French, German, Russian, and English.

Both systems used a methodology of science and both were naturalists. Both regarded healing more than making a diagnosis and prescribing within a limited area. Healing to them meant being aware of the patient's inner and outer environment and treating the individual, not the disease. The aim was to restore harmony and ease for discord and disease. The basic difference was the wave theory and the relationship of parts to the whole of the Chinese and the atomistic theory, Karma, cause—effect of the Hindus. The Ayurvedist and the Chinese agree on the life force principle and the five elements and both agree that balance is health and imbalance disease; that food, temperature, seasons, planets, etc. all affect the five elements and the life force; further, that the pulse is the measuring gauge of the body's balance. Both have three of the five elements in common: Fire or Pitha, Earth, and Water or Kapha. The Ayurvedists add Ether and Air or Vayu and the Chinese, Wood and Metal. The Ayurvedist has five types of protomatter, and each atom contains equal parts of the other four plus the radicle of the atom in question: a chain of being—cause and effect. The Chinese are not interested in atoms, but are concerned with the dialectical relationship of each element to the others.

Table 1

A Comparison of the Views Expressed in Chinese and Ayurvedic Cultures Bearing upon the Pulse

Legend: 5E—the five elements   K—Kapha: equivalent of water
Y-Y—Yin-Yang   V—Vayu: equivalent of air
     P—Pitha: equivalent of fire

Chinese Beliefs	Ayurvedic Beliefs
1. 5E are dynamic, not static forces.	1. Same.
2. 5E are earth, fire, water, wood, metal.	2. 5E are earth, fire, water, air, ether.
3. Life force, Chi Hua, is manifested by Y-Y which is carried in body by meridians.	3. Life force, Prana, is transmitted through body by Chakras.
4. When Y-Y are deranged, disease or death results.	4. When the Tridhatus become Tridoshas, disease or death takes place.
5. 5E compose all processes and all substances.	5. Same.
6. 5E are aligned and associated in symbolic correlation with everything else in the universe which can be worked into a five-fold arrangement; reflects correlative thinking.	6. The same, but not to the extent prevailing among the Chinese.
7. Key words are order and pattern.	7. Key words are duty and law.
8. Things behave in a particular way because their position in the ever-moving cyclical universe is such that they are endowed with intrinsic natures which make that behavior inevitable for them and not because of a prior action or impulsion of other things; relationship (Compare with DNA).	8. A trace of similar or parallel thinking in Sva-Dharma or Intrinsic Dikavosune, but emphasis and belief in Karma and Reincarnation make cause and effect inevitable.
9. Nothing is uncaused but nothing is caused mechanically.	9. Nothing is uncaused, but causes are mechanical and preordained.
10. Scholars of almost every shade spoke of the regularity of natural processes, but had in mind, not government by law, but the mutual adaptation to community life.	10. Not true here; scholars stressed law and duty to the gods and community.

11. Nothing is created in the world. The world was not created. Ideals involve neither god nor law.

11. World was created by a supreme being. Individual is responsible to and is required to follow the laws of the gods, especially in medicine.

12. There is a right and a wrong way of living, but that has nothing to do with the gods. Man must follow the pattern of nature to be in harmony with himself and the universe.

12. There is a right and a wrong way of living, and it is inextricably bound up with God. To be in harmony with oneself, one must worship and obey the law of God.

13. There are no good or evil forces, only impersonal forces.

13. There are good and evil forces.

14. 5E should be studied with relation to the time and the culture of the Chinese, not with Western terminology.

14. Same.

15. All tastes are composed of the 5E.

15. Same.

16. Medicine deals with the Chi Hua; all the energies — chemical, neutral, thermal, etc.—are ancillary to Y-Y.

16. Medicine deals with V.P.K. which are three types of energy in the body, but does not deal directly with Prana.

17. 5E theory became more and more bound up with pseudo-science, such as fate calculations.

17. Same.

18. Tastes affect Y-Y.

18. Tastes affect the Tridhatus and Tridoshas.

19. There are five tastes.

19. There are six tastes; five are the same as the Chinese, but astringent is added. The Hindus combine two elements to give the five tastes: Fire and Earth give sour; Water and Fire give salty; Ether and Air give bitter; Fire and Air give astringent.

20. All matter is composed of 5E and Y-Y.

20. Rasa or all matter contains the following five properties: a) taste; b) 20 gunas, 5 important; c) and d) Veerya and Vipaka: physiochemical reactions; determine and predict effect of medicinal substances in physiological and pathological states; nutrition in all its aspects; e) Prabhara represents isomers.

21. Have wave theory of matter; not atomistic; one form of protomatter does not create another; polarity is present in all things; a shifting hierarchical relationship goes on all the time; change constantly occurs.

21. The Tanmatra, the atom in Western terminology, is built up by two kinds of proto matter: the "proton," with a specific energy, equivalent to modern positive electricity, and the "electron" charged with negative electricity. Modern physics has one type of proton and electron. Ayurvedic has five types of protons and electrons which are in a definite proportion for each tanmatra. Each is derived from the one which is higher in the scale. All matter is derived from one source according to this view.

22. Chi Hua and seminal essence are represented in every cell of the human body (unlike Western medicine where the seminal essence is believed to be in the reproductive apparatus). Chinese consider Chi Hua present in every cell and the reproductive apparatus is an outlet for life force.

22. Prana and the seminal essence are in every cell of the body with this remarkable theory: once the seminal essence is used up, old age ensues. Hence the Hindu belief in asceticism is intended to conserve the seminal essence and Prana.

Table 2

A Comparison of the Five Elements as Interpreted by Chinese and Ayurvedic Medicine

Legend: C—Chinese; H—Hindu.

1. **Earth**
   C: produced edible and nutritive vegetation; its physical characteristics are squareness, form, concreteness; its taste is sweetness; its organ is the stomach; its physio-psychological function is thought and flesh.
   H: is gross, heavy, capable of causing friction, rough, hard, inert, dense, sturdy, opaque; excites the sense of smell; organ is the nose; physio-psychological function is smell and consciousness; taste is sweet.

2. **Water**
   C. soaking, dripping, descending, dissolving, liquidity, fluidity in solution; physio-psychological function is hearing, bones, and marrow; dangers are precipitousness, mental abnormality; its taste is saltiness; its organ is the kidney.
   H: liquid, viscous, cool, soft, inert, slippery, fluid; excites the sense of taste; organ is the tongue; its physio-psychological function is taste, feeling, pleasure, pain.

3. **Fire**
   C: heating, burning, ascending, heat, and combustion, brightness, light; its physio-psychological function affects vision and pulse; its taste is bitterness; its organ is the heart.

   H: hot, penetrating, subtle, light, dry, clear, rarified, and luminous; capable of evoking visual sensation; organ is the eye; its physio-psychological function is form and will.

4. **Wood**
   C: accepting form by submitting to cutting and carving instruments; solidity involving workability; movement, speed; its taste is sour; its organ is the liver.

4. **Air**
   H: light, cool, dry, transparent, rarified, impinging, rough, capable of causing friction; capable of evoking tactile sensation; organ is the skin; its physio-psychological function is touch and thought.

5. **Metal**
   C: accepting form by moulding when in the liquid state and the capacity of changing this form by remelting and remoulding. Its physio-psychological function is strength, force, expansiveness, speed; its organs are lung, skin and hair; its taste is pungent.

5. **Ether**
   H: imponderable, light, rarified, elastic, capable of vibration, sound, capable of evoking auditory sensation; organ is ears; its physio-psychological function is sound and intuition.

Despite the detailed information listed in Table 2 above, the five elements should not be literally interpreted as air, fire, etc., but as dynamic states of matter, five powerful forces in ever-flowing cyclical motion, not passive motionless substances. The association of the five elements with taste in the two cultures cannot be written off as correlative thinking, but as an attempt to explain a chemical relation, which is not a static, but a dynamic process; which affects not only a part, but the total organism. An example of this interplay of change may be cited for one element: When bitterness is associated with fire, the process implies the heat used in preparing draughts or potions from medicinal herbs and plants which are bitter or else the hotness or bitterness in foods and in spices-like the chili added to Mexican food or the curry in Indian preparation.

Further, the Chinese analyzed these dynamic changes within and among the shifting five and devised a set of relationships which will be treated later in this study. But for the purposes of synthesizing, they set up guides or rules—called Mutual Conquest, Production, and Masking. It is noteworthy that a very early effort was made by these people to correlate the functioning of the five elements with the viscera and parts of the body, with the sense organs, and with the state of mind. The text **Huang Ti Su Wen Nei Ching, Pure Questions of the Yellow Emperor; Canon of Internal Medicine** set up this relation probably in the Early Han or Warring States period.

Chinese interpretation of the five elements led to organismic inter-relations, to the rearrangement of the five into the action of mutual order, the action of masking or the action of rearranging the elements, and this patterning or programming thus directed them to the twelve classical pulses which related to organs in the body because they regarded the elements as waves, cycles and relations not as energy forces in a physical, a chemical or any particularized sense. Their energy or life force was Yin-Yang with its polarity. When India spoke of Prana as a life force, it did not use Prana pragmatically as did the Chinese their Chi Hua. The Indians, unlike the Chinese, viewed their five elements as atoms that led to cause and effect with the consequent divisioning of the elements into energy fields; for example, they use the energy force of Vayu as the equiva-lent of nervous energy and Pitha as the physio-chemical-electrical force of the body which is oxidation and metabolism. Hence atomicity was carried over into their readings of the pulse as **energies, not as organ relation-ships.** This statement capsulizes the chief difference between the Indian and Chinese interpretation of the pulse.

The Indian view of pulse, energy, and element was an outgrowth, consciously or unconsciously, of their conditioning by their religious philosophy which led to atomicity. The slanted view of the elements by its chief philosophical schools will unmistakably clarify this religio-philosophic-medical interrelationship.

Charaka, one of the basic authorities for Ayurvedic medicine, held a view similar to the Vedantists': that each of the gross Bhutas or Mahabutas (elements) is a peculiar ultra-chemical compound of the orig-inal five subtle Bhutas. In this sense, every substance is made up of the five but for purposes of chemical analyses and synthesis of their chemical contituents, the substances belong to one of the elements not to all five. Compounds of the different elements may combine to form complex sub-stances and these in turn become more complex and advance onward in progressive transformation, as is especially the case with organic sub-stances and products.

The Buddhists omit ether and recognize only four essential types of matter which are 1) air defined as having impact or pressure; 2) fire, as having color and touch sensibility; 3) water, as having in addition to color and touch, the aspect of taste with its characteristic viscosity; and 4) earth, as having these above three and smell as well with the char-acteristics of dryness or roughness.

The Jains' contribution to atomic theory relates to their analysis of atomic linkage or the mutual attraction of atoms in the formation of molecules. They hold that the different classes of elementary sub-stances, the five elements, or the Bhutas are all evolved from the same primordial atom.

The Nyaya-Valseshika theory lists five atoms, but only four are significant. It divides atoms into eternal, ultimate, indivisible, and infini-tesimal. The four kinds of atoms are earth, water, fire and air; they possess mass, numerical unit, weight, fluidity or viscosity, velocity, color, taste, smell or touch; not produced by the chemical operation of heat.

Ether has no atomic structure and is absolutely inert being posited only as the substratum of sound, which travels wave-like in the air. Only the four elements unite or separate in atomic or molecular form. The orthodox view is that earth, atoms, and heat must be present whenever chemical transformation takes place.

The Five Element Theory: Chinese, Ayurvedic, and Greek

The pre-Socratic school of Anaximander (560 B.C.) promulgated four elements—earth, fire, air, water—as well as a fifth, the non-limited, which was a kind of substratum for the others. This view could be contrasted with the Indian theory Nyaya-Valseshika.

In the ancient Orphic formulation, however, there had been only three elements, and this thinking was perpetuated by Ion of Chios (430 B.C.) and others. This speculation should be compared with the Tridosha theory of the Indians as applied in Ayurvedic medicine.

According to Pherecydes of Syros (550 B.C.) the elements warred with one another. They could be compared with the Chinese theory of Mutual Conquests but while the Chinese regarded the elements as dynamic forces, Pherecydes and Empedocles (450 B.C.) viewed them as static or small, stationary upright posts. It was Aristotle who gave the four elements—fire, air, water, earth—the aspect of movement together with the qualities of hot, cold, moist, and dry—which were taken over by the West to become the standby in European science and medicine. This view should be compared with the Buddhist interpretations.

Philolaos of Tarentum added a fifth element—holkus, the hull, because he thought there ought to be some connection between the elements and the five known figures of solid geometry; Plato identified the fifth with ether. The concept of the ether of Plato and Aristotle is not the same as the Hindus' Akasha which has two forms—original or non-atomic and derivative or atomic. Akasha is their link between the infra-atomic particles and atoms; further, Akasha is, in some respects, the ether of the physicists and, in other respects, it is the proto-atom. Akasha is all pervasive; is devoid of the properties of impenetrability which characterizes even the infra-atomic potential; unites the Tanmatras, which are explained in the section on Ayurvedic beliefs.

Earlier in this chapter, the observation was made in a footnote that the two historians of medicine Royle and Garrison reported that Hippocrates and Aristotle were indebted to the Hindu physicians and to Indian **Materia Medica**. A contrast of the Greek and Indian treatment of the four and then the five elements as they evolved would reveal that the Greeks appeared to have borrowed mainly from the Indians the concepts of the element theory as well as from the Persians and possibly from the Chinese, but without fully understanding the concepts and the philosophical slants.

With respect to the Chinese, it would seem that they were not influenced by the flow of information from other cultures in so far as the five element theory is concerned because they were the only people to put the five element theory into use in the forms of relationships, not atomic particularities. Let the independent inventionists and the diffusionists concern themselves with aspects of who borrowed from other cultures. That problem is not pertinent to this treatment of pulse diagnosis.

The opening pages of this study phrased the question: Why did the Chinese who were 1500 years ahead of the West in scientific development fall behind to be overtaken by the West? The answer may lie in the fact that the West through Leibniz on to Kant and Hegel took over the Chinese theories and applications and gave them new life whereas the Chinese were content to rest on correlative thinking. The Chinese had the right theories with the doctrine of dialectic and with their views of binary arithmetic and the on-off principles but the wrong applications. Confucianism and Buddhism fossilized their thinking, and they were unable to break out of the trap of ancestor worship and reverence for the old. Dogmatism, not observation; rote, not experimentation, became the way of life.

The Indians had a trace of dialectics, but were hampered by their doctrine of Karma and Reincarnation; perhaps one could also add the monistic principles inherent in their religious interpretations of Atman-Brahman, the many becoming the one; for these all led to a cause-effect relationship, not to an organismic inter-relationship. The four basic tenets of the Hindus were Dharma or duty and law, Artha or power and success, Kama or love, and Moksha or liberation and these four resulted in a rigid, stifling, and a **permanently inherited** caste system[12] that killed initiative and led to resignation and vegetation. Authority took the place of reason and experimentation; progress was no longer possible if it conflicted with the ancients. Utopia had been reached, and there was no place to go but backwards. The Hindus of today are living in the myth of yesterday's spirituality without its knowledge, interest, and drive. Their zombie culture is going through the stimulus-response conditioning of thousands of years. Despite this fact, the ancients were right about the pulse although their descendents went to sleep for more than the twenty year nap of Rip Van Winkle and for a longer period then Brunnhilde's trance.

With respect to the advances and regressions of both the Chinese and the Indians, one may add that the West took over by the twentieth century, dropped concepts of atomism as well as cause and effect, the Greek heritage, adopted the dialectic and the binary theories together with waves and polarity which the Chinese had evolved, and used them without the Oriental restrictions of correlative thinking, symbology, etc. They made the new break-through in physics and in some of the physical sciences, but not in medicine, where both theoreticians and practitioners still lag behind. The one great advance of the Orient in medicine was

---

[12] The Indians have presumably banished the caste system since Gandi's reforms. But the Westerner who has lived in India for any length of time and is acquainted with the social climate of the country as well as with the writings on this touchy subject knows that customs die hard.

Further, critics may assert that China too had its class system in its Bureaucracy and in its Confucian paternalism. But there was no inflexible rule about Karma. The bureaucratic system with its competitive examinations was open to all—rich or poor, prince or pauper. Advance was possible.

in its readings of the pulse. Chinese, Ayurvedist, as well as the Unani physicians provided a solid foundation and firm ground work for diagnosis, for treatment, and, what is more significant, for preventive medicine. The most important requirement of the art of healing is that no mistakes or neglect occur, and in that respect there should be no doubt or confusion about interpreting the readings of the pulse. The Chinese phrase an attitude toward the art of healing which East and West could make axiomatic. The Yellow Emperor states:

> How excellent that I now know the essentials of the pulse, the final destiny of everything below heaven, the five colors and that changes which the pulse might undergo can be calculated and prefigured. And it is strong and wonderful that Tao, the right way, is in each of these and combines them into one entity.

One premise in the **Nei Ching** also permeating Chinese thought is that the ailing are rebellious against the laws of the universe. Thus all should be instructed in the ways of right living. Their adage, which dictates classifications of the healer, is that, "The superior physician serves the nation because he keeps the people well. The middle-grade physician serves the individual when he disobeys the Tao. The inferior physician treats physical ailments because he cannot cure." Thus whether he be Ayurvedic, Unani, or Chinese, the Oriental physician seeks to keep the person well—a form of social insurance protecting the state. The inferior physician treats symptoms of disease. Is Western medicine forgetting the purposes of the superior physician and concentrating on the duties of the inferior so that the true principles of healing are vitiated?

Chapter II

The Yin and Yang and the Five Elements

The Chinese method of taking the pulse in its twelve classic ways for diagnosis and healing evolved out of their two basic philosophic precepts: the theory of the Yin and the Yang and the doctrine of the five elements. A Westerner tends to be sceptical when he reads how they correlated the pulse readings of the body with the climate, the seasons, the wind directions, color, taste, odor, sound, planets, and the movement of the spheres since he disdains the thought that a microcosmic force reflects back or is interdependent upon a macrocosmic force. But he will quickly note the modernity of their persuasive reasoning about the interpenetration of the influences without and within the body as they affect the pulse. Such a weighting of all valences provides new techniques for the present-day physician in the West as he reads about the pulse and opens up other vistas for the medical horizons of the future. The Chinese in this phase of their medicine approach the total organism where man is viewed in a holistic environment with the inner and the outer creating a fluctuating hierarchical relationship of kinetic and potential energies.

The Chinese method, removed from the atomistic practices of modern Western medicine, geared its reading of the pulse to the organismic theory of the total man, to the two types of energy and to the cybernetic principle of on and off which binary arithmetic has given to the West, now projected in its twentieth century automation practices. Long before the contributions made by Norbert Weiner and by the feed-back principle to modern living, the Chinese devised their own cybernetic machine and in their discovery of the magnetic compass anticipated the West by centuries. In their readings of the pulse they interpreted the electrical field forces of the body and of the cosmos; for the doctor with his sensitively alert and knowingly educated fingers on the pulse read the total organism like a ticker tape reflecting the rising and falling cyclic rhythms of the body, the mind, and the spirit of the total man in its relations to the organs within and to the external surround without. The computing machine of today with its switching devices and its feed-back for automatic maintenance of a predetermined plan of operations has been regarded as an ideal model of the animal central nervous system. Within the central nervous system of the higher living organism, the neurons themselves seem to act according to the principles of binary arithmetic:

the all or none reaction, as the physiologists describe it. The Chinese were familiar with this view and projected it in the popular **I Ching.**

One of the latest conceptions of the workings of the law of the universe—according to the scientists working in the field of thermodynamics who seek to apply Einstein's theory of relativity—is that the universe is going through reversible processes at a definite rate and that there is an unending succession of expansion and contraction, a movement described by one of their theoreticians, ". . . like a limitless breath acting on the universe in an unknown manner." This statement could have been made by an ancient Chinese philosopher explaining how the theory of the Yin and the Yang and how the Chhi, or the life force— known also as breath, pneuma, or vapor—are applied through the five elements; further, it reflects their theories of kinetic and potential energies undergoing ceaseless change and working within the framework of an all or none principle of binary arithmetic.

The theory of the five elements signified five powerful forces in ever-flowing cyclical motion. The term element as used in their terminology must not be confused with the Western definition of element since to the Chinese, the five elements were not static substances nor passively inert items. The English translation of element was unfortunate but has remained: ideograph for a cross road implied movement and signified a relationship among substances undergoing change. The enumeration of wood, fire, water, earth, and metal was a provisional classification of the basic properties of material based on the premise that these properties would be manifested only when they were undergoing change. This image was then interwoven with their earlier theory of the Yin and the Yang—the negative and positive forces of polarity or the female and the male principle of eternal dualism in the world. These two laws must be visualized as they ceaselessly play about in relating to each other's actions and changing their positions as they move back and forth in their manifestations. The image of an orchestrated movement is reflected in their physicians' reading of the pulse and of disease.

The Yin and the Yang: Evolution of Views

Fourth-Third Centuries B.C.—Mythological references

Second Century B.C.—Contrast with Indian views on love

Ho-Chhi Festivities—Definition, male-female relationship, material immortality

I Ching—Hexagrams, binary arithmetic

First Century A.D.—Wang Chung: Lucretius of China

Eleventh-Thirteenth Centuries—Shao Yung, Lu Chiu Yuan, Wang Yang-Ming, Wang Chhuan-Shan, Chu Hsi

Seventeenth-Eighteenth Centuries—Tai Chen

The etymology of the terms Yin and Yang is connected with darkness and light and refers both to the forces of nature and to the sex differences between men and women; with the passage of time, these early concepts had many other connotations and denotations added to the basic ideograph. Yin signifies shadow and clouds to Yang's sunrays and heaven; Yin the idea of femaleness, cold, rain, dark, that which is inside; Yang, the idea of maleness, sunshine, heat, spring, and summer months, brightness, and strength; Yin refers to the shady side of a mountain and Yang, the sunny side.

Warner's **A Dictionary of Chinese Mythology** defines Yin and Yang in the following way:

> The negative and positive principles of universal life. These words mean originally the dark and bright sides of a sunlit bank, and occur on the Stone Drums (eighth century B.C.). By the time of Confucius, they had acquired a philosophical significance as two aspects of the duality which Chinese thinkers perceived in all things. Traces of the dual notion occur in the "Great Plan" of the **Shu Ching**, but the actual words Yin and Yang as used in this sense first occur in the pseudo-Confucian commentaries on the **I Ching**.
>
> In this way, Yang came to mean Heaven, Light, Vigour, Male, Penetration, The Monad. It is symbolized by the Dragon and is associated with azure color and oddness in numbers. In Feng-shui, raised land forms (mountains) are Yang.
>
> Similarly Yin stands for earth (the antithesis of Heaven), Darkness, Quiescence, Female, Absorption, The Duad. It is symbolized by the Tiger and is associated with orange color and even numbers. Valleys and streams possess the Yin quality.
>
> The two are represented by a whole and a broken line respectively, thus: _____ Yang; ___ ___ Yin. Groups of three such lines are known as "trigrams", groups of six as "Hexagrams", and the **I Ching** is classified under the sixty-four possible hexagrams.
>
> In connection with the five elements (or natural forces), the Yin and Yang have been for at least two thousand years used to interpret the processes of nature and they are the fundamental feature in the theories which underlie Feng-shui, astrology, divination, and medicine. . . . But Yin and Yang are themselves supposed to have proceeded from a "great Ultimate", **T'ai Chi.**

These theories of Yin and Yang are combined with the five elements to signify that there are only two fundamentals operating in the universe, one now dominating and then the other, in a wave-like succession. Since change in the process is inevitable, all—man, society, and nature— respond.

In their readings of the pulse, one traces this interpretation of their basic premises in the practices of a succession of scholars—Taoist or Confucian. The theory of the Yin and the Yang as two fundamental forces began about the beginning of the fourth century B.C. The common view that the philosophical use of the term goes farther back even to the second millenium is now quite untenable says Joseph Needham.[1]

The first appearance of these words as philosophical terms "One Yin and one Yang; that is the Tao" appeared early in the third century

---

[1] Joseph Needham, **Science and Civilisation in China: Physics and Physical Technology,** with the Collaboration of Wang Ling and the Special Cooperation of K. G. Robinson. At the University Press, 1962, vol. 4, p. 6. This systematic and authoritative history of the science, scientific thought, and technology in the Chinese culture-area is an indispensable and basic reference work.

B.C. (in the Appendix of the **I Ching**) with the general sense that there are only these two fundamental forces in the universe, **one now dominating, now the other, in a wave-like succession.** But a term was added which was destined to play a significant role in Chinese thought: **Chhi** and its relationship to the Yin and the Yang. The **Tai Te Ching** promulgated that all living creatures are surrounded by Yin and envelop Yang and the harmony of their life processes depends upon a harmony of these two chhi.

In their cosmogonic myths, no attempt is made to explain a deity or a supreme being, for the Chinese mind did not think in such terms. Imperial majesty corresponded to a polar star, the focal point of universal evermoving pattern and harmony not made with hands, even those of God. And the pattern was rationally intelligible because it was incarnate in man. The autochthonous idea of a supreme being, if it ever had existed in Chinese mythology, had early lost its qualities of personality and creativity since there was no need for an Author of Nature or for a Supreme Being to give to man the gift of life, love, fire, air, or water. The Chinese world-view depended upon a different concept: the harmonious cooperation of all beings arose not from a superior god external to themselves, but from the fact that all were parts in a hierarchy of wholes forming a cosmic pattern and they obeyed the external and internal dictates of their own natures.

An example may be cited to indicate the reflections of basic hypothesizations in the mythological accounts furnished by East and West of how primitive man obtained fire. The Western world's mythological inheritance is the Greek Titan Prometheus who gave man fire. When angry Zeus withheld it from mankind, Prometheus, man's saviour, stole it: according to one version, from the workshop of the lame god Haphaistos; according to another version, from the hearth of Zeus himself on the summit of Olympus; according to a third version, he plucked the fire from the sun. But whatever the origin, Zeus avenged himself by having Prometheus nailed to the highest summit of the Caucasus and had an eagle daily devour his liver, which regenerated itself at night so that the torture could continue endlessly. The prophecy that the priests of the chains of Zeus would tremble and that the punishment would end was answered in the Nietzschean remark, "Could it be possible! This old saint in the forest has not heard that God is dead!" and in the **Prometheus Unbound** by Shelley.

For the Chinese, no gods hold sway to punish or to reward or to become symbols of salvation, death, resurrection, liberty, bondage, freedom, despair, or guilt. In their mythology, there is no story of creation, no grandiose imagery of cosmic dissolution as appears in the mythologies of India, for their world is a much more solid form than the Indian cosmic mirage. Finally, there is no sign of the denial of the fundamental drive of the will to live. The Chinese have maintained an extraordinary confidence both in themselves and in the uses of prosperity, progeny, and long life. The world even in their mythology is solidly under foot, and the primary myths are concerned with the task of building up the country not with the relationship of man to a vengeful deity. In the period of the earliest men, The Lords of the Birds' Nests tell of people who lived in birds' nests in order to avoid the dangers threatening them on the ground, and they were followed by The Lords Called the Fire Drillers. Eating raw food, the people were ruining their stomachs. Some sages invented the fire drill and taught them how to cook. Then the rulers as well as the people availed themselves of the natural conditions and of the constrained spaces which land and water circumscribed. In this account, two basic Chinese themes are announced: a sage, not a god or a supernatural entity, helped man. Respecting natural conditions is a virtue and if one makes use of them, he is considered competent. Both ideas reflect in the Chinese reading of the pulse. The psyche is under control and there is no thought of guilt, death, resurrection, punishment, salvation, and emancipation as have evolved in the neurotic patterns familiar to the West.

In tracing the doctrine of Yin-Yang, one finds specimens of ancient Chinese naturalist thinking of the second century B.C. wherein their thought refused to separate man from nature or the individual man from the social man. Rather, they affirmed that the same force in the microcosm and in the macrocosm is evidenced in the human body. Though variants of this idea have appeared in all cultures and in all philosophies since the Mesopotamians, the contrast only between the Chinese and the Indian will be made as pertinent to the study of the pulse. The Chinese differed from the Indian in their acceptance of sex; they did not uphold the doctrine of asceticism, for the Chinese maintained material immortality in this body on this earth; nor did they uphold a belief in Karma or in Reincarnation coupled with the four basic Indian ideals: Dharma, or duty and law, Artha or power and success, Kama or love, and Moksha or liberation. The Chinese may be said to have in the Tao, an equivalent of the Indian Dharma, but this state was achieved through the healthful sexual relations that the Yin-Yang principles reflected in the Ho-Chhi festivals and in one's daily life: personal and social.

The Yin and the Yang interpretations of the second century B.C.— as described in the **Ta Tai Li Chi** text—treated sex and the interchange of energies as an important aspect of living and as a means by which to achieve immortality. If there is harmony between the Yin and the Yang, peace and quiet prevail. If Yang conquers, clouds and rain—the Chinese poetic term of sexual intercourse—result; if Yin prevails, ice is formed. In this micro-macrocosmic reflection, man cannot be separated from nature nor the individual personal man from the social. The sage is man on the higher level, one who can command gods and spirits that are not transcendent beings, but imminent, natural forces. Human society is the highest product of nature here and now in this world.

Some scholars are of the opinion that there was a connection between the Yin-Yang theory and the social manifestations of sex differences in early Chinese society and in the seasonal festivities where the young people chose their mates and danced in formations which symbolized the eternal duality in Nature. When this duality, a doctrine of polarity, was applied to the Yin and the Yang as supreme examples of all polar opposites and correlations, the term used was **Ho** and the celebrations of this duality were labeled Ho Chhi festivities.

The Taoists considered that sex, far from being an obstacle to the attainment of material immortality, could be made to aid it in important ways. Techniques practiced in private were called "the method of nourishing the life by means of Yin and Yang", and their basic aim was to conserve as much as possible of the seminal essence or ching by "causing the ching to return." At the same time, the two great forces—incarnated in separate human individuals—were to act as indispensable nourishment for each other. In this polar concept of Yin and Yang is the idea of chemical reactions as well as their concept of eternal life.

The early Toaists were captivated by the idea that it was possible to achieve a material immortality and to become, in their terms, a **Hsien** or a true man. The **Hsien** was one who lives forever with a youthful body in a paradise here on this earth. There was no thought of death, salvation, resurrection, asceticism, or liberation from the wheel of suffering. The perfected body had to be prepared like an embryo in a womb by a lifetime of actual practices intended to nourish the **Chhi.** Among their six different techniques for becoming a **Hsien,** the respiratory technique will be briefly recounted here primarily to contrast their views with the Indian practices of asceticism which have filtered through to the West. The Chinese purpose in developing the technique of breath control, unlike the Yogi's purpose, was to seek to repeat the respiration rate of the foetal life in the womb and to keep inspiration and exhalation as quiet as possible. They thus induced asphyxiant symptoms: buzzing in the ear, vertigo, and sweating. (Incidentally, chapter 55 of the **Tao Te Ching** sums up their concept of this happy state.) Scholars have concluded that these techniques for **Hsienship** were an indigenous development of ancient pneumatic physiology and not derived from contacts with Indian Yogiism, which begins with a different premise: to seek liberation. When the Indians explained life's four stages (Dharma, Artha, Kama, and Moksha), they related the belief that asceticism was the doorway to liberation with the physiological-philosophical corollary that the seminal essence exists in all the cells of the body, but only in a limited supply, and that once this essence is exhausted, the body ages. Here the Indians' belief in asceticism as one of the direct paths to liberation differed from the Chinese belief and practices in the Ho-Chhi festivals. The Chinese, like the Indians, believed that the seminal essence existed in all the cells, but the doctrine of **Hsienship** or material immortality led to a different interpretation of the function of sex.

The Ho-Chhi festivals have been interpreted by some scholars as strongly Taoist in character because they were originally primitive tribal mating activities in which sex itself played a vital role, but in which community solidarity remained a strong undercurrent. One Buddhist whose criticism of these festivals may have been influenced by the Indian caste system reported that the men and women united in an improper way not because of their sexual practices, but because there were no distinctions made between the nobility and the commoner. China never devised a rigid caste system, like the Indian, and the gods worshipped during the Ho-Chhi liturgies seem to have been the cosmic gods of the five elements and the spirits or forces supposed to reside in and control the parts of the human body. The control of the sexual forces in the body relates to the reading of the pulse (triheater); thus their concept of the total organismic man led various scholars to add that this sexuality continued until later times and even beyond Tantric Buddhism and Lamaism. (A few historians even affirm that there is a Taoistic origin for many Tantric ideas and practices. See Needham.)

The Ho-Chhi festivals then evolved into ritual dances held under the full moon with the playing of the dragon and the tiger (sexual symbols) and ended in public or group sexual unions of the members of the assembly in chambers along the temple courtyard. Couples were instructed in the techniques contained in the manual **Huang Shu.** The Chinese, unlike the Indians, were aware that the proper consummation of sex· was a prerequisite for health, a fact which twentieth century psychology— psychiatry is finding to be true. Sexual frustration or overindulgence leads to depletion of physical and emotional energies, as the neurotic in Western culture reflects. In contrast, the proper use of sex leads to relaxation and regeneration. With respect to medical diagnosis, after the completion of the sex act, the neurotic pulse is an abnormal one, as the Chinese physician knows, and the "sexual pulse" is known as the healthy pulse, for it relaxes and replenishes the body energies, the proper use of Yin and Yang. Thus the physician can tell from the pulse whether the sexual act was really consummated or gone through as a mechanical process or as a form of masturbation. The proper use of sex leads to relaxation and regeneration. The neurotic uses sex incorrectly to relieve tension momentarily but then builds up more tension, a vicious cycle, as the Chinese well understood. Here is evidence of too much Yin or too much Yang, depending on the individual, and a good application of the **Masking** principle. In the sexual act, the orgasm for the male—the ejaculation—is the crest of the Yang cycle; for the female, the orgasm is the crest of the Yin cycle. The interpretation made by some Western religions that the female is passive in the sexual act goes contrary to the Yin-Yang principles (Shades of Ho-Chhi).

Making the Ching—or seminal essence—return became a part of the Chinese mode of expression and belief. And at one point, Taoist public ceremonies as well as ordinary conjugal-life exercises together with private exercises for cultivating the **Hsien** led to liturgical developments called "The Pure Art of Equalizing the Chhi's or Uniting the Chhi's of Male and Female." Needham observed that they may have originated in 200 A.D. and remained in common practice until 400 A.D., that the private practices continued into the Sung period for the Taoists who were attached to the temples and apparently until the last century for lay people in general, all the more so as they were approved and counselled by the medical profession. As late as 1950, when a secret society was being dissolved in China, there were allegations of group sexual intercourse pursued as a way to health and immortality (not immorality).

The Ho-Chhi festivities related to Chhi, a term which may present difficulties for the Westerner to grasp since many different connotations have been built about it by the customs and traditions of the centuries. Perhaps it would be wise to use the Chinese term since no single word can convey the significance the image has for the Chinese.

Chhi could be a gas or a vapor; an influence as subtle as ethereal waves or radio active emanations as used in the modern sense. It could be likened to pneuma or prana. In ancient China, Chhi was said to be derived from three sources: earth, heaven, or breath. But Chhi, more rarified than steam or breath, could also signify an emanation or a spirit. The accounts of 600 B.C. describe six forms of Chhi: Yin, Yang, wind, rain, darkness, brightness, and their incorporation produced the five flavors; their blossoming made the five colors, and they manifested themselves as the five notes. Thus if sound, flavor, and color were different forms of Chhi, the concept of Chhi was related to the vapors of the cooking pot and specifically to its fragrant steam. One authority observed that Chhi meant (in Chou times) vapor, air, breath, vital principle, temperament, and as a verb—to present food, to pray, to beg, or to ask. One who is not aware of the wide connotations would miss the multi-ordinal meaning associated with the Ho-Chhi festivals for the understanding of the self in its Yin-Yang social as well as individual aspects.

In the hands of the Neo-Confucians, Chhi came to mean matter. Chu Hsi who took over the established conception of the formation of things by aggregation of the universal "matter-energy", noted that the Chhi condenses to form solid matter. What was added at this time was the association of the condensation process with Yin and the dispersion process with Yang. The Yin female or negative principle became associated with contraction and the Yang male or positive with expansion.

At this stage of defining terms, it is necessary to introduce the word Li as some Neo-Confucians used it in preference to Tao and others, to Chhi. Westerners who seek to equate Chhi and Li with Aristotelian form and matter would find this usage is not acceptable since there is no place for the term soul in Chinese philosophy. (See Needham.)

Li is not soul-like or animate, but Li is Chhi potentially. Li as matter is potentially form. One asks whether Li is the Neo-Confucian equivalent of the Taoistically inspired word Tao as he reads the description of the term in the Neo-Confucian philosophical dictionary of 1200 A.D.: Li is roughly the same as Tao and it was explained that Tao is what prevails at the human level. In comparison with Li, Tao is broader and Li more profound. Li has the definite meaning of unchangeableness so that although the Tao has run through all the centuries—in a principle of variable human organization—the Li has never changed. Li then is formless, is a natural and inescapable law of affairs and of things; it is a patterning, standardizing, and modelling law. It conveys the idea of certainty and fixity and unchangeableness. (Compare this interpretation with the Indian Akasha.)

The distinction between Li and Chhi was not at all the same as that between soul and body, for souls are composed of subtler kinds of Chhi and the very arrangements of the parts of the bodies in space and in time with all their interactions were Li in manifestation and effect. In the world of Li and Chhi, there was no god of pure form and pure actuality; there were invisible[2] organizing fields or forces existing

---

[2] Compare with the Burr Northrop theory: the invisible architect and the field force theory.

at all levels within the natural world. No god head and no supreme being entered into the matter; only the distinction between Li and Chhi not as between body and soul but as the arrangements of parts of bodies in space and in time with all their interactions.

In Chinese Acupuncture, the doctor works with the life force which in their medical terminology, is termed Chi Hua, a concept alien to the Western physician. In reading the pulse, the doctor interprets the life force by means of the twelve classical pulses, a procedure detailed in another portion of this study.

No undertone of good or evil nor any moral condemnation of the Yin-Yang[3] sexual practices of the Ho-Chhi festivals or any other similar practices appeared in China. Some authorities sought to determine whether or not the Chinese gave this idea of light and darkness to the Persian Manicheans and Zoroastrians or whether the Chinese derived their theory from them. The present opinion, as summarized by Needham, is that Iranian dualism was derived from Chinese Yin-Yang sources. A sharp contrast to the Iranian dualism of good and evil is furnished by the Chinese belief that health, happiness or good order could be achieved only by attaining and maintaining a real balance between the two equal forces. As a people, they chose to find an underlying harmony and unity in all things rather than struggle and chaos. The fundamental concept of Yin and Yang is that they are two independent and complementary facets of existence and the aim of their philosophers was not the triumph of light over shadow, or of good over evil, but the attainment in human life of perfect balance between the two principles. The basic concept is repeated: operations in process of change; any static condition is derivative or only momentarily implicit.

As a matter of physiological significance of consequence to their medicine, the Chinese recognized the importance of women and accepted their equality with men on the conviction that health and longevity needed the cooperation of the sexes. This attitude led to admiration for certain feminine psychological characteristics and the incorporation of the physical phenomena of sex in noumenal group catharsis—free, it is to be stressed, from asceticism and from class distinctions. The Taoists of ancient China were the supreme representatives of social solidarity and of all that was opposed to division and separation. The physiology of the Taoists might have been primitive and fanciful, but they had a much more adequate attitude to the male, the female, and the cosmic background than the paternally repressive austerity of Confucianism or the other-wordliness of Buddhism, for which sex was neither natural nor beautiful. In this respect, the Yin-Yang principle and practice had universal parallels with other cultures in its understanding of the power of love.

At this point of recounting the historical role played by the Yin-Yang theory in Chinese culture, its influence on the **I Ching** or the **Book of Changes** and its significance in medical and scientific thought

---

[3] Some authorities, like Wang and Wu, link Yin and Yang to the Egyptian worship of Osiris and Isis and even to the Even and Odd of Pythagoras.

should be reviewed. The West is familiar with Jung's introduction of the **I Ching** through the Wilhelm translation. Symbolic hexagrams were used, each of which was composed of six lines, a whole line _____ corresponding to Yang and a broken line __ __ coresponding to Yin. Each of the hexagrams was primarily Yin or Yang, and it was possible to derive all sixty-four of them in such a way as to produce alternating Yin and Yang, components of which never became fully separated. But at each stage, only one of them was manifested.

Of interest to the West is the principle of segregation manifested in the Yin-Yang interplay of the **I Ching** hexagrams as the yarrow sticks are thrown, from which three analogies have been deduced: with genetics —the interplay of dominant and recessive factors in the genotype—with embryology and with chemistry—steps of purification that finally lead to the separation of substances. The **I Ching** scholars correctly observed that no matter how long the purification of substances might be carried on, there would still remain the positive and the negative combined together, even though in appearance one or the other might dominate. Thus some elements of "field thinking" and of the structure of the world as modern science knows it were prefigured in the speculations of these early Chinese.

The **I Ching** originated from peasant omens and from the practices of divination about the eighth or the sixth centuries B.C., according to Needham who reported that the dates to be assigned to the book are still a disputed sinological question, but that no mention of the book existed before the third century B.C. With the passage of time and with additions made by successive scholars, the **I Ching** became a "repository of concepts" and to its sixty-four kuas, all the concrete happenings of man, of society, and of nature could be referred. Thus the **I Ching** came to project a phenomenon of conceptualization, an achievement without parallel in any other culture; its framework of reference has been described as a "Cosmic Filing System" and also as the "administrative approach" to natural phenomena, an organization for "routing ideas through the right channels to the right department", a particular view that may have grown out of the bureaucratic social order characteristic of Chinese civilization, very different from any Western historical movement of the past.

Chinese thought was influenced by the five-element theory and the two force theory of the Yin and the Yang, ideas favorable to the development of scientific thought, but the tremendous filing system and the symbolic correlations that evolved from the **I Ching** together with the phases of correlative thinking had both a healthy and unwholesome effect on Chinese thought. Especially in the **Book of Changes** does the Western reader note its devastating effect on Chinese culture. Yet out of its system grew an organismic thinking which manifested itself through its symbolic correlations, its use of dialetics and its tabulation of forces. No single book could better illustrate the dialectic character of the correlative thinking pervading Chinese thought: namely, no state of affairs is permanent or immutable; every vanquished entity or defeated force will rise again; but every prosperous or victorious force carried within itself the seeds of its own destruction. (Shades of Hegel and Marx!)

What started out as an auguristic text became increasingly more abstract as it evolved into a filing system of coordinated correlations, a filing system which placed one in a position connected by "proper channels" with everything else. Of special interest to the twentieth century reader is what happened on this path from omen to concept along which the scholars traveled. Shao Yung stumbled on the idea of binary arithmetic in his arrangement of the hexagrams, principles which anticipated automated devices and the cybernetic feed-back of today together with the signal response by the body operated within the nervous system. Incidentally, when Leibniz communicated with Jesuit missionaries in China, he discovered between 1698 and 1701 that the I Ching could be interpreted with the binary system so that the Chinese influence was responsible in part for his conception of an algebraic language in the same way as the **Book of Changes** foreshadowed binary arithmetic. These signals and these devices reported in the order system of the I Ching were also the substance of the Chinese readings of the pulse.

A noteworthy contribution was made in 82-83 A.D. to the theory of Yin-Yang by Wang Chhung, called the Lucretius of China. He accepted the Yin-Yang dualism and the five element theory and held to a naturalistic view in which spontaneity was his key word. Maleness and femaleness set up principles where heaven was synonymous with Yang and earth with Yin. He believed that calamity came if Yin and Yang were at variance and that they both worked in waves which reached a climax and then receded. Wang Chhung also took over from the Taoists the ideas of rarefication and condensation.

By the time of the Neo-Confucianists in the Sung Dynasty (960-1126 A.D.) the ideas of the two fundamental forces in the universe as an hypostatization of the two sexes was well established. The five theoreticians who will be discussed for their changes in the Yin-Yang theory never departed from this fundamental: Shao Yung, the two idealists Lu Chiu Yuan and Wang Yang-Ming, the materialist Wang Chhuan-Shan and Chu Hsi, one of the great Chinese thinkers.

Shao Yung explained the two primary manifestations of the Tao as motion and rest. Motion generated Yin and rest generated Yang. Then Yang or rest generated two new entities—softness and hardness. Thus the world picture drawn by Shao Yung was extremely concrete and physical. Motion and rest, softness and hardness were then taken over as basic conceptions by the Neo-Confucianists. The greatest idealist of the Sung period was Lu Chiu Yuan, an opponent to Chu Hsi. He placed the Neo-Confucian principle of organization, termed Li as was explained in respect to Chhi, within the experiencing mind and his system was opposed to Chu Hsi's. The influence of Buddhism penetrated China, but the Chinese always continued to affirm the duties of man in the world today and to deny the Buddhist doctrine of salvation as escape from the world. The second idealist was Wang Yang-Ming who stressed inborn intuition apart from which there could be no knowledge. He is said to have anticipated the idealism of Berkely by some two hundred years and the categorical imperatives of Kant.

The materialist approach of Wang Chhuan-Shan led him to occupy himself with the origin of the generative forces of nature, and he observed that reality consisted of matter in continuous motion, but that **Li** was no more important than **Chhi** or that organization in the universe was no more important than matter or energy, an equivalent perhaps to the principle of dynamic equilibrium. The forms remain, but their material composition is in the process of continual change. And thus Wang Chhuan-Shan intuitively understood metabolism. Had his speculations about matter and energy been pursued, they could have led to a Chinese Einstein theory of relativity $(E = MC^2)$.

Perhaps the greatest of all Chinese thinkers is Chu Hsi (1131-1200) whose contribution to the philosophy of organism is significant. But at this stage his additions to the Yin-Yang theory should be clarified. He associated condensation with Yin and the dispersion process with Yang; thus expansion went with the Yang, a male or positive principle, and contraction with the Yin, female or negative. The result was that after the Sung, these doctrines of expansion and condensation became part of the universal background of Chinese thought. But Chu Hsi built upon his country's use of correlative coordinative thinking which he reslanted in the direction of organismic conceptual thinking. He has been compared with Aristotle, Aquinas, Leibniz, and H. Spencer; Needham labels him "The supreme synthetic mind in all Chinese history" when he explained how Chu Hsi developed a philosophy that was more closely akin ". . . to the philosophy of organism than to anything else in European thought." The Sung Neo-Confucianists attained by insight a positive analogous to that of Whitehead without having passed through the stages corresponding to Newton and Galileo.

Thus by the end of the twelfth century, the Sung philosophers had established the conception of the entire universe as a single organism with Chhi as its organization center but with no particular part of it permanently in control. The world was a series of integrative levels of organization, the whole at one level becoming a part on the next. Thus two facts were significant: the existence of a universal pattern or field determining all the states and transformation of matter-energy and the omnipresence of this pattern. The motive power could not be localized at any point in space and time and the organization center was identical with the organ itself. Here is profound insight into the negative and positive aspects of matter which have as protons and electrons become today the components of all material particles. Perhaps their language did not have our type of clear-cut appraisal, our full comprehension, but they had a true insight into these relations long before the West even dreamed of their possibilities. Then they added that nature worked in a wave-like manner; that each of the two forces rose to its maximum and in turn fell away to leave the field to its opposite; moreover, they generated each other—like thesis and antithesis—with motion and rest occurring in alternate periods, the motion rising to a maximum degree and then falling—a scientific abstraction with which the West is very familiar.

When Needham contrasted modern Western organismic thinking with the Sung Chinese precepts, he pointed out that Western philosophy of organism was not a product of European thinking and he showed how Leibniz and his doctrine together with his theory of binary arithmetic may have been influenced by these systematic Neo-Confucian forms and ideas; he concluded that "Chinese bureaucratism and the organicism which sprang from it may turn out to have been as necessary an element in the formation of the perfected world-view of natural sciences, as Greek mercantilism and the atomism to which it gave birth." The history of Chinese thought provides another comparison: The Sung philosophers of the tenth to the twelfth centuries could be paralleled with their thinkers of the fifth to the third centuries B.C. (Warring States) whose writings revealed glimpses of dialectic logic long before Hegel.

Up to the seventeenth century, the flow of techniques and inventions had been mainly from East to West, but during the seventeenth and eighteenth centuries, the reverse took place when the post-Renaissance science of the Western world was brought to China by the Jesuits. Despite the theological aspects of this influence, certain writers maintained the indigenous Chinese tradition of naturalism; among them were Tai Chen and Huang Lü-Chuang. Three writers—Yen Yang, Li Kung, and Tai Chen— were concerned with reappraising Han thought; realizing to what extent Sung Neo-Confucianism had been impregnated with Taoism and monism, they set out to structure a materialistic monism with all foreign elements removed from Chinese theories. But here only the contribution of Tai Chen will be reviewed. He returned to the older conception of the Tao which had the order of nature as explained by the Yin and the Yang and the five elements. He rejected the concept of Li as a mental entity and affirmed that Chhi alone accounted for all phenomena: the instincts, the emotions of man, and his highest manifestations. In reassessing Li, he reassigned to the word the old meanings of pattern, organization, and structure in nature, smothered by the Buddhists and by the supernaturalism which had almost transcendentalized **Li,** and once again affirmed that **Li** was immanent in Chhi (matter-energy); further, he removed **Li** from all positive social laws and vulgarizations of the meaning by which the word had been used to inculcate obedience to legal laws. He criticized Buddhist introspection and meditation which Vulgar Neo-Confucianism had taken over together with its belief that man's natural desires were essentially evil and should be suppressed, to praise reason which is exemplified in every manifestation of man's being, even in the baser emotions. For Tai Chen insisted that the qualities of fellow-feeling, righteousness, decorum and wisdom are all extensions of the fundamental instincts of nutrition and sex or the natural urge to preserve life and postpone death and that they could not be sought apart from these urges. Virtue would not be suppression of desire, but their orderly expression and fulfillment. Thus **Li** was never a private illumination nor a private opinion. (See Needham.)

The theory of Yin and Yang was established as a hypothesis put forth to explain all things in nature. One explanation of this dual power as given by Noriyuki Sugihara[4] follows:

1. The Creation of Heaven and Earth

The universe before heaven and earth were created was called Chaos from which static Yin and dynamic Yang were engendered. Static Yin remained in earth and dynamic Yang went into heaven. In this way the phase of all things in nature was determined. A phase is what strikes our five senses and is divided into dynamic and static. The dynamic phase strikes our senses as motion, heat and cold, light, sound and smell while the static phase does this as form, hardness, and colour. The dynamic phase is engendered by the consumption of Yin and Yang and the static is formed by the collection of the two. Either phase is not engendered or formed by one of the two components of Yin and Yang. That is, Yin or Yang itself does not strike our five senses.

Chaos was a world of nothingness, from which Yin and Yang were engendered. At first this world was shapeless like an astronomical nebula, and with the creation of Yin and Yang it changed into the present world.

Heaven and earth are terms used [by man]. . . . Yang is dynamic and becomes heaven centrifugally, and Yin is static and becomes earth centripetally. Yin or Yang in this case is not pure. . . [each contains an element of the other but in the overall picture one is dominant and the other recessive as the case may be]; Yang $>$ Yin or Yang $<$ Yin. Heaven is Yang $>$ Yin on the whole, but individually it is either Yang $<$ Yin or Yang $>$ Yin. Therefore the representative of Yang (Yang $<$ Yin) is the sun and that of Yin (Yang $<$ Yin) is the moon and stars. Earth is Yang $<$ Yin on the whole but individually it is either Yang $<$ Yin or Yang $>$ Yin. Yang: Yin is infinitely various; hence a great variety of creatures on the earth.

2. The Change of Phase

Yang vanishes and Yin appears, and Yin vanishes and Yang appears. There is no appearance without vanishment, hence vanishment leads to appearance.

In heaven the sun, the representative of Yang, vanishes and the moon and stars representing Yin appears. On the earth, for instance, when we strike a match, its stick vanishes and fire appears; then fire vanishes and ashes are felt. The stick of the match is static, fire is dynamic, and ashes are static. That is, the change of phase is static $\rightarrow$ dynamic $\rightarrow$ static.

In medicine the Yin-Yang theory was so vast a hypothesis that it was subdivided into five arrangements or five elements: wood, fire, earth, metal, and water. How it is applied to healing would be too vast a subject and would require a text by itself. However a short summary will be attempted to give the reader an idea of the Chinese bases for healing.

In the arrangement of the elements, certain laws emerge of which two will be discussed here together with their explanation of the five flavors.

---

4 Noriyuki Sugihara, "On Oriental Medicine," Reprinted from **Acta Scholae Medicinalis in Gifu,** vol. 12, No. 4, December 31, 1964, pp. 286-7.

1. The Law of Creation

Wood creates fire, wood burns and fire is created; fire creates earth, fire vanishes and earth (ashes) is left; earth creates metal, earth is refined and metal is obtained; metal creates water, metal attracts water; water creates wood.

2. The Law of Subjugation

Wood subjugates earth by taking nourishment from the earth; earth subjugates water by absorbing it. Water subjugates fire by extinguishing it. Fire subjugates metal by smelting it. Metal subjugates wood by cutting it (axe).

3. The Five Flavors: An Explanation

Man lives between heaven and earth by taking and consuming Yin and Yang which is taken in the form of food and drink. In eating and drinking man knows five flavors: sour, bitter, sweet, pungent and salty. These, in turn, are created from the five elements as follows. Wood creates sourness; wood when dried up by distillation creates acetic acid which is sour. Fire creates bitterness by burning ash which is bitter. Earth creates sweetness by making a tuberous root sweet. Metal creates pungency; when metal is refined, it gives off a pungent odor. Water creates salt; sea water contains salt.

The five flavors in turn create the five viscera. Sourness creates the liver, bitterness creates the heart, sweetness creates the spleen. In Oriental medicine no mention is made of the pancreas; perhaps it was overlooked because in some animals the pancreas looks like a net. In Acupuncture, the spleen is regarded as discharging the function of the pancreas, which produces insulin that suppresses sugar in the blood. Hence there is a relationship between the sweetness and the pancreas or the spleen in Chinese medicine. Pungency creates the lungs. Salt creates the kidneys.

The five viscera create the five tissues: muscles, blood, flesh, skin and hair, and bone-marrow. Muscles create the heart; blood, the spleen; flesh, the lungs; skin and hair the kidney; bone-marrow, the liver. In like manner the five Ho, the five Yungs, and the five Chu are created. They deal with composition and function. This theory is adopted for the diagnosis of disease: e.g.; the five viscera are within the body so their function cannot be directly known from without by observation. (It can by palpation; see Amber's book on **Nu Reflex Therapy**). The five Ho are without the body so their function can be known directly. Jaundice can be observed by the color of the eyes and skin. The five colors, five sounds, five voices, and five odors are used in diagnosis: for example, if one's face is pale, it shows that the liver is weak and if one's odor is tainted, the lungs are not functioning properly.

The Five Elements

The statement was made earlier in this chapter that the five elements—water, earth, fire, wood, and metal—were to be regarded as invariable principles; the term could mean a natural norm, a rule, or a law from its early derivation. These were not so much a series of five types of fundamental matters since particles do not come into the picture, but five types of fundamental processes. The Chinese avoided substances and clung to relations. One example would be fire going through a process of heating and burning, ascending, providing heat for combustion with the resulting taste of bitterness. Thus this theory sought a classification of material things and their basic properties which could be manifested only when they were undergoing change and therefore these powerful forces were in an ever-flowing cyclical motion. They were not passive.

Though the Chinese do not have the concept of the five tanmatras for their explanation of the physical nature of the atom as does Ayurvedic philosophy, both cultures use the doctrine of the number five for their classifications and both, under different terminology, break matter down into component parts. In both traditions these five elements or these five tanmatras were inevitably associated with the tastes as influencing the pulse beats, an association that suggests an awareness of the fundamentals of chemistry and nutrition in both cultures. The Chinese five element theory was later bound up with fate calculations and with pseudo-science (which the Westerner rightly sloughs off as a mass of superstition and thus erroneously condemns the total achievements). But in their observations of how the five elements related to the body, taste, pulse, rhythmic rise and fall of the organs at their zenith and nadir points during the twenty-four hours of the day, the Chinese doctors revealed unusual insights into the body, generalizations which were incorporated in their **materia medica** on the pulse. In this respect the Chinese contribution to civilization and to modern medicine deserves greater praise, more discriminating perception, and direct pragmatic utilization.

A key to the reading of the pulse is that the theory of the five elements was a universal commonplace of Chinese thought by the sixth century and as a stabilized part of the philosophic framework was woven into the doctrine of polarity—the Ho principle combined with Chhi—of the Yin and the Yang. Thus these five elements came to be associated with every conceivable category of things in the universe which it was possible to classify in five tables; with the passage of time came growing artificiality and arbitrariness. But this pseudo-development did not fully apply to the study of medicine where they related the five elements to the five viscera, the various parts of the body, the tastes and the seasons. It took some time to get away from this type of correlative thinking especially in medicine, for there were more than five organs in the body. Once this breakthrough occurred, they went on to the twelve classical pulses, or fourteen as some moderns affirm, and these were communicated in the later editions of the **Nei Ching** with observations on the twelve classical pulses by Wang Shu Huo. Could the algebraic reasoning of the Chinese have led the medical practitioners away from the primitive arithmetic of the figure five to the figure twelve, a system more advanced than our system based on the figure ten?

The most important medieval book setting forth the main principles of the five elements was the **Wu Hsing Tai I**, written by Hsiao Chi in 594 A.D. Since this dealt more with scientific matters than with fate calculations, it stabilized four types of relationship of the five elements, only two of which will receive treatment here. Omitted will be the cosmogonic order and the "modern" order of the five elements. The symbols used in the analysis will be W. for wood, M. for metal, E. for earth, F. for fire and w. for water.

The arrangement of the elements in **Mutual Production** was W.F.E.M.w., an order dictated from the second century B.C. and occurring with twice as great a frequency as any other order in Chinese texts. In the **Mutual Conquest** theory, the elements were arranged W.M.F.w.E. and could be best explained as an example of Chinese reasoning about these elements by beginning with the last of the series—earth. Wood conquers Earth because it can in the form of spades, dig it up and shape it. Metal conquers Wood since it cuts and carves it. Fire conquers Metal since it can melt and volatilize it. Then water conquers fire by extinguishing it. Earth conquers water or constrains it and completes the cycle.

From these two orders were evolved two others: **Control** and **Masking.** In the system of **Control,** a given process of destruction is said to be "controlled" by the element which destroys the destroyed; for example, W. destroys or conquers E., but M. controls the process.   M. then destroys W., but F. controls the process.   Fire then destroys M., but w. controls the process; w. destroys or conquers F.,   but E. controls the process.   E then destroys w. but W. controls the process. These conclusions following logical paths of Chinese thought have been found applicable in many experimental sciences today, as Needham has wisely pointed out: in the kinetics of enzyme action; in the oecological balance of animal species; in the digestion of an oxidase by a protease and the consequent inhibition of the reaction which it would otherwise have catalysed; and in the enzyme phosphorylase which breaks down glycogen to hexose molecules.

Dialectic thinking is reflected in the Chinese principle of **Control** as related to **Mutual Production** and to **Mutual Conquest.** The corollary that the controlling element is always that one produced by the destroyed element, the idea being that something which acts upon something else and destroys it, but in so doing is affected in such a way as to bring about later its own change or destruction has been familiarized to us through the teachings of Hegel and Marx.   Modern science has also found that not all agents can act with impunity: enzyme proteins in living cells themselves suffer biologically important changes.

The second principle refers to the **Masking**[4a] of a process of change by some other process which produces more of the substratum or produces it faster than it can be destroyed by the primary process. The order is W.F.E.M.w. which differs from the order of **Control** (W.M.F.w.E.): for example, W. destroys or conquers E., but F. masks the process, etc. Here are examples of competing processes which illustrate the deductions from the cycles of production and destruction that are a commonplace of modern science.

The five element theory gradually came to be associated with every conceivable category of things which could be classified in five and with time came a set of many symbolic correlations, some of them arti-

---

[4a] Syphilis, the great imitator, is a good example of masking.

ficial and some fruitfully observant of natural phenomena and their interrelations; the observations made by the astronomers for the correlations between the elements and the denary and duodenary cyclical signs will be discussed with the celestial stems as they affect the pulse. The symbolic correlations set up by the medical group are incorporated in what is regarded as the most ancient surviving Chinese medical text— the **Huang Ti Su Wên Nei Ching** and will be used extensively for its account of the pulse and for its five elements in relation to mind and body.

Correlative Thinking

The term correlative thinking will be explained by way of its use in military warfare, by the senior citizen and the young child, by the psychiatrist, and by religion and myth before it will be applied to Chinese medical practices. If it is used correctly, it is a valuable tool in any discipline.

The Office of Strategic Services headed by Donovan had a Department of Research and Analysis—familiarly known by its abbreviation as **R and A**—which used as one of its principal approaches the correlative hypothesis of Bacon; this simply meant applying in one field what worked in another. The British had its own **R and A** which worked closely with the American. One example of its application is the generalization that swarming hornets, not the lion, rule the jungle. Translated into naval warfare, it means that several light craft of high speed will defeat a slower craft of heavier firepower. Bluejays fighting a snake attack in numbers: some assail the snake's body as a diversion while others attack its eyes. When the snake is blinded, it is killed. The Japanese bluejayed the mightiest ship of the British navy, the Prince of Wales, and a warship of the Repulse class, north of Singapore. The Japanese planes came out of the morning sun. The giant battlewagons never had a chance. They were torpedo-stung to death.

In essence, Research and Analysis, composed of scholars, used thought in the abstract, but it produced some remarkably cogent applications to modern war. The British **R and A** reasoned that what worked by sea would work by land. German armor was treated as a reptile and the British air force as bluejays. Special equipment was put under the wings of a fighter squadron. There were four rockets under each wing, and each had the fire-power of a five inch cruiser. When General Patton plunged from Normandy down to Brittany, his line of supply was three miles from the sea at Avranche. The enemy threw in its full armor: 250 tanks to cut Patton's line. This was the chance the R.A.F. was waiting for. The rocket planes attacked the enemy armor like bluejays attacking a snake. When the battle ended, 175 German tanks were "flamers" and more than 35 were "smokers." The bluejays killed the snake.

Other examples of correlative thinking are to be noted among children and senior citizens and even in the conversation of normal well-adjusted people who disregard rules of formal logic. With a better understanding of correlative thinking, the psychologist and the psychiatrist could make contact, the first step toward a "cure", with the emotionally disturbed.

Still another illustration of this type of reasoning is derived from religion and mythology as it explains, for example, the moon and its mystique; the changing rhythms of thought-shifting symbols are recounted not in a cause-effect relationship but in a totality conceptualization. The term moon from its Sanskrit root means to measure and the moon is thus a universal measuring gauge of "living time" bound up with life and nature, with rain and tides, with sowing and the menstrual cycle; its symbolism links the moon with sea, rain, fertility, plant life, man's destiny through the mysteries, the initiation rites, and death. The moon also unifies and hence moon forces or rhythms are the lowest common denominators of an endless number of phenomena and symbols wherein the universe is seen as a pattern subject to certain laws and as a space where things can be seen to correspond and fit together and all perceived by an intuition in its totality. No part exists without its whole; and the example frequently cited in proof is the spiral, the age-old symbol of the moon. The spiral thus relates to the phases of the moon, the erotic elements springing from the vulva-shell analogy, the water elements, and fertility as seen in the horn and the double volute motif. When a woman wears a pearl, she is united to the power of water in the shell. The moon too has a shell as its symbol and thus eroticism, birth, and embryology all are interpreted as created by the rays of the moon. No symbol has only one meaning. Instead, everything hangs together and connects in a cosmic whole. To the primitive, the lunar symbol was the power of a ritual that placed the individual at the center of these forces increasing his vitality, making him more real, and guaranteeing him a happier state after death. Every act has a character of totality. Thus the powers of the moon are not revealed by analytical exercises, but by an intuition that is an orchestration of symbols: The moon appears and disappears; the snail shows and withdraws his horns; the snake sloughs his skin and lives eternally; the bear appears and disappears with the seasons. Here is a cosmic reality with meaning and harmony to be explained not by the word "because" or "therefore", but by the term "in the same way." And thus, "in the same way" does the pulse measure the changing rhythms of the organs of the body which have their high and low tides of energy and the changing levels of mind and spirit as they affect the individual in sickness or in health.

The proto-scientific ideas of the Chinese involved two fundamental forces in the universe: the Yin and the Yang, negative and positive projections of man's own sexual experiences, and the five elements of which all process and all substance were composed. With these five elements were associated in symbolic correlation everything else in the universe which could be placed into a fivefold arrangement. Around this central fivefold order was a larger region comprising all the classifiable things which went into some other order: a numerology which some people label Chinese superstitious nonsense. Is this type of thinking, which has been labeled "coordinative" or "associative" thinking, superstition or a reflection of primitive thinking? This intuitive association has its own logic and causality in its own thought forms; in coordinative as distinguished from subordinative thinking, concepts are not of different ranks, in a cause-effect relationship, but in a side-by-side patterning wherein one influences the other not by mechanical causes but by interrelations that become larger patterns.

Out of this reasoning grew a theory of symbolic correspondences; things behaved in particular ways because their position in the ever-moving cyclical universe was such that they were endowed with intrinsic natures or qualities which made that behavior inevitable. They existed in dependence upon the whole world-organism and reacted upon one another and in relation to each other as though moving in sound waves or by vibrating resonation. Thus the correspondences in this correlative or coordinative relationship existed in a closely knit universe in which only things of certain classes could or would affect other things in the same class. This causation was not done at random. Nothing was un-caused, but nothing was caused mechanically. Harmony was the basic principle of living and of the world. Here was an ordered universe in which all things "fitted" exactly.

From a chronological view, coordinative thinking may be primitive, but it is not "participative." When the five element system was established with its categorizations, Chinese thought developed an organic view of the universe as a hierarchy of parts and wholes; a conviction that the universe and each of the wholes composing it had a cyclical nature under-going alternation so that the idea of inter-dependence assumed signi-ficance as did alternation. Social and world order rested not on authority or god, but on a conception of rotational responsibility; not on a creator or a deity, for nothing is created in the world and the world was not created. Chinese ideals projected no belief in god and no adherence to a law or to a dharma; instead they registered the alternation of aspects, not the succession of phenomena. If two aspects seemed to be connected, it was not a cause and effect sequence but a pairing in the relationing; the **I Ching** stated the pairing as "echo and sound" or "shadow and light."

Algebra has been described by Whitehead as the mathematical study of patterns, and algebra was characteristic of Chinese mathematics; the entire effort of their mathematicians was how to fit a problem into a pattern and solve it. Thus the Chinese discovered the principles of magnetism and devised a theory-practice of field physics. By the first century A.D. the Chinese were familiar with the principles and the prop-erties of a magnet long before the West and they invented the south-pointing carriage, the first cybernetic machine, again long before the West[5]. One may even go so far as to say that the idea of the Tao which appeared early in Chinese history was really a field of force[6] wherein all things oriented themselves according to it without having to be instructed or forced to do so and without being mechanical. The same cosmic field forces manifest in the **I Ching** hexagrams where Yin and Yang act as positive and negative poles; indeed the Chinese stumbled upon the field force of their own planet when they devised the compass.

[5] It is the authors' opinion that the Chinese did not use the cybernetic machine because it would have disrupted their sociological order. Politically and economically, they were not ready for it. Cybernetics needs a cybercultural environment to flourish, a society of abundance, not scarcity, a society where the machine does not create unemployment, but leisure.

[6] An interesting study would be a comparison of the field force theory by the eminent gestalt psychologist Kurt Lewin with the story of the Tao .

The statement made by Needham about Chinese civilization specifically applies to the nervous system and to the pulse. "In such a system causality is reticular and hierarchically fluctuating, not particulate and singly catenarian. . . . At one time one gland or nerve centre may take the highest place in a hierarchy of causes and effects, at another time another, hence the phrase 'hierarchically fluctuating.' "[7]

It is useful at this point to remind the reader of similar developments of the field force theories. The Burr-Northrop studies at Yale University showed that the electrical potential found in the human body is directly related to an electrical pattern; this pattern dictates the nature of the organism, but it is not an inflexible form. Rather it is a patterning principle in the sense that it evolves and changes. As the patterning evolves, so the organism evolves, assumes form, grows, matures, remains constant; then the organism builds new cells, but always organizes them after the original design. The organism is recreated, but always with the pattern dictated. The patterning here is a dynamic process, not a static entity. The patterning is determined in the sub-atomic field and given the same environment, it evolves with fidelity.

The East always recognized and the West has begun to recognize that the law of life is motion, a rhythmic cyclic pulsation of radiant energy which always tends to restore balance and harmony, as Maryle De Chrapowicki stated in the twentieth century, as the Burr-Northrop investigations revealed, or as the ancient Chinese asserted. One "takes his pick" of which he chooses to praise, but he must begin to have an open mind in seeing that man stumbles on natural laws regardless of what the anthropologists attribute to diffusion or independent invention. (For a fuller discussion, see Amber's **Color Therapy,** pp. 38-39.)

The Chinese Beliefs Applied to the Readings of the Pulse

According to the system propounded in the **Nei Ching,** man was subdivided into a lower, a middle, and an upper region and each of these regions was again subdivided three times, each subdivision containing an element of heaven, an element of earth, and an element of man. This scheme of subdivisions was concurrent with another scheme according to which each of the three main subdivisions was held to be composed of one part of Yin and one part of Yang: i.e., the human body was regarded as consisting of three parts of Yin and three parts of Yang. Since treatment of a specific disease or a specific organ depended largely on its location within a particular part of Yin or Yang, knowledge of these subdivisions was very important for diagnosis as well as for treatment. Disease was therefore the upsetting of the natural balance of the Yin and the Yang, the negative and the positive forces that animate all life, whose pattern is the same in the universe—whether micro or macroscopic.

In ancient China, there were men who understood and lived in accordance with Tao, the right way. They patterned their action upon the Yin and the Yang in harmony with the arts of divination. They were temperate in their eating habits, kept regular hours and lived simply.

---

[7] J. Needham, **op. cit.,** vol. 2, p. 289.

Thus they maintained the union of body and mind. The leaders (who were not priests) taught those beneath them to restrain their desires, to live with peace in their hearts without fear and to toil with a minimum of fatigue. The **Nei Ching** then went on to detail the four classes: spiritual men, sapient men, sages, and men of excellent virtues (their highest rank) and to relate all their activities to their manifesting balance between Yin and Yang and harmony with the Tao in the following:

Spiritual men were the earliest. They mastered the Yin and Yang and controlled the universe. They lived in accordance with Tao, the right way. **Sapiens** followed. They preserved their virtue and upheld the Tao and lived in accord with the Yin and the Yang and in harmony with the four seasons. They retired from the world of affairs that they might save their energies and preserve their spirits. They roamed the universe and at last they attained the state of the spiritual man. Then came the **sages** who attained harmony with heaven and earth, adjusted their desires to worldly affairs. They harbored no hatred or anger in their hearts. While they were indifferent to customs, they did not separate themselves from the activities of the world. They did not over exert themselves either at physical labor or with strenuous meditations. They regarded inner happiness and peace as fundamental and contentment as the highest achievement. It was said that their bodies could never be harmed nor their mental faculties be dissipated. Next came the **men of excellent virtues** who followed the rules of the universe and emulated the sun and the moon. They studied astronomy (astrology); they foresaw Yin and Yang and obeyed them; they followed the ancients' way and tried to maintain their harmony with Tao.

The theory of Yin and Yang and its relationship to the five elements are bound up with explanations of Chhi and Li and elucidations of Chi Hua or the life force; all play a counterpuntal theme about the function of the doctor when he reads the pulse in relating the man to the disease. What is the Chinese theory about disease? The **Nei Ching** observes the principles in nature and the four seasons are the beginning and the end of everything and they are the cause of life and death. Those who disobey the laws of the universe will give rise to calamities and visitations, while those who follow the laws of the universe remain free from dangerous illnesses, for they are the ones who obtain Tao, the right way. Yin and Yang must be respected to an equal extent. The interaction of Yin and Yang, the negative and positive principles in nature, is responsible for disease which befalls those who are rebellious to the laws of nature. In health, the two principles are in harmony. Disease is disharmony. To cure disease, they must be brought into harmony.

The physician who uses Chi Hua or life force in diagnosis and treatment knows that it has two forms: potential Yin and kinetic Yang and that a vibration consists of the interchange of the two from inception to climax: the kinetic energy decreases, being converted to potential. From climax to reversal, potential energy decreases and becomes kinetic. From reversal to anti-climax, kinetic energy decreases becoming negative potential and from negative potential, it returns to positive kinetic energy at the inception of the new vibration. The positive kinetic energy is upper Yang; positive potential energy is lower Yin; negative kinetic energy is lower Yang; negative potential energy is upper Yin.

Since the Chinese physician's problem was and is to keep man in balance and to heal him if he is in a state of imbalance or disharmony, he utilizes the pulse in two ways that are markedly different from the Western physician's use: first, as a reading of the relationship of the organs to each other and then as an indication of the actual state of each organ. Since he has been trained to know and to trace the condition of each organ as it reflects very precisely to the pulse, he is able to read the twelve classical pulses, six on each wrist: three superficial and three deep.

For the narrator of medical history, it is interesting to trace the way in which the Chinese became increasingly adept in their readings of the pulse. Their classic treatise on internal medicine and supposedly the oldest medical book extant is **Huang Ti Su Wên Nei Ching (Pure Questions of the Yellow Emperor; The Canon of Internal Medicine)** by an unknown writer. Upon it is built most of the medical literature of China; so important is it to medical men that even at present, thousands of years after its writing, is it regarded as one of the world's great medical authorities. Tradition assigns the writing of this volume to the time of Huang-Ti with the legendary date as 2698 to 2598 B.C., but recent scholarship places it in the Chhin dynasty (221 to 207 B.C.) or the Han Dynasty (202 B.C. to 220 A.D.). Whatever the date, there is no denying that the Chinese had assigned these pulse readings of the various organs for the physician to follow in his diagnosis.

The lungs are found at the Ts'un right; the stomach at Kuan right; the heart at Ts'un left; the liver at Ku'an left; and the kidneys at Ch'ih left.

The five Tsang or Yin organs were perfectly localized upon the wrists by this time. It was Wang Shu Huo[8] who wrote the **Meh Ching** or "Classic of the Pulse" that established the concept of the deep and superficial pulses. He showed that the deep pulses were the Yang organs and the superficial, the Yin organs.

Basic to the pulse reading of the organs is the physicians' use of the Chi Hua principle, their term for the life force. Earlier in this chapter, the relationship of **Chhi** to **Li** had been established but now the **Li** and **Chi Hua** should be interrelated as though they were one force for at one time they act as a creative force and at another time as matter. The fact that matter is bound-up energy (the key to atomic physics) was unknown to the Chinese philosophers, but only one theoretician came

---

[8] Wang Shu Huo (265-317 A.D.), author of **Mei Ching** or **Mo Ching,** was the Court physician during the Western Chin dynasty. The work consists of 10 volumes and is a summary of all the traditional methods and knowledge on this subject together with his own comments and observations. A spurious work called **Mo Chueh, or The Secret of the Pulse,** which appeared at about the period of the five dynasties (907-960 A.D.) has often been mistaken for the genuine work of Wang Shu Huo.

Hervieu, a French missionary, mistook the **Mo Chueh** for Wang Shu Huo's **Mo Ching** and translated the greater part of it into French in 1735. Du Halde also included it in his **Descriptive Geographique Historique Chronologique Politique de l'Empire de la Chine.** Brookes translated the French version into English. Chang Shih-hsien of the Mings was also misled and wrote an illustrated commentary on the **Mo Chueh** entitled **T'u Chu Mo Chueh** in which form it has been used to the present day. Reprints of the original classic of Wang Shu Huo's still exist though they are scarce. As Chinese doctors lay great stress on the pulse, the **Mo Ching** is regarded as one of the standard works on medicine.

close to understanding this intimate relationship—Wang Chhuan-Shan—when he observed that **Li** was no more important than **Chhi** or that organization was no more important than matter or energy. Perhaps others had speculated in a similar way, but if so, the methodology and technology for unlocking this energy eluded all.

The pragmatists who used and still use this knowledge that Li and Chi Hua could act as a creative force at one time and as matter at another were the medical practitioners, for they were and are aware that energy influences matter and organization or form. They accommodate to this in their belief that Chi Hua, the life force, influences matter and that there is an apparatus in the body—the meridians—that carries the energy to every cell. This life force is not conducted by the circulatory or the nervous systems. Among their enumeration of the twelve organs, the Chinese have two classifications—the tri-heaters and the heart constrictor—which are unknown to the West; these two organs[9] carry the energies: thermal, neural, electrical, etc. The Acupuncture points are some of the control centers of the body, but that is a story different from this account. The pulse is another of the body's master signals, an extremely important flashboard to which the organs send their pulsating vibrations—numbers, intensities and frequencies—or on which the organ reflexes are constantly flashed whether or not the individual reads and interprets them for the proper diagnosis and healing. The body flashes its own vibration signal lights to the pulse and perhaps it would be best to end this chapter with Goethe's famous phrase, "Mehr licht, mehr licht."

Chinese Bibliography in Three Parts

Primary Sources for Chinese Medicine

Every selection of material is dictated by the writers' purpose. Basic to this study upon the pulse are the five texts which will be treated, before other writings are enumerated, in the following chronological order:

1. The Yellow Emperor or the **Nei Ching**; the Yellow Emperor's **Manual of Internal Medicine** and later called **The Spiritual Pivot.**
2. Pien Ch'iao, the **Nan Ching or the Classic or Difficulty** (81 passages of the Yellow Emperor's **Nei Ching** explicated).
3. Wang Shu Ho, the **Mei Ching**, the **Classic of the Pulse.**
4. Chang Chung-Ching, the **Shang-han-lun** or **Essay on Typhoid.**
5. Sun Ssŭ-Mo, **the Sun-chen-jên ch'ien-chin-fang, A Thousand Golden Remedies.**

1. The Yellow Emperor, an unknown writer, **Huang Ti Nei Ching Su Wên, Pure Questions of The Yellow Emperor; the Canon of Internal Medicine,** ch. 1-34 translated from the Chinese by I. Veith, with an Introductory Study, Williams and Wilkins, Baltimore, 1949. (Her translation is to be read with caution since her knowledge of Chinese medicine is superficial.)

---

9 The tri-heaters represent a composite function which synthesizes the absorption of all energies. They are placed in the category of Fu which are the organs of intermittent physiology; are concerned with nutrition and excretion (digestion) ; are Yang by nature. It is only through the intermedium of the tri-heaters that the organism can absorb and transfer the vital energy necessary to life. They are concerned with respiratory, digestive, and sexual functions.

This is regarded as the oldest medical book extant and is also a Chinese classic; here the ancient Chinese views on physiology and pathology are explained. It is written in the form of a dialogue between Huang Ti and the Minister of his court. Though authorship is ascribed to the Yellow Emperor, it is believed that he was a legendary figure probably invented by the Taoists; for each successive ruling house or dominant philosophy was inclined to place an essentially invented character at the head of the list of ancient culture-heroes in order to heighten its own prestige.

Traditions assign the writing of this volume to the time of Hung-Ti with the legendary dates as 2698 to 2598 B.C., but recent scholarship, as seen in Needham's study, places it in the Chhin dynasty (221-207 B.C.) or to the Han dynasty (202 B.C to 220 B.C.). A word about Chinese historiography and modern interpretations would be in order at this point. **The Annals of the Bamboo Books**, a collection of bamboo tablets said to have been discovered in 281 A.D. in the tomb of Hsiang, King of Wei who died in 295 B.C., are a safe source for the history of China before 841 B.C. Among the discoveries in the tomb were the text of the **I Ching** and the **Annals** from the time of Huang Ti to 298 B.C. If the **Nei Ching** is placed in the third century B.C., where would Pien Ch'iao and his study of the pulse be placed if he is a fifth century physician and if his work discussed eighty-one difficult passages of the **Nei Ching**?

The authors discussed this matter of dates of texts with several Chinese and Japanese historians, and one scholar, in particular, observed that there was always a change of dates in order to bring Western thought in closer agreement with Eastern developments. He cogently remarked, "At the rate they are going, Christ will be older than Buddha." It is also interesting to note that if the modern dates are accepted, then the time of the Yellow Emperor was also the time of the Persian Darius the Great and the Indian Chandragupta who established the great Maurya Empire and who, in his youth met with Alexander the Great.

Mention should be made, among the other issues, of the edition by Wang Ping entitled **Huang Ti Ni Ching, Ling Shu, The Yellow Emperor's Manual of Internal Medicine; the Spiritual Pivot (or Gate or Driving Shaft or Motive Power)**. This is useful as a medical text and may be called the "Gray's Anatomy of Acupuncture."

2. Pien Ch'iao or Pien Chhio, the nickname for a Chinese physician named Ch'in Yueh Jen, is called the Chinese Galen. He lived in the state of Cheng possibly in the first half of the fifth century B.C. and was probably the author of the **Nan Ching**, one of the most popular treatises on medicine, and some say that he discovered the Chinese theory of the pulse. The fact that Diogenes, who flourished in the second half of the century, had some knowledge of the pulse has led some scholars to ask whether or not Diogenes knew of his work

The **Nan Ching** or **Classic of Difficulty** is a medical treatise explicating eighty-one difficult passages selected by the Yellow Emperor from the **Nei Ching**. No mention of it is found in the **Annals of Art** of the Han dynasty. The Sui and T'ang **Annals** state that the book was composed by Pien Ch'iao and that a commentary on it was written by Lu Kuang, the Court physician. It may be inferred from this that the **Nan Ching** was published before the period of the "Three Kingdoms." Many centuries earlier than the Ptolemaic School of Anatomy at Alexandria, Pien Ch'iao dissected cadavers and also elaborated a "Science of the Pulse." The Alexandrians carried out dissection though Galen and his teachers never dissected the human body. (A curious story is told about this semi-legendary physician. He performed an operation in which the hearts of two men were transplanted, a process which exchanged their minds while leaving their appearance and will-power unaltered.) No less than eleven commentaries were devoted to the Nan Ching before the Ming dynasty.

The text of the Nan Ching may be found in the Ku-chin t'u shu chi ch'eng, vol. 842. Many separate editions exist. F. Huebotter has made a German translation of it (November 1924); hitherto unpublished.

Criticism: A. Wylie: Chinese Literature, [1876 (1902) 97; with information on later commentaries]. H. A. Giles: Biographical Dictionary (155, 1898). F. Huebotter: Berühmte Chinesische Aerzte (Archiv fur Geschichte der Medizin, t. 7, 115-128, 1913). Contains an annotated translation of chapter 105 of the Shih-chi, Pien Ch'iao's biography. L. Wieger: La Chine (41, 57, 449, 1920). F. Huebotter: Guide (10-15, Kumamoto, 1924; includes brief analysis of the Nan Ching; Isis, VII, 259).

3. Wang Shu Ho (265-317 A.D.) was court physician and author of the Mei Ching or Mo Ching or Meh Ching, The Classic of the Pulse. His work consists of ten volumes of a summary of all traditions, methods, and knowledge and his is the principal manual of the pulse. He was the first to discuss adequately the energy systems of the body, as can be seen from his explanations of the tri-heaters and the heart constrictor. Reprints of this standard work still exist. His book was translated into English by Mei Yi Pao to be included in The Ethical and Political Works of Mo Tzu, Probsthain, London, 1929. In this volume is found the book on the pulse. The reader is also referred to the translations by Alfred Forke, "Moti . . . etc." Mitteilungen d Seminar f. Orientalische Sprachen (Berlin, 1922), Bei Bande, vols. 23-25.

A spurious work called Mo Chueh or The Secret of the Pulse which appeared about 907-960 has often been mistaken for the genuine work by Wang Shu Ho. Hervieu, a French missionary, mistook the Mo Chueh for Wang Shu Ho's Mo Ching and translated the greater part of it into French in 1735. Du Halde also included it in his study. Brookes translated the French version into English. Chang Shih-hsien of the Mings was also misled and wrote a commentary entitled T'u Chu Mo Chueh, in which form it exists to the present day.

In 1313, Rashid al Din al Hamdani, a Persian physician and patron of learning, included the Mo Ching in his encyclopaedia of Chinese medicine for circulation in the Arab world.

4. Chang Chung-Ching was also called Chang Chi or Chi Chung-ching. This sage of Chinese medicine was born either in Nan-Yang, Honan, or in Tsao-yang-hsien, Hupeh, and lived at the end of the second century. He was called the greatest physician of his time. He wrote a treatise called Chin Kuai yu han yao lüeh fang lun, Synopsis of the Golden Chamber. This is a classic in three volumes dealing with disease and dietetics wherein many plants were enumerated. His Shang-han-lun or Essay on Typhoid is a famous classic which ranks with the Nei Ching and which enjoyed as long a popularity in the Far

East as Galen's work in the West. It is divided into ten chuän, of which the first deals with the pulse and the others with various fevers and suitable prescriptions. Published in 217 A.D., the original manuscript was lost and what has come down to us is a compilation by Wang Shu Ho, the great authority on the pulse, about 265-317 A.D.

The **Shang-han-lun** consists of ten volumes, but the name is a misnomer since it does not restrict itself to typhoid fever alone; it treats other diseases as well. There are 22 essays and 397 rules of treatment; 113 commentaries have been written on this book, but most of them have been lost. The best edition extant is one by Hua Shou of the Yuan dynasty entitled **Nan Ching Pen I.** In the Ming dynasty during the reign of Ching Te (1506-1521 A.D.), Chang Shih Hsien published an edition containing diagrams and annotations which have remained popular to this day. Dr. Hubatler has translated the **Nan Ching** into German.

Criticism: E. Bretschneider: **Botanicon sinicum** (Part 1, 41, Shanghai, 1882). Puschmann: **Geschichte der Medizin** (Bd. I, 38, 1902, B. Scheube). M. Courant: **Catalogue des livres chinois de la Bibliothèque Nationale** (t. 2, 81-83, 109, 1910). Berthold Laufer: **Sino Iranica**, 205, 1919 (Isis, 111, 301). F. Huebotter: **Guide** (16-18, Kumamoto, 1924; Isis, VII, 259).

5. Sun Ssu-Mo. Born in Hua-yuan, Shensi, he died at a very old age in 682. He was a Taoist, and his medical works were influenced by his religious training. He was the author of many Taoist medical works, and two of the most important will be mentioned. His **Yin-hai ching-wei** is a treatise on eye disease, but the most important of his works was his compilation of **Sun-chen-jên ch'ien-chin-fang, A Thousand Golden Remedies**, which was a general encyclopaedia of medicine in thirty volumes. This was divided as follows: (1-4) women's diseases; (5) children's diseases; (6-21) special pathology and therapeutics; (22, 23) swellings, ulcers, hemorrhoids; (24) antidotes; (25) emergency cases; (26-27) dietetics; (28) pulse; (29,30) acupuncture and moxibustion. He describes an ulcer of jealousy as a soft chancre; he is one of the early psychosomatic physicians.

There is also a **Supplement** of thirty volumes, likewise called **Ch'ien chin Fang**, in which appear several chapters of incantation and exorcising magic. Sun Ssŭ Mo does not mention Chang Chung Ching's famous **Classic on Typhoid** in his first work. But thirty years later he devoted two volumes to the subject in his **Supplement**. He has been immortalized as one of the deities with the name of Sun chin-Jen.

When the Imperial Medical School was reestablished in 1191 A.D., the Supplement to the **Thousand Golden Remedies** was one of the texts utilized. The others were the **Su Wên** or **Canon of Medicine, The Pulse**, Chao's **Pathology**, the **Essay of the Dragon Tree**, and books on surgery, acupuncture, and moxibustion.

Alphabetical Arrangement

Chang Chung Ching, see supra, item 4.

Ch'ao Yuan Fang was a Chinese physician who wrote a treatise on theoretical medicine, the **Ping-Yuan hou-lun**, between 605 and 609. Its 50 parts contain descriptions of seven kinds of genito-urinary troubles, of impetigo contagiosa, of "sandlice", of scabies; part 27 deals with hair diseases; part 28, with eye diseases; part 31, with tooth complaints; parts 39 to 42, with women's complaints; parts 43 to 44, with midwifery; parts 45 to 50, with children's diseases, but there is little reference to the pulse. See F. Huebotter: **Guide** (26-28, Kumamoto, 1924).

Chien-chênor, in Japanese, Kanjin; a Chinese physician who came to Japan in 755 and seems to have been the most important physician of that time in Japan. He died in 763 at the age of 77. The earliest hospital of any importance was founded at Nara in 758. See entry under Japanese medicine in secondary bibliography.

Chuang Tzu means the philosopher Chuang. His name was Chou and his surname Chuang; hence he is sometimes called Chuang Chou. Born in 330, in the State of Wei, modern Anhui, he was a Chinese philosopher, the greatest representative of Taoism and one of the most original thinkers of his country. He defended the doctrines of Lao Tze, laying stress on **the relativity of all things**, the unreality of the tangible world, the value of spiritual freedom, the preeminence of wu-wei. (He has been compared to Heraclitos and also to Plato.) He wrote the work which is now generally called the **Canon** (or the **Classic**) of **Nan Hua, Nan Hua Ching.** (Nan Hua is the name of a hill in Ts'ao-chou fu, Shantung, where he lived in retirement.) This work bears said title only since its canonization, under the T'ang emperor Hsuan Tsung, in 742.

Text: Frederick Henry Balfour: **The Divine Classic of Nan-Hua with Copious Annotations in English and Chinese** (Shanghai, 1881). Another translation by James Legge in the **Sacred Books of the East,** vols. 39-40, 1891 (together with the masterly commentary by Lin Hsi-chung dating from the first half of the seventeenth century). See also Lionel Giles, ed., "Musings of a Chinese Mystic," in **Wisdom of the East** (London, 1906, 112). Extracts were translated into German by Richard Wilhelm (Jena, 1912, 202 p.; Isis, I, 119, 1919). Criticism: H. A. Giles: **Chuang Tzu, Mystic, Moralist, and Social Reformer** (London, 1889); **Chinese Biographical Dictionary** (1898, 202-3).

Hsiao chi wrote **Wu Hsing Ta I, Main Principles of the Five Elements,** c. 600. This was the most important medieval book on the five elements.

Hsi Yuan Lu chi tsing or **Fatal Spots**; a standard work in forensic medicine (1241-1253 A.D.). To be compared with the Marmars, the Indian points.

Huang Fu was a physician and Confucianist who was called Shih An; he flourished under the Chin dynasty (215-282 A.D.). His most famous work is a treatise on Acupuncture, called **Chia-i-ching,** which became the fountain head of other works on the subject, but it was itself based upon older works. It is divided into 128 chapters and 12 chüan as follows: (1, 2) anatomy, physiology; (3) the 354 spots for acupuncture; (4) pulse, etc; (5) places where acupuncture is forbidden; (6-12) pathology ending with women's and children's diseases. See F. Huebotter: **Guide** (21-2, Kumamoto, 1924).

Huang Ti, see Yellow Emperor, supra, item 1.

Hua To or Yuan was born in Po-hsien Anhui and flourished probably between 190 and 265 A.D. A Chinese surgeon, he wrote **Hua T'o chung-ts'ang-ching.** The volume in its present form is certainly not his. The present edition was prepared by Teng ch'u ch'ung during the Sung dynasty. Chapters 1-11 deal with the pulse and physiology; 12 to 49, with pathology; and the rest, with special therapeutics. Hua To produced general anaesthesia by means of a wine of unknown composition called ma-fei-san or ma-yao.

This text is included in the great encyclopaedia **Ku-chin t'u-shu-chi-ch'eng.** The edition was revised by the Japanese physician Genko Hori, c. 1750. The biography was translated from Chinese sources by F. Huebotter, See **Meth. der Deutschen Gesellschaft für Naturkunde Oestasiens, Tokyo.** F. Huebotter: Guide (18-21, Kumamoto, 1924).

I-Ching was a Chinese Buddhist monk who traveled to India. He was born in 615 and died about 712. He is significant for his interest in medicine and three chapters of his book (27-29) deal with medical matters. He mentions the Ayurvedic medical systems and speaks well of Indian physicians, but remarks the best herbs are found in China, a country that has never been surpassed for the healing arts of acupuncture, cautery, and skill of feeling the pulse.

See J. Needham, **Science and Civilization in China,** Cambridge, At the University Press, 1954, vol. 1, pp. 208-211. J. Takakusu (translator), **A Record of the Buddhist Religion as Practised in India and the Malay Archipelago** (671 to 695) by I Tsing, Oxford, 1896. A. Barth, "Critique of Chavannes and of Takakusu", **Journal des Savants,** 1898, 261, 425, 522.

Kuo P'o was born in Wen hsi, Ho-tung, in 276 A.D. and was murdered in 324. A Taoist lexicographer, philosopher, astrologer, and occultist, he is the reputed founder of **fêng shui** (i.e., wind and water); he became famous as a soothsayer and for his practice of **fêng shui,** which is a development of the oldest cosmogonical ideas of the Chinese. His was a new application of their immemorial dualism, symbolized by Yang and Yin, the positive and negative, male and female principle of universal life. It is the "art of adapting the residence of the living and the dead so as to cooperate and harmonize with the local currents of the cosmic beath." It is misleading to translate **fêng shui** by geomancy; it is comparable to Western astrology, though very different. It is a complicated and very comprehensive discipline which obtained as much prestige in the Far East as astrology in the West. There are two collections of his predictions: the Tung-lin and Hsin-lin.

See H. A. Giles: **Chinese Biographical Dictionary** (Shanghai, pp. 408-9, 1898); **History of Chinese Literature** (138, London, 1901). S. Couling: "Feng Shui," Encyclopaedia Sinica, 175, 1917.

Li Chi, Book of Rites, Book 9, Sec. 26: "Li Yun"; 26—Translated by J. Legge, The Chinese Classics, vol. xxvii, Book 7, Sec. 3, pp. 380-381.

Ling Shu, see supra, item 1.

Li-Shih-chen, see secondary sources.

Pen Ts'ao, see Ying Kung.

Pien Ch'iao or Pien Chhio, see supra, item 2.

Shêng chi Tsung Lu or **Imperial Encyclopaedia of Medicine**—consists of 200 volumes and was compiled by a staff of physicians under imperial order and published about 1111 A.D. It deals with every branch of the healing arts known in China at that time, some of which are acupuncture, moxibustion, massage, emotional pathology, medical astrology, dieting, fasting, hydrotherapy, and the elixir of life. It was reprinted in 1300 A.D.

Sun Ssŭ Mo, see supra, item 5.

Su Wên, see supra, item 1.

Takakusu, J., see supra, I-Ching.

T'ang Pen Ts'ao, see Ying Kung.

Thai Hsi Ching, Manual of Embryonic Respiration, Date and author unknown. See Needham, for reference to TT/127, p. 605.

Tsun Sêng Pa Chien, Eight chapters on putting oneself in accord with the life force, 1591 A.D., Ming, Kao Lien. Abbreviated translation by Dudgeon.

See "Kung Fu or Medical Gymnastics," Journal of Peking Oriental Society, 1895, vol. III, 341, 376, 440, 454, 494, 516.

Wang Ping was a Chinese physician who wrote in 761 the earliest commentary in twenty-four books on the Huang-ti Nei-ching Su Wên, the Yellow Emperor.

See A. Wylie: Chinese Literature (96, 1868, 1902). L. Wieger: La Chine (462, 495, 1920); Histoire des Croyances (305-309, 1922. An analysis of the Su Wên). F. Huebotter: Guide (6-9, 30, Kumamoto, 1924).

Wang Shu Ho, see supra, item 3. Also Shu-Ho or Shu-Huo.

Wang Tao was a Chinese physician who was the author of a very comprehensive medical treatise published in 752 entitled Wai-t'ai-pi-yao or Important Secrets of the Outer Terrace. Its 40 parts include every branch of medicine and therapeutics and even a brief summary of veterinary art. The text available at present is very doubtful.

Criticism: F. Huebotter: Guide (31, Kumamoto, 1924).

Wang Wei-Te by order of the Emperor made in 1027 two copper figures of the human body to illustrate the art of acupuncture with 367 places being indicated. He wrote a treatise on the subject entitled T'ung-Jên chên-chiu ching.

See A. Wylie: Chinese Literature [101, (1867) 1902]. J. D. Ball: Things Chinese (8, 1904. Ball says that one of these plates is still extant, but he does not say where; however, he gives various references). "Acupuncture," Encyclopaedia Sinica, (7, 1917). L. Wieger: La Chine (466, 1920). Max Neuburger: Geschichte der Medizin (vol. 1, 105, 1906).

Wu Wei-Ping, Chinese Acupuncture, translated from Dr. J. Lavier's French Edition by Philip M. Chancellor, Health Science Press, Sussex, England, (1962-6).

Yellow Emperor, see supra, item 1.

Ying Kung, ed, T'ang Pen ts'ao.

The T'ang emperor Kao Tsung in 650 ordered the revision and completion of the materia medica, Pen ts'ao, then in use, which was the one edited at the beginning of the sixth century by T'ao Hung Ching on the basis of earlier works. This revision was directed by a high official Li-chi, also styled Ying Kung. Thus originated the T'ang Pen ts'ao of Ying Kung. A few years later, a new revision was edited by another high official, Su Kung. This was the new

Pen ts'ao of the T'ang, t'ang hsin pen ts'ao. Its substance was classified under the following headings: minerals, man, quadrupeds, birds, insects, fish, cereals, vegetables, fruits, trees, herbs, and natural objects not employed in medicine. It was contained in 20 books with one for the index plus 25 books of illustrations and 7 books explaining the illustrations.

L. Breitschneider: **Botanicon Sinicum** (part 1, 44-45, Shanghai, 1881).

Secondary Sources for Chinese Medicine

Bagchi, P. C., **INDIA AND CHINA; A Thousand Years of Sino-Indian Cultural Relations**, Hind Kitab, Bombay, 1944; second edition, 1950.

Boddhe, D., "Dominant Ideas in the Formation of Chinese Culture," **Journal of the American Oriental Society**, 62, 1942, p. 293. "The Chinese View of Immortality. Its Expression by Chu Hsi and Its Relationship to Buddhist Thought," **Review of Religions**, 1942, p. 369. "Dominant Ideas (of Chinese Thought) in China," in **China**, ed. H. F. McNair, University of California Press, Berkeley, 1946, p. 18.

Chamfrault, A. and Ung Kang-Sam, **Traité de Médecine Chinoise; d'après les Têxtes Chinois Anciens et Modernes**. Coquemard, Angoulême, 1954, 1957. vol. 1: Traité, Acupuncture, Moxas, Massages, Saignées. vol. 2: Les Livres Sacrés de Medecine Chinoise (Nei Ching, Su Wên and Ching, Ling Shu):

Chang Tzŭ-Ho was a Chinese physician who flourished during the Chin dynasty. His main work is the **Ju mên shih ch'in**, a treatise on internal medicine. (His medical theories were apparently the same as those of Liu Wan-su.) The first books contain generalities and the seven that follow deal with special pathology and therapeutics, but in number 14, he touches upon the prognostic signs taught by the ancient physicians.

Franz Huebotter: **Guide** (Kumamoto, 34, 1924; Isis, 7, 259); **Die chinesische Medizin** (22, 349, Leipzig, 1929; Isis, 14, 255-263).

Chekashige, M., **Alchemy and Other Chemical Achievements of the Ancient Orient; the Civilization of Japan and China in Early Times as Seen from the Chemical Point of View (and Metallurgical)**, Rokakuho Uchida, Tokyo, 1936.

Chien-chen, see Japanese Medicine below.

Forke, Alfred, **The World-Conception of the Chinese; Their Astronomical, Cosmological and Physico-Philosophical Speculations**, Probsthain, London, 1925. A Chinese and a German translation of this work appeared in 1925 and in 1927. "Lun Heng", **Philosophical Essays of Wang Chhung**, Pt. 1, 1907, Kelly and Walsh, Shanghai; Luzac, London: Pt. II, 1911 (Reimer edition, Berlin). **Mittelungen d Seminar f Orientalischen Sprachen**, (Berlin) Beibände 10 and 14. Originally published 1906, vol. 9, 181; 1907, vol. 10, 1; 1908, vol. 11, 1; 1911, vol. 14, 1. "Mo Ti des Sozialethikers und seiner Schüler philosophische Werke," Berlin, 1922, **ibid**, vols. 23-25. "Wang Chhung and Plato on Death and Immortality," **Journal of the Royal Asiastic Society, North China Branch**, 1896, vol. 31, p. 40.

Fujikawa, Yu, **Japanese Medicine**, tr. from German (1911) by John Ruhrah, M.D., with a chapter on the recent history of Japan by Kageya W. Amans.

Groot, Jan Jakob Maria de, **The Religious System of China**, Brill, Leiden, 1892, N. Y., 1912, 6 vols.

Gutzlaff, Rev. C., "The Medical Art among the Chinese," **Journal of the Royal Asiatic Society of Great Britain and Ireland**, London, John W. Parker, West Strand, MDCCCXXXVII, vol. IV, p. 168.

Hollis, H., "Chinese Medical Art," **Medical Library Association Bulletin**, 1944, vol. 32, pp. 318-323.

Huang Man (Wong Man), "The Nei Ching, the Chinese Canon of Medicine," **Chinese Medical Journal**, 1950, 68, I (Originally Inaug. Diss. Cambridge).

Huard, P., **Structure de la Medicien Chinoise**, 1957, 88 p.—and Ming Wang, **La Medicine au Cours des Siecles**, 1959.

Huebotter, Franz, **Die Chinesische Medizin**, 1929, Leipzig; Isis, 14, 255-263.

Hume, Edward H., The **Chinese Way in Medicine**, Baltimore, Johns Hopkins Press, 1940. "The Square Kettle," **Bulletin of the Institute of the History of Medicine**, 1934, II, pp. 547-557.

Japanese Medicine, see Part III of this bibliography.

Johnson, Obed, A., **A Study of Chinese Alchemy**, Shanghai, 1928.

Jung, C. G., see Wilhelm, Richard.

Latourette, K. S., **The Chinese, Their History and Culture**, N. Y., 1932, vols. 1 and 2.

Li-Shih-chen (1518-1593) was a naturalist and a pharmacist who made the greatest scientific achievement of the Ming period with his book, the **Pên Tshao Kang Mu**, which was finished in 1578 and appeared in 1596. About 1,000 plants and 1,000 animals are exhaustively described in sixty-two divisions as are the following: distillations, smallpox inoculations, therapeutic uses of mercury, iodine, kaolin, etc. In his classifications of fire, Li-Shih-chen makes a distinction between the essential heat-production of the body and the heat connected with muscular movement and, as Needham points out, he foreshadows our categories of basal metabolic rate and total output which is Yin. The heat of the viscera and generative organs he classified as Yang as he did meditation—fire of maintaining a high body temperature under continued exposure to cold—as performed by Yogis and certain Shamans.

Lu Wan-Su was a Chinese physician during the Chin dynasty. A good many medical treatises are ascribed to him and their titles show that his writings were inspired by the old classics like the **Nei Ching**. His medicine was dominated by a theory equivalent to the Western one of the micro and macrocosmos. Everything in man as well as in the larger universe is regulated by the two antagonistic and complementary principles yang and yin: that is, the male and female principles. Each of the five tsang or viscera corresponds to one of the five elements. Criticism: Franz Huebotter: **Guide** (Kumamoto, 33, 1924; Isis, 7, 259); **Chinesische Medizin** (22, 349, 353, Leipzig, 1929; Isis, 14, 255-263).

Morse, William Reginald, **Chinese Medicine**, N.Y., 1934, Clio Medica.

Needham, Joseph, **Science and Civilisation in China**, Cambridge, At the University Press, 1954, vol. 1: **Introductory Orientations;** 1956, vol. 2: **History of Scientific Thought;** 1962, vol. 4: **Physics and Physical Technology.**

Osgood, Elliot, **Breaking Down Chinese Walls** — A Doctor's Viewpoint, 1908, 217 p.

Radhakrishnan, S., **India and China**, Hind Kitab, Bombay, 1947.

Sarton, George, **Introduction to the History of Science,** Published for the Carnegie Institution of Washington, Publication No. 376, Williams and Wilkins Co., Baltimore, vol. I, 1927; vol. II, 1931; vol. III, 1931.

Sugihara, Noriyuki, "On Oriental Medicine," reprinted from **Acta Scholae Medicinalis in Gifu,** vol. 12, No. 4, Dec. 31, 1964.

Tibetan Medicine, see secondary bibliography.

Whitney, W., **Notes on History of Medical Progress in Japan,** Yokohama, 1883, pp. 245-469. Reprint, **Asiatic Society of Japan,** tr. v. 12.

Wiener, P.P., "Notes on Leibnitz' Conception of Logic and Its Historical Context," **Philosophical Historical Review,** 1939, vol. 48, p. 567.

Wilhelm, R., Jung, C., **The Secret of the Golden Flower; A Chinese Book of Life** (incl. tr. of the Thai I Chin Hua Tsung Chih) Eng. ed., tr. C. F. Baynes, Kegan Paul, London, 1931. **The I Ching or Book of Changes,** The Richard Wilhelm Translation Rendered into English by Cary F. Baynes, Foreword by C. G. Jung, Routledge and Kegan Paul, Ltd., London, 1960, 2 vols.

Williams, C. A. S., **Outlines of Chinese Symbolism, An Alphabetical Compendium of Antique Legends and Beliefs as Reflected in the Manners and Customs of the Chinese.** A limited edition of 250 signed copies with 200 illustrations in Chinese style, consisting of stone lithographs, woodcuts, photogravures, color plates and hand colored prints, Peiping, China, Customs College Press, 1931. **Outlines of Chinese Symbolism and Art Motives,** Shanghai, 1932, pp. 185.
Outlines of Chinese Symbolism and Art Motives, Shanghai, 1932, pp. 185.

Wong K. Chimin, "Chinese Medical Literature," **Chinese Medical Journal,** 1918, XXXII, p. 154. "Chang Chung-King, the Hippocrates of China," **ibid.,** 1924, XXXVIII, p. 940. "The Pulse Lore of Cathay," **ibid.,** 1928, XLII, pp. 884-897; reprint of same in the **History of Chinese Medicine.** "Some Famous Ancient Drugs," **The People's Tribune,** Shanghai, 1936, Dec. 1, pp. 333-338. "Chinese Medical Superstitions," **National Medical Journal,** China, 1916, II, p. 8.

Wong, K. Chimin (Licentiate of Medicine and Surgery, Hongkong, Formerly Lecturer on Medical History, National Central University; Chief Medical Officer, Shanghai-Ningpo Railway; Ex-President Chekiang Medical and Pharmaceutical Association, etc.) and Wu, Lien-Teh M.A., M.D. (Cantab); Dr. M. Sc. (Tokio); Hon. Litt. D. (Peking), (LL.D., Sc.D., Director and Chief Medical Officer, Manchurian Plague Prevention Service; Director, National Quarantine Service; Ex-President of the National Medical Association of China: Author of A Treatise of Pneumonic Plague, Etc.) **History of Chinese Medicine Being a Chronicle of Medical Happenings in China from Ancient Times to the Present Period,** Tientsin Press, Ltd., Tientsin, China, (1932). (This book should be read with care since one must bear in mind that the authors are prejudiced in favor of allopathic medicine.)

Secondary Bibliography on Japanese and Tibetan Medicine: Chinese Origins

Japanese Medicine

The Japanese names for the five basic Chinese texts translated and utilized are briefly listed below; an explanatory note is added under the entry for Chang Chung-Ching:

1. **Kon-ki** is their name for Chang Chung Ching's **Essay on Typhoid** (see supra, item 4) also **Kin-ki**.
2. **Sho-kanron** is their name for Chang Chung Ching's **Synopsis of the Golden Chamber** (see supra, item 4).
3. **So-mon** is their name for the Su Wên, the Yellow Emperor's **Manual** (see supra, item 1).
4. **Rei-sui** is their name for the **Classic of the Marvelous Pivot**, a later issue of the Yellow Emperor's **Manual** (see supra, item 1).
5. **Nan-kyo** is their name for Pien Ch'iao's **Nan-Ching** or the **Classic of Difficulty** (see supra, item 2).

Chang Chung-Ching. See supra, item 4 with reference to the **Shang-Han-lun** or **Essay on Typhoid** and the **Chin kuei yu han yao lueh fang lun, Synopsis of the Golden Chamber.**

These two treatises were among the first Chinese medical works to be imported into Japan, their Japanese names being respectively **Kin-ki** and **Sho-kanron.** The other Chinese works upon which Japanese medicine was primarily based or founded are the **Su-Wên** and the **Ling Shu** or **ch'u ching—Classic of the Marvelous Pivot** of the **Huang Ti Nei Ching** by the Yellow Emperor (see supra, item 1) and the **Nan-Ching** or the **Classic of Difficulty** (see supra, item 2). The Japanese names of these three works are respectively **So-mon, Rei-sui,** and **Nan-kyo.**

Texts: There are many Chinese and Japanese editions of the **Shang-han-lun.** Commentary: E. Bretschneider: **Botanicon sinicum** (part 1, 41, Shang-hai, 1882). Puschmann: **Geschichte der Medizin** (Bd. 1, 38, 1902, B. Scheube). M. Courant: **Catalogue des livres chinois de la Bibliothèque Nationale** (t. 2, 81-83, 109, 1910). Berthold Laufer: **Sino Iranica**, 205, 1919; Isis, 111, 301). F. Huebotter: **Guide** (16-18, Kumamoto, 1924; Isis, VII, 259).

Chien-chên or, in Japanese, Kanjin was a Chinese physician who came to Japan in 755 and died in 763 at the age of 77. The earliest Japanese hospital of any importance was founded at Nara in 758 by order of the Empress Komyo, who had become a nun at the time of the abdication of her husband Shomu in 749. The foundation may thus be ascribed to Buddhist influence.

See Y. Fujikawa: **Geschichte der Medizin in Japan** (10, 97, Tokyo, 1911).

Kwanroku was a Buddhist physician who came from Kudara to Japan in 1602 during the reign of the Empress Suiko (593 to 628) and taught medicine to a few Japanese students. In 1608, the Empress sent a number of young Japanese physicians to China. The direct influence of Chinese upon Japanese medicine may be dated from that time.

See Y. Fujikawa: **Geschichte der Medizin in Japan** (6, 97, Tokyo, 1911).

Wake Hiroyo was a Japanese educator and physician of the late eighth century who wrote an important treatise on materia medica called **Yakkeitaiso** in two volumes. It is derived from the Chinese work **Hsin-hsiu pen ts'ao** by Su King (see supra, Ying Kung, ed. **T'ang Pen ts'al**); it deals with 254 drugs, borrowed from the three kingdoms of nature, explaining their preparation, preservation, use, and effects. He was the chief of the medical department (ten-yaku-ryo) of the imperial court, the head of the university (Daigaku-betto) which he endowed, and about the year 800, he founded a private school—Kobun-in—with a large library. This was the first free school in Japan.

See E. Papinot: **Historical Dictionary** (293, 734, 1909); Y. Fujikawa: **Geschichte der Medizin** (20, 1911).

Yasuyori Tamba was a Japanese physician who compiled about 982 the **Ishinhō,** the oldest Japanese treatise on medicine which is still extant in its original form. It is essentially derived from the **Ping-yuän-hou-lun** of the Ch'ao Yuäng-fang (see supra) (first half of the seventh century) and other Chinese works. It is divided as follows: (1) generalities; (2) acupuncture; (3) diseases of pneuma; (4) internal diseases; (5) skin diseases; (6) eye, ear, and teeth diseases; (7) hands and feet; (8) abscesses and tumors; (9) wounds; (10) pediatrics; (11) gynaecology and obstetrics; (12) hygiene; (13) sexual hygiene; (14) dietetics; (15) materia medica.

See Y. Fujikawa, **Geschichte der Medizin** (13, 20, 21, 1911).

Tibetan Medicine

Tibetan medicine is linked with Buddhism and with the adaptation of the Sanskrit alphabet to the Tibetan language. In 632, Song-tsen, King of Tibet, sent Tun Mi to India to investigate both Buddhism and Sanskrit. This alphabet was thus introduced and the Tibetan language was then for the first time reduced to writing. Tibetan civilization received its first impulse from India and subsidiarily from China, but the Chinese influences became gradually more important. The common kinship of Tibetans, Chinese, and Mongolians asserted itself against Hindu leadership. Hindu teachings reached Tibet through Nepal, the population of which is essentially Mongolian. Thus even Hindu influences were not purely Hindu, but were already colored by Mongolian conceptions. From China came tea, butter, cheese, barley-beer, ceramics, and water-mills.

With reference to medicine, two terms are important: **Kanjur** and **Tanjur.** They are linked to Buddhism and Tibetan scriptures, the equivalent of the Chinese **Tripitaka.** The **Kanjur,** meaning **Translation of the Word,** is a translation of 108 volumes from the Sanskrit to form the Buddhist Canon of the Tibetans made between the seventh and thirteenth centuries, but the greater part of which was translated in the second half of the ninth century. There are two editions of the **Kanjur:** the older is printed in Western Tibet; the other and later is printed in Eastern Tibet.

This enormous Canon was supplemented by a Commentary more than twice as large called the **Tanjur** which is divided into two classes: the Sanskrit Tantra on ritual and ceremonies and the Sutra on science and literature. The Sutras are of interest since they contain works which are neither specifically Buddhist nor even religious, even as the Christian Bible does not contain only

religious texts, but many others of secular interest. The early sacred writings
of these people are the true equivalents of our modern encyclopaedia; they
included the whole of knowledge. And some five volumes of the **Tanjur** are
devoted to medicine.

In addition to the **Kanjur,** which had some medical information, and
to the five volumes on medicine in the **Tanjur,** there is an independent medical treatise entitled "rGyud-bsi" (sic) meaning "The Four Tantras." Native
traditions record that a Tibetan interpreter translated it in Kashmir with
the assistance of a physician-pundit and presented it to King Ti-song De-tsen.
It is divided into four parts: (1) arteries, veins, nerves, and pulses; (2) "explanation" of the body and causes of diseases; (3) "instruction" as to the
treatment of diseases; (4) "external" treatment, etc.

Texts: Alexander Csoma de Körös published an English analysis of it
on the basis of the Tibetan summary prepared for him by his Lama instructor
(**Journal Asiatic Society of Bengal,** vol. 4, 1835; reprinted in the **Tibetan
Studies, Journal Asiatic Society of Bengal,** vol. 7, 1911, extra No., 47-65).
See also Heinrich Laufer: **Beitrage zur Kenntnis der Tibetischen Medizin**
(2 parts, 90 p. Berlin and Leipzig, 1900. Elaborate study of Tibetan medicine
arranged in systematic order, all the facts relative to each medical subject,
say physiology, special pathology, diagnostic or balneology being put together;
this very important investigation was carried out with the philological
assistance of the author's brother, Berthold. Only 200 copies were printed.)

E. H. C. Walsh: "The Tibetan Anatomical System" **JOURNAL R. AS.
SOC.,** 1215-1245, 1910, 1 large plate. This deals mainly with an anatomical chart
kept in the Temple of Medicine at Lhasa, which, together with its connected
monastery, forms the medical college of Tibet. Every Tibetan doctor is
taught his anatomy from it. It is called **Pyang-khok las thig:** i.e., the chart
divided by lines; it is divided into a number of squares to identify the locations
of particular organs. A facsimile of the chart is attached to this memoir.)

K. Sudhoff: "Die Anatomischen Ganzfiguren in Tibetanischer Uberlief-
erung" (**Archiv. für Geschicht der Medizin,** vol. 8, 143-145, 2 fig., 1915.)

Chapter III

AYURVEDIC HEALING PRECEPTS

Indian medicine is really Ayurvedic medicine, for Ayurveda signifies the science of life which includes among other aspects, the subjects of medicine, philosophy, cosmology, biology, pharmacology, astronomy, and physics. But Ayurvedic medicine in applying its precepts always walks the path of the Tridoshas. Before an account is made of their doctrine of the five elements, their structuring of the atom or their divisioning of matter, the Indian theory of the Tridoshas should be briefly related as it evolved from the philosophic beliefs and religious practices. What mode of reasoning led the Ayurvedists to use the Tridoshas of Air, Fire, and Water as the three basic forces for health and disease in their healing beliefs? Without an intimate knowledge of these three, no pulse could be taken.

The Tridoshas in Indian medicine represent the extension of the Hindu triad of Gods, and this "Trinity" (the gods Brahma, Vishnu, and Siva) represents Creator, Preserver, and Destroyer. Thus the theory concerns itself with the internal and external conditions and with the production or the loss of equilibrium of the three elements in the human body. With the Tridoshas, man is more than a mass of bones, flesh, skin, and chemicals; he is a living organism and all parts of his body vibrate with life. Thus this theory embraces the whole man and the environs.

Some authorities claim that Tridosha is the crown of the Indian medical science. Nothing can transcend the three forces which permeate the whole world and all names and forms must be traced to their basic powers before they can be of any use to the physician, who is grounded in their applications to the body. Though both India and China have a theory of the five elements, the classifications of the five differ; the Indians see the five as omnipresent in the Tridoshas so that they empower their Trinity with the five. The Chinese add two elements—Wood and Metal—and never smother the five elements in their Yin-Yang or Wave theories of shifting relations so that they were able to develop an organismic theory of constantly changing relations by the impersonal aspects of the Yin-Yang. The Indians sought to correct the imbalances of the body when the three forces were deranged (see Amber's **Color Therapy** for a fuller discussion). Thus the five elements were inextricably a part of the three forces (called Tridoshas when in disharmony) which functioned upon the seven systems in the human body. The Tridoshas are termed Vayu for air, Pitha for fire, and Kapha for water. When they work in perfect harmony, a state of balance or Tridhatus manifests as health, strength, and longevity for the individual. It is the Ayurvedic belief that the three forces, each with the five divisions of activities, account for the human energies manifesting in the body as chemical, electrical, mechanical, nervous, psychic, thermal, and the like.

Whether the Chinese borrowed from the Hindus and the Iranians or they from the Chinese is not the concern of this study. Neither will the question begun in the nineteenth and continued into the twentieth century in Indian medical literature be debated: namely, "Is allopathic medicine an off-shoot of Ayurvedic and of its worst aspects?" Let the theoreticians of the future engage in this polemic. The concern here is with a comparative evaluation of the philosophic precepts and their technological reflections in reading the pulse to diagnose the illnesses of man as propounded by the Ayurvedic school of indigenous medicine.

The Ayurvedist arrives at his conclusion through a scientific methodology known as Darsanas, a term which means that by which truth is manifested, that which deals with demonstrable doctrine. Consequently Darsanas means a science[1] where the facts of natural phenomena are collected and classified and where their mutual relations are then determined; these are followed by a description of their sequence and the knowledge generalized. For them, the understanding of nature's phenomena could be arrived at by perceptual observation, conceptual knowledge, or intuitional experience. One of their foremost medical authorities—Charaka, who dates from the second century B.C.—enumerates this series for the physician:

1. Direct observation.
2. Application of deductive, inductive, and analogical reasoning to analyze the facts observed.
3. Paying due regard to known authoritative knowledge on the subject under study or, as an alternative, commencing and following the study with direct observation.
4. Submitting the facts of observation to crucial analysis with the help of deductive, inductive, and analogical reasoning.
5. Validating the conclusions reached in the process by experimentation.

Their methodology also included preventive and curative medicine. With reference to prophylactic procedures, the doctor advised the patient how he should conduct himself during the day or at night, during the seasons of the year, and at the various stages of life. In curative medicine, the diseases of the body were classified and the areas of treatment then mapped out in the following way:

1. Shalya — surgery.
2. Shalakya — diseases above the neck: eyes, ears, nose, etc.
3. Kaya Chikitsa — constitutional diseases such as fever, diarrhea, bronchitis, etc.
4. Kaumara Bhritya — division which treats of children's diseases, pregnancy, and post-parturition.
5. Bhuta Vida — diseases of the "Super-Physics" (Metaphysics).

---

[1] The Indian term for the methodolgy of science is Vaiseahika-Nyaya.

6. Agadutantra — poisons and their antidotes.
7. Rasayna — rejuvenating the worn out bodily tissues and so preventing
the effects of age on the system.
8. Vajeekarana — remedies which restore the impaired and dissipated
virile powers.

The Ayurvedists have their theory of the five elements, like the
Chinese, but the elements are differently classified in both cultures. They
also list five aspects of the atom, termed tanmatras, five properties of
matter, and five subdivisions for each dosha. The differences in their interpretation of the five elements, atoms, and properties of matter can be
disregarded for the moment in order to note the significance of the
number five in these Eastern cultures and the similarity in their use of
this number. Anthropologists have demonstrated that primitives used
arithmetic to the base five; and in the section of the I Ching, an explanation was tendered of how the Chinese use of the symbols was possibly a
degeneration of this ancient form of arithmetic. The relationships developed by correlative thinking, the use of the base number five, and the
symbology growing out of a series of interrelations provide an interesting
comparison of the healing practices in both cultures. The Chinese, it is
true, in their symbology presented correlations that strain the modern
readers' patience. But their use of the base number five in relation to the
elements and to the body proved helpful in the observations of man's
illness and in the interpretation of the pulse. The Ayurvedists—also
using the number five, but resting on a monistic theory—were led to
note the energy flow of the body and the disturbances in the body, but
they did not stress the organ or organs' relationships. Both Ayurvedic and
Chinese cultures sought to restore balance and both knew how to direct
the energy flow of the body to correct disturbances, but then the two
cultures parted to travel along different paths. The Ayurvedists do not
pinpoint the organ or organs out of balance. The Chinese—guided by the
Yin-Yang theory, by polarity and waves that reflect themselves in an
on or off principle of shifting relations—give a detailed account of organ
to organs, of part to part and part to whole, of adjusting and balancing
the body part of the whole to emphasize this rule: a changing relationship
and a cyclical rhythm must be continually interpreted since they are
constantly being manifested. The Ayurvedists never developed this type
of organismic relationship. Did their one-ness, unity, or the Brahman
principle constrict their viewpoint?

Five Elements

According to Ayurvedic, all matter is made up of five elements,
but these five are not to be confused with the Tridoshas, their term
for the three forces in disease or disharmony. The five elements, however, appear in various combinations in the Tridoshas. The elements
with their physical characteristics are listed below together with their
symbols: what is to be noted is that the same names are given to the
tanmatras, the five atoms in Ayurvedic physics:

1. Ether or Akasha: possesses penetrability; contributes to the finer
etheric essence which is life in the body as we know it; light, rarified,
elastic, vibration or capable of sound; symbol-AK.

2. Air or Vayu: is the driving force which sets the other elements in motion; is the motor force in the body; possesses impact; exerts mechanical pressure; is the carbohydrate; is a gaseous state, light, cold, dry, transparent, rarified, impinging; symbol-V.

3. Fire or Tejas: possesses heat and light; gives metabolic heat to body; is the hydro-carbon; light or radiant matter; hot, penetrative, subtle, light, dry, clear, rarified, and luminous; symbol-T.

4. Water or Ap: is the womb or medium through which the other elements cohere to form compound substances; is the liquid state; possesses viscous attraction; yields to pressure; is watery part of the organic fluids; viscous, cold, soft, slippery, fluid; exciting the sense of taste; symbol-AP.

5. Earth or Prithvi: is the primordial force or matrix for the formation of all substances; is the fundamental unit of matter, the nucleus or radicle around which the other four elements are grouped in a definite ratio and form; possesses cohesive attraction, tactile qualities; is sensitive to touch; its compounds supply the hard, formed matter of the body, like bones; is the nitrogen compound in the foods; is the solid state; heavy, rough, hard, inert, dense, opaque; excites the sense of smell; symbol-P.

The Five Tanmatras—Ayurvedic Physics of the Atom[2]

In Ayurvedic physics there are five atoms termed tanmatras, and they may be said to correspond to the proton of modern science; but where Western science has only one type of proton, Ayurveda lists five. When the Hindus speak of their tanmatras as being specific kinds of energy, they mean motion, for to them energy is motion and motion signifies matter. The five tanmatras possess something more than quantum of mass and energy; they possess different physical characteristics; some of them penetrability; others, powers of impact and pressure: still others, radiant heat; and some, capability of viscous and cohesive attraction. In intimate relations to these physical characteristics, they also possess the potentials of the energies represented by sound, touch, color, taste and smell; but being subtle matter, they are devoid of the peculiar forms which these potentials assume in particles of gross matter, like the atoms and their aggregates. The potential lodged in subtle matter must undergo transformations by new groupings or collocations to be classed among sensory stimuli. The tanmatras are infra-atomic particles charged with specific potential energies. The Ayurvedic classifications and formulae are given below and they should be appraised in their three relations— a position in space, in the time series, and in the causal series:

1. Akasha: a mono-tanmatra; is protomatter charged potentially with the energy of sound; possesses the physical vibration of energy; is the root of all protomatter, but is not itself a tanmatra; is the link between the infra-atomic particles and the atom; is sound stimulus; possesses penetrability. The formula is AK_1 (V.T.AP.E) AK_1 being the radicle.

2. Vayu: a di-tanmatras; is protomatter charged potentially with the

2 The Sankhya-Patanjala system accounts for the universe or cosmic evolution.

energy of tactile powers; its particles possess the physical energy of impact or mechanical pressure in addition to that of vibration and serve to form the radicle of the air-atom (Vayu). The formula is V_4 (AK, T, AP, E) V_4 being the radicle.

3. Tejas: a tri-tanmatras; is protomatter charged potentially with the energy of radiant light and heat; in addition to those of impact and vibration energy, it serves to form the radicle of the light and heat corpuscle; is color stimulus. The formula is T_4 (AK, V, AP, E) T_4 being the radicule.

4. Ap: a tetra-tanmatras; is protomatter charged potentially with the energy of taste; it possesses the energy of viscous attraction in addition to those of heat, impact, and vibration; afterward it develops into the atom of water; is taste stimulus. The formula is AP_4 (AK.V.T.E.) AP_4 being the radicle.

5. Prithvi: a pancha-tanmatras; is protomatter charged potentially with the energy of smell; its particles are charged with the energy of cohesive attraction in addition to those of viscous attraction, heat, impact, and vibration; it serves to form the radicle of the earth-atom; is smell stimulus. Its formula is E_4 (AK, V, AP, T) E_4 being the radicle.

Because these five elements can combine in innumerable ways, substances are formed to exhibit characteristics according to the preponderance of one or more of the five elements. For this reason, each substance possesses and exhibits a multiplicity of tastes and for the same reason, the imbalance of the Tridoshas in varying degrees and proportions creates a multitude of diseases. All matter contains these five inherent properties:

Five Properties of Matter: Individually Explained
1. Five Rasas or the six tastes
2. Twenty Gunas or the twenty qualities of matter
3. Veerya or energy, power, and efficiency
4. Vipaka or chemical reaction
5. Prabhas or isomers

Five Rasas or the Six Tastes
All matter is composed of six tastes which affect the human organism. They are sweet, sour, pungent, astringent, saline, and bitter. The Ayurvedists state these five properties determine the six tastes:
1. Nature and physio-chemical constituents of the substance tasted.
2. Structure and function of the chemo-receptors in the tongue and mouth—the taste receptors or the taste buds: exteroceptors[3], proprioceptors[4], and introceptors[5].
3. Area in the cerebrum to which the sensory impulses are carried, interpreted, and then projected back to the tongue.
4. Reflexes produced through the sympathetic and para-sympathetic pathways in the near and distant organs—such as salivary, gastric, or intestinal glands, etc.

----

[3] Stimulated by forces outside the body.
[4] Stimulated by forces inside the body.
[5] Stimulated by substances or conditions within the Gastro-Intestinal system.

5. Mind: The psychological factors in regard to taste.

All substances are then further divided into three classifications:
1. Samana or Palliative: This group alleviates the disturbed doshas and restores them to their normal functions.
2. Kopana or Provocative: This group provokes or disturbs the equilibrium of the dosha or doshas.
3. Swastyahitam: This group is beneficial and necessary for the maintenance of health.

Twenty Gunas or Qualities of Matter

The ultimate factors of the universe are 1) essence of intelligence—stuff; 2) energy; and 3) matter characterized by mass or inertia. These Gunas are conceived to be real substantive entities—not, however, as self-subsistent or independent entities, but as interdependent movements in a very real or substantive existence. Energy does not possess inertia or gravity and therefore is not material, but it possesses quantum and extensity and is conceived to be substantive in this sense. The gunas though assuming an infinite diversity of forms and powers, can be neither created nor destroyed (See Montage in last chapter.)

Ayurveda lists twenty gunas of all substances, but the first five as listed below are important; their origins are cited but those of the other fifteen are not:

1. Laghu is light and its action is Lagaven, that which creates activity. Its origin is ether (Akaseeya).
2. Guru is heavy and its action is Bruhana or tonic. Its origin is earth (Parthva).
3. Snigda is oily or viscous and its action is Kledhan, that which produces moisture. Its origin is water (Apya).
4. Rooksha is harsh and drying and its action is Soshana, that which dries. Its origin is water (Vayu).
5. Teekshana is sharp and active and its action is Sodhana, that which cleans. Its origin is fire (Tejasa).
6. Manda is dull and slow moving; its action pacifies (Samana).
7. Hima Seetha is cooling and its action condenses (Sthambhana).
8. Ushna is heating and its action induces perspiration (Kedhan).
9. Sleekshana is smoothness and it stimulates growth (Ropana).
10. Khar Parush is rough, harsh, and coarse and it satisfies (Lekhan).
11. Sandhara is thick, dense, or solid and it nourishes (Prasadhan).
12. Drava is liquidity and its action dissolves or mixes (Vilotana).
13. Mrudhu is softness and it relaxes (Slethana).
14. Kathena is hardness and it is a fastener or a hardener and it solidifies (Drudeekarana).
15. Sthira is static or immobile and it supports (Dharana).
16. Sara is fluidity and it produces motion or excitement (Prenana).
17. Sookshma is subtle and it penetrates and analyses (Vivarana).
18. Sthoola is gross and it covers and protects (Samvarana).
19. Visadha is clear or transparent and it cleans or clears (Kahalana).
20. Pichhola is slimy or gelatinous and it forms a coating (Lepana).

Veerya or Energy, Power, and Efficiency

It means power, potency, and efficiency. Charaka, one of the outstanding Ayurvedic authorities, defines the word "as the power which performs work or action." There is no action which is not due to Veerya. In chemical changes, energy is liberated or absorbed usually as heat and occasionally as light, electricity, or work. There are two types of Veerya: potential energy and kinetic.

Vipaka or Chemical Reaction

It means chemical reactions of different kinds, like digestion. It is the physiological process of metabolism and directs the course of digestion of different food elements.

Veerya and Vipaka deal with physio-chemical reactions, the effects of foods and medical substances in physiological and pathological states.

Prabhas or Isomers

There are isomers having the same formula but different properties and reactions on the body. This conception is important in nutrition and in pharmacology. The isomeric modes of each substance have specific colors, tastes, etc. due to the physio-chemical characters of compounds. These result from the collocation in unequal proportions of the different forces latent in the atoms of the component substances.

Tridhatus (Homeostasis), Tridoshas, and the Individual Properties of the Tridoshas with a Prefatory Note on Fire as an Example in Mythology and in Healing

The powers of fire, water, and air, the Tridoshas, are omnipresent and are taken for granted by modern man whose life is so mechanized that striking a match turns on the flame in a gas range or turning the ignition key and pressing a pedal start his car. He has lost sight of the glory or the disaster these forces generate unless he is stopped short by some catastrophe. Seldom does modern man realize how he himself projects these forces in his own interior self except to remark, "I'm hot" or "I'm thirsty." But from primitive man onward, these forces have always been the subjects of myths, folklore, medicine, magic, alchemy, and religion. The reader does not need to be reminded that the powers of fire, water, and air are present in every man—be he hero, saint, priest, laborer, or farmer of yesterday or today; the pulse of each one can be read in the same way and in accord with these principles as they affect the body in disease or in health.

Since it is manifestly unwise as well as impossible in this study to show how mythology, folk literature or comparative religion interpreted these forces to project man on the road to peace in understanding himself and his world, fire was singled out in Chinese mythology for special treatment of one of the elements and then related to their belief in nature rather than in a transcendent or a supreme being. A comparison was there made with the Western myth of Prometheus, his gift to man, his punishment by a vengeful deity, and out of that complex, the concern with fear, guilt, salvation, resurrection, freedom, etc. Here fire as a force will be reviewed as one of the cosmic powers which the Indians interpreted, applied in their medicine, and apotheosized in the practice of asceticism to achieve liberation. Avoidance of sex in one country could be contrasted with the acceptance of sex as practiced in the Ho-Chhi festivities. Both cultures, like all cultures, identified fire as one of the cosmic forces. But out of the Indian stories woven into the social-religious-medical matrix came interpretations that vitalize some of the tabulated generalizations of the Tridoshas that will be the substance of this study as they relate especially to the pulse.

Did the early priest-physician of India familiar with the secrets of the initiates understand the cosmic forces, in this case fire, and use them for magic and for healing? They were remarkably accurate observers. The legends, myths, and parables recount endless stories that delight and inform the public, but that are now being reassessed. Here is a forgotten language articulating insights into healing which became the traditions of the physician-priest who imparted his wisdom and his learning to the inner group. The secret of fire as an excess of extreme warmth is characteristic not only of some Indian ascetics but of all religions; this power was known to and experienced by the mystics, the magicians, and the healers from ancient times and recounted most vividly for others to learn. The monks of India and Tibet today take seven seeds of black pepper early in the morning (as was observed in 1964); but primitive sorcerers and magicians likewise drank salted or peppered water or ate exceedingly hot-flavored herbs to heighten their inner heat. The Shamans and the sorcerers, supposedly masters of fire, swallow burning embers or walk over fire. The obverse form of this power is to exhibit resistance to cold. The ascetics of the Himalayas because they could control this magical heat performed feats of resistance to cold that amaze Westerners. Some of these ascetics have been observed drying wet sheets in sub-zero temperature by heat from their own bodies in contests of body mastery and body control. Obviously, they knew which foods produced heat or cold and how to control respiration so as to project heat or cold, and they thus built up a schemata of pulse interpretations with the Tridoshas.

Indian Yoga and Tantrism both stress the tremendous heat that is generated when one awakens Kundalini and then uses the various Chakras. There is no equivalent for this force Kundalini in Western medicine, but the Chakras are dynamic moving energies which represent more than does the term endocrinology that today is principally chemical (see author's **Color Therapy** for the Chakras and Kundalini). The progression of Kundalini through the body reveals itself by the fact that the lower parts become ice-cold. In renouncing asceticism, Tantrism avers that this heat is obtained by the transmutation of sexual energy, but the Yogis and the Buddhas maintain that the force is derived from the ascetic practices and Tapas. Both schools of thought teach control of heat as a form of magico-religious power. The Buddha is said to "burn" when he practices asceticism or his Tapas, a term which originally meant extreme heat but which in time came to denote strivings for asceticism. Through the creative powers of the Tapas, the ascetic could become clairvoyant. The Indian myth of the cosmic god Prajapati states that he created the world by "heating" himself up through asceticism. He created the world by magical perspiration, as do certain gods in the cosmogonic stories of the North American Indians.

The Tantric myth of creation—relevant for showing the way the Shakti-Tantrics denied asceticism—projected the creative powers of the woman or the Great Goddess. (It was earlier pointed out that some authorities believe Tantrism was Chinese in origin.) Tantric mythology explains that the world was created and ruled by two polar principles—Shiva and Shakti. Because Shiva represented absolute passivity, all movement, all life, and all creation became a manifestation of Shakti so that in Tantrism, Shakti manifesting in multiple forms of the Great Goddess is active in Woman and is the universal force which creates the world. Tantrism built upon cosmic forces and ancient fertility cults personified in the Great Mother of Pre-Aryan India since Neolithic times; in slanting anew this mythology ritual, it furnished a technique for awakening the Kundalini, which is accompanied by the release in the body of tremendous heat. The birth of the Great Goddess may be a denial of the Prajapati story: The gods were being threatened by the demon Mahish. Seeking the assistance of Vishnu and Shiva, all the angry gods came together and sent out their combined energies in the form of a fire flaming from their mouths. These fires and flames became a huge cloud which took the form of the Goddess Shakti with her eighteen arms who then crushed Mahish and saved the world. Prajapati or Sakti, male or female, both used fire!

The heat aroused by violent and excessive emotion, like the combined fury of the gods, can be interpreted as fire in different ways. The student of comparative religion and mythology regards these stories of fire released through Kundalini as a sacred or magico-sacred power. The soldier or the warrior sees in the Shakti story the energy of the atom bomb and the mushroom cloud. The Indian Yogi says this fire came through asceticism; this fire led the way to Shanti, his word for a state of peace, tranquility, absence of passion and suffering in order for him to reach the non-conditioned state of mind of samadhi. Further, the true Yogi will try to overcome the temptations of the magical power (siddhi) that results from the misuse of heat and fire. The philologist casually remarks that the word Shanti is derived from the root Sham which originally included the meaning of extinguishing the fire, cooling down of anger, or quieting the heat aroused by demonic power. The engineer uses fire to stoke his furnace and sees no magical religious connotation in this cosmic energy as the flames mount up and no parallel between the processes of oxidation in his body and the flames in the furnace. An ancient Greek regards the fire as Prometheus' gift to man; the ancient Chinese says that the sages directed the fire drillers to teach man how to make a fire. The physician sees a power that can be used in healing and abused for killing. Soldier, warrior, priest, physician, engineer, ancient Greek or ancient Chinese, all use the same force. The modern Westerner does not pray when he turns on the electrical current or switches on the light. Modern medicine may have to reappraise these forces that are the bases of chemistry and physiology to pattern them in new combinations.

Another line of presentation—the historical—may be cited to show how fire was viewed as a force and therefore how it could be related to medical practices.

The monument of Sardanapolis, near Tarsus, relates the story of the Assyrian ruler Ashurbanipal whose brother Shamashshumukin revolted, but when his city could not hold out, Shamashshumukin burned himself to death along with his wives, his children, his slaves, and his treasures. The same tragedy was repeated at Nineveh by Saracus or Sinsharishkun, the last king of Assyria; his fiery death marked the end of Nineveh and of the Assyrian empire. But the three different accounts of the death of Croesus, King of Lydia, must be prefaced by an explanation of the Persian belief in fire.

Since the Persians revered fire, it was sacrilegious for the people to defile this sacred element with the pollution of a dead body. To the Iranians, fire was the earthly form of the heavenly light, the eternal, the infinite, the divine, and to them, death was the main source of corruption and uncleanliness. Hence they took stringent precautions to guard the purity of the fire from the defilement of death. To burn a corpse was a heinous crime punishable with death. Down into modern times, the death penalty was inflicted on all who threw a corpse or cowdung on a fire or on one who blew on fire with his breath. (Here the Iranians differ dramatically from the Hindus who burn their dead—as one can readily recall the Ghats of Benares-Varanasi. Both peoples regard the dead as unclean.)

The story of the destruction of Croesus by the Persian Cyrus the Great must be viewed with care. Herodotus reported that Cyrus caused a great pyre to be erected on which he placed the captive monarch in fetters. Fire was applied to the pyre, but at the last moment Cyrus relented and a sudden shower extinguished the flames so that Croesus was spared. In the light of the Persian view of the sanctity of fire, it is difficult to believe that a Persian king would have commanded his subjects to perpetrate a deed alien to their beliefs. Two other accounts of his death may provide a truer version of the relationship between these two rulers; these are evidenced in the account by the Greek poet Bacchylides, born forty years after the event, and by an artist's painting of the scene on a red-figured vase. Bacchylides reported that Croesus unable to brook the thought of slavery caused a pyre to be erected for himself and his family, but the bright flames were extinguished by Zeus. In like manner, the vase-painter represents the burning of Croesus as a voluntary act, not as a punishment inflicted on him by the Persian king. The demeanor of the king is solemn and composed and he appears to be performing a religious rite, not suffering an ignominious death.

Thus Croesus prepared to meet death like a king or a god in the flames. Here he followed in the tradition of Hercules; of Zimri, king of Israel; of Shamashshumukin; of the last king of Assyria; and of the Carthaginian king Hamilcar. What was the special reason for electing to die by fire? To be burnt alive was regarded as a solemn sacrifice and also as an apotheosis which raised the victim to the rank of a god. The ancients regarded fire as a purgative so powerful that properly applied it could burn away all that was mortal of a man, leaving only the divine and immortal spirit behind. Jamblichus wrote, "Fire destroys the material part of sacrifies, it purifies all things . . . and, in virtue of the purity of its nature, making them meet for communion with the gods. So, too, it releases us from the bondage of corruption, it likens us to the gods, it makes us meet for their friendship, and it converts our material nature into an immaterial."

Thus one can understand why kings and commoners who claimed or aspired to divinity should choose death by fire. It opened to them the gates of heaven. The quack Peregrinus ended his career in the flames at Olympia; the Sicilian philosopher Empedocles leaped into the crater of Etna in order to establish his claim to godhood. They both did what Indian Fakirs and magicians did in antiquity and what certain Buddhists are doing today. People are more concerned with appraising these acts as extremes of fanaticism or of vanity or a mixture of the two, but what is required is an understanding of how these beliefs are a conscious or an unconscious response to the hidden language of the body. When historical incidents report of death and transfiguration through fire, they project a wisdom that can be applied to healing. The sceptic may wonder how or why, but for one who is familiar with the forces of the body as they spell out health, disease, and death, they speak a different tongue: FEVER, WHICH IS EXCESS FIRE, IS THE BODY'S METHOD FOR PURIFICATION.

Only in the body, human or otherwise, is the spectacle of fire burning in water ever present and always in action as a process. An historical account for the death of kings in the past or a report of miracles performed today in the laboratory are the two extremes of what in reality is a commonplace in the body as it functions or enacts its life-processes. When man learns the secret of fire burning in water, he will learn the secret of immortality—if he wants or esteems it—and, what is more important, the secret of health. Air is a controlling agent. For the Chinese, the doctrine of material immortality or **Hsienship** was based on a breath that simulated foetal life. For the Indians, the Yogi link to Samadhi was by way of breath control and asceticism which eventually related to control of the Chakras and of Kundalini. For the Westerner, the chemical changes of oxidation explain what happens in the body but do not account for how it happens. This body process may be rephrased from a medical view in this way:

One has altered function or disease in the bodily processes
        if water puts out fire;
        if water is evaporated by fire;
        if air increases fire excessively;
        if air diminishes fire so that it is curtailed.

In the further consideration of these factors, one accommodates to time, place, seasons of the year, and conditions of the body. What is normal, for example, in the foetus is not normal outside the body. What is normal on top of the mountain is not normal at sea level. As the Orientals say, climate, atmosphere, and seasons are all important and here they differ from the Westerner who is only now beginning to include these factors in his consideration.

To what extent do the stories recounted by myth, folklore, philosophic precept, religious practice, and history reveal the forgotten language of the past with its insights into healing? What happened when the doctor-priest with his accurate observations stopped growing so that the literature of healing became indurated and even fossilized. No new rearrangements of the old forms into new patterns were permitted because tradition and practice did not allow the Ayurvedist physician to take liberties or to change. They became static. One may observe that growth occurs only when old ideas or precepts are rearranged into new forms by new approaches in thinking. The cosmic laws of the universe are there, always available, but man is not always ready to tune in on the right application. As an example, one may observe that electricity existed since the world began, but not until the twentieth century was the power released by pressing a button. What happened to arrest the interpretation of the Tridoshas in Ayurvedic medicine despite their insights in reading the pulse? Was the limitation to be found in their religion, in their blind worship of traditional ways, in their adherence to the past? Did their monistic theory, their belief in Karma and Reincarnation lead to a cause-effect relationship that could not accommodate to change? The Chinese method of the dialectic if used correctly can minimize this type of induration and fossilization. Twentieth century physics correctly uses the dialectic early enunciated by the Chinese to make extraordinary advances in technology and in knowledge. The misuse of the theory or its limited application does not negate the fact that the modern physician must replace the harness with a jet motor in utilizing the same cosmic laws with respect to healing. The Ayurvedic principles of the Tridoshas project an acknowledged cosmic power which the West seeks to measure by instruments, a static device not applied in a dynamic way. Thus both sides make advances and mistakes—West as well as East. But the forces of the universe remain for man to direct in healing. What follows will be an account of how the Tridoshas manifest themselves in health and in disease.

Theory of the Tridhatus (Balance) or Homeostasis

Guiding Maxim: When the elements are in balance, then the body is in balance.

Ayurvedic maintains that "Man is a miniature world in himself and as in the macrocosm so in the microcosm." Thus the conclusion is reached that in the universe three factors work in harmony: wind—which includes electricity and magnetism, heat, and humidity. By harmonious working of these factors, the integrity of the universe is preserved and when the cosmic harmony is upset or disturbed, the universe goes into chaos. The same factors when applied to the human body become the Tridhatus of the Ayurvedic physicians. Their viewpoint is entirely different from the Western physicians' whose field of investigation rests principally upon the premise that matter constitutes the physical body. To the Indian doctors, LIFE animates every particle of the body. Here more than matter is the scope of thought. The science of the pulse cannot be determined by or rest upon dead matter. It can flourish only by practice on the living body in health or in disease.

Ayurvedic then observes that the correct and moderate functioning of the mind and the sense organs with a due regard for the seasons of the year and the stages of the individual's life preserves perfect harmony and results in a sound body and sound mind[5]. Conversely, the absence of or the excessive indulgence with respect to the individual's 1. season of the year as well as stages in life (Kala), 2. mind and intellect (Buddhi), and 3. pursuit of the sense organs (Indryasthanan) are the three-fold causes of disease—mental and physical. These causes are internal. External causes—like injuries, accidents and the like—bring on disharmony in the working of the fundamental vital forces and hence produce disease and pain. In other words, even traumatic causes become ideopathic. Ayurvedic recognizes another cause which is foreign to Western medicine: Karma Vipaka or the result of the dynamic action of one's previous births which determine heredity and environment in the present birth.

Diagnosis of Disease

The keynote of the causation of all diseases that victimize the human body is the disturbed harmony of the Tridhatus. When this disturbance occurs, the body manifests some physiological and pathological changes or symptoms, characteristic of one or the other of the particular disturbed dhatus. The physician must therefore know which particular dhatu or which combination of dhatus are affected and what changes it or they have wrought on the system. This he can determine by careful observation of the different bodily organs and excretions, by examination, by contact, and by inquiry. He also notes the following facts in relation to disease:

1. etiology; 2. incubatory symptoms; 3. developed symptoms; 4. previous treatment and its results; 5. the present stage of the disease.

Three stages are differentiated in the career of a disease:
1. easily curable; 2. difficulty in curing—can it be arrested or suppressed? 3. incurable.

By observing and noting some peculiar symptoms (called Arista Lakhanam), it is possible to prognosticate the probable if not the exact moment of the death of the patient.

In addition to the above procedure, the Ayurvedists have elaborated and adopted a science of reading the pulse, their own sphygmology, as a method of diagnosing and prognosing the disease. There are several treatises on the science, chief among them being Kanada's **Nadi Vignana** and Ravana's **Nadi Pariksha.**

These methods, in short, sum up the measures used by Ayurvedic physicians in diagnosing as well as in prognosing disease.

The principle involved in the treatment of diseases is the restoration to harmony of the disturbed fundamental vital principles of Vayu, Pitha, and Kapha and including in the new approach, the circulation of the

---

[6] The authority Vagbhata cites these terms for the sound body and sound mind: Sannyek Yogastu Vigneyo Arogyasya Eka Karanam.

blood. In other words, they follow the rational law of "Medicatrix Naturae", in contradistinction to the allopath's "Contraria Contrarus Curantor", and the homeopath's "Similis Similibus Curantor"—both of which can be freely translated to read "Opposites Heal" and "Like Heals Like."

The Tridoshas

When these three forces Vayu, Pitha, and Kapha are in balance, the body is also in a state of balance or Tridhatus. But should any or all of these three be thrown out of balance, their discord causes disease or a dosha. Their term Tridosha means three for tri and fault for dosha, a Sanskrit word that refers to the three forces Vayu, Kapha, and Pitha when they are deranged or out of balance. The nearest Western equivalent could possibly be pathology although the Indian definition is much more inclusive than the allopathic. When the harmony of these three fundamental and vital forces is disturbed by some strainer—internal or external—they will undergo a complete change. Instead of continuing to be preservers of the bodily system, they will then be transformed into doshas or faults which will generate morbid substances in the body called, in Indian terminology, **morbifit diathesis**[7]—the root causes of all bodily and mental illness. These doshas taking hold of any one or more of the seven systems bring on various kinds of imbalance (disease) by generating in the body accumulations which affect the other systems adversely in ascending or descending scale. These seven systems are known as chyle, blood, flesh, fat, bone, marrow, and sperm.

The three Ayurvedic terms have their counterparts in Unani medicine, where the following are used: Hawa for air or Vayu; Khun (blood-fire) for fire or Pitha; and Balgam (phlegm-water) for water or Kapha. A fourth element, Shonita, is added, however, to their acceptance of these three forces, an element signifying the circulation of the blood. Of some interest to the reader is the fact that in South India (where Tamil is spoken, a language which is proud of its being least "Sanskritized" and which maintains the belief that its language is older than Sanskrit according to some authorities) a fourth element is also used in their medical practices and beliefs. In the Ayasthya system, called the cult of the Thathwar, their fourth element is termed **Sleshma** and is associated with the manufacturing and disposal of phlegm. This cult affirmed that the sixty-four functionings are told by sixty-four different systems with their sixty-four pulse readings. Any change in balance presents other combinations of pulse readings.

But for the comprehension of the basic patterns of belief that dictate the interpretations of the pulse, the three elements as promulgated by Ayurveda are completely adequate for the purposes at hand if the reader knows that modern Ayurvedic practice includes **Shonita** and **Sleshma** in their effects on the body.

---

[7] Significant terminology:
When the body is in balance or in Tridhatus, Vayu is Dhatavodeka, Pitha is Dharanat, and Kapha is Sarangadhara. When the body is out of balance and doshas are created, Vayu is Sarira, Pitha is Dhushanat, and Kapha is Dosho Sarangadhara. When **morbifit diathesis** accumulates in the seven systems, Vayu is called Malaka, Pitha is called Malnikaranam, and Kapha is called Malaka Sarangadhara.

Whether there be three elements according to one school, four according to another, or five in pragmatic application, one needs to understand after the enumeration of the forces generating "morbifit diathesis" on a seven fold system of the body, that these forces have polarity. Without this frame of reference, much insight into the readings of the pulse would be vitiated. All these are dynamic forces, but disease is also a dynamic force. Thus disease or disharmony in every case is the result of some imbalance which is reflected in a disturbance of the body's polarity. Since they are not static, they must be thought of as constantly moving, acting upon and affecting the body and, in turn, being acted upon by one another as well as by the seasons, by foods and the like. "Prana" (the Indian term for the life force which the Chinese term Chi-Hua and which is not to be confused with the Western term oxygen) is omitted from this group since it is more inclusive than these three. These human energies are chemical, electrical, mechanical, nervous, psychic, mental, and thermal.

With reference to the polarity of these forces, Vayu or air represents the neutron, is the nerve force in the body, and splits up the atom into electrons and protrons. Pitha or fire represents the electron and controls the enzymes, the hormones, and the metabolic as well as the circulatory systems[8], all of which impart to the body heat necessary for its preservation and functioning. Kapha or water represents the proton, controls all the mucous surfaces of the body, and is similar to protoplasm.

Vayu or air has the following relationship to the other two doshas:
1. When it joins with the electron or Pitha, **atomic heat** is produced because Vayu has a high affinity for mixing (called yogavaki).
2. When it joins with the proton Kapha, **atomic cold** results.
3. When, on the body level, it combines with Pitha, fever results; with Kapha, chills.

The Tridosha concept is as modern as Selye's theory. Despite the differences in terminology, the concepts are the same: e.g., the stress syndrome, the alarm reaction, the stage of resistance and exhaustion— all were recognized and explained in Ayurvedic and Unani medicine long before the time of the Greeks and certainly at least two millennia before Western allopathic medicine rediscovered them. Further, the concept of how the human organism works in balance, called homeostasis by Cannon, was also recognized by them as their term indicates: Dosha-Dhatu-Mala Vignana.

What Selye called stressors are known as four types of changes affecting the individual in the external environment:
1. the seasonal and climactic variation known as Kala;

---

8 Ayurvedic and Unani medicine describe the process or the function. The Western terms like the circulatory, the digestive, or the nervous system are not used by them, as one would naturally expect, but the reader must learn how from their description to correlate Eastern ideas with Western terminology and concepts.

Does the term nerve impulse really tell what it does or what it is? It is recognized for being a metabolic living event, a chemical reaction, a sequence propagated along a nerve fiber. One is reminded of Bertrand Russell's statement that "Electricity is not like St. Paul's Cathedral. When we have told how things behave when they are electrified, we have told all we have to tell." In the same way, it is as difficult to explain the Tridoshas as it is to explain the nervous and electrical phenomena.

2. the physical force of the universe known as Artha;

3. the volitional forces and other cosmic influence known as Karma: not recognized in Western interpretation of stressors;

4. the cognitive organs or the exteroceptors known as Gnadendruya.

The body reacts to these four stimuli or changes in the external environment (stressors) through the Tridoshas. The neural modulator is Vayu; the chemical modulator with its hormones, enzymes, vitamins, and minerals is Kapha; and the effector, or balancer which responds with counterchange, the adapter mechanism of the body which restores equilibrium or homeostasis is Kapha. The fourth stressor Gnadendruya acts as the regulator among the other three—Kala, Artha, and Karma—to maintain homeostasis (known as indriuya samyata). When the liminal threshold is too high (atiyoga) or too low (hinayoga or ayoga), imbalance occurs (mithyayoga) and internal stress results (doshavaish-amya).

The survival of the organism and its recovery from internal stress are largely determined by the integrity of the Tridosha mechanism and its capacity to rehabilitate itself or to achieve a steady state or an equilibrium (known as samyata). This is what Selye calls the stage of adaptation. The time interval between imbalance (dosha-vaishamya) and the restoration of the balance (dosha-samyata) constitutes the different phases of the stress syndrome (kriyakalas of the roga). If the organism does not succeed in attaining balance, exhaustion, the last stage of the General Adaptation Syndrome (G.A.S.), takes place and the organism succumbs or dies.

The Individual Properties of the Three Doshas[9]

According to the ancients, there are eighty air-diseases, forty fire-diseases, and twenty water-diseases or a total of one hundred and forty, and each one has its own characteristic pulse beat. Before the pulse beats for the various diseases can be described, the individual properties of the Doshas must be reviewed.

Vayu or Air (Hawa in Unani Nomenclature)

Vayu is the primary moving force or the driving force of the living body and without Vayu, the other two Doshas could not move; hence it is concerned with the production of somatic and psychic processes which are predominantly dynamic in nature: sight, speech, hearing, perception in all its physical and psychic manifestations, and the like. It may be said that Vayu sets and keeps in motion all the other forces which by themselves are incapable of action.

According to Vagbhata, one of the authorities, Vayu or Vata (the terms are interchangeable) in its normal state is said
to govern   1. enthusiasm (mental state);
            2. respiration;
            3. motor activities of the body—mental, vocal, and physical.

---

9 See Montage in the last chapter of the book.

to regulate 4. the natural urges by way of the spino-cerebral or the vegetative reflexes which can be volitionally[10] inhibited or provoked;

5. the proper circulation and function of the sevenfold dhatus, their term for tissue elements explained earlier under the seven systems of the body;

6. the functioning of the sense organs;

to manifest
itself   7. in any inflammatory state as pain; no pain is possible without Vayu.

Respiration is necessary for life. The inhaled air is contained in the lungs, joins, mingles and intermingles inside the system to produce heat and fire (oxidation or Vatha). When the process of oxidation is being maintained in a normal state, this condition is termed Vatha Thathwa.

According to Ayurveda, Vayu or air is light, cold, dry, mobile, and piercing. It is prompt in action and flows through the body in swift currents. It is the source of the life force in the individual and is equivalent to the Jiva-atman or the individual soul. As a vital force, it is present in every cell of the body. It is self generated and is regarded as identical with the divine energy of universal life. Vayu is the creator, preserver, and destroyer of all living things.

Like the other two elements, air is given a separate residence in the human body. Its abode is the intestines, loins, thighs, bones, and feet. Since Vayu supports Pitha and Kapha, then the five principles associated with each of these elements mean that Vayu as a force supports these last two forces with their ten manifestations. Vayu thus controls their combined functions as well as its own five—in all a total of fifteen. It is air or Vayu that makes man and animals move, see, hear, and think.

Vayu or air, like Pitha and Kapha, manifests its characteristics in five different ways:

1. **Prana or Vital Air** is situated in the cavity of the mouth and the heart. It protects life from destruction and enables food to go into the stomach. It is this type of air that throws out the child from the womb at birth.

2. **Udana or Upward** is found in the upper part of the body and especially in the throat. With the help of Udana, man talks, sings, coughs or sneezes.

3. **Samana or Even Air** is located in the region of the intestines. It splits up the food into waste matter, like urine and stools, from the food that nourishes the body. Anabolism and catabolism are its functions.

4. **Vyana or Diffused Air** is found throughout the organism. Vyana supplies serum (rasa) to all parts of the body, keeps the joints

---

[10] In Western terminology, the vegetative system is automatic and cannot be controlled volitionally. The Yogis claim it can be done through practice. Western man is now beginning to understand that through the new brain, the old brain can be controlled (the autonomic nervous system). New Thought, Zen, and other movements today all seek to control by techniques of breathing and suggestion.

lubricated and is responsible for perspiration and for the flow of the blood.

5. **Apana or Downward Air** is located in the lower intestines and is responsible for forcing the foetus into the womb. Apana regulates the waste matter of the body and helps to expel it.

When the five kinds of air mentioned above are in harmony, they keep the body in good health and are responsible for the regulation of the nervous, respiratory, and digestive systems. Too much or too little of one or more of these five will cause disease—local or general, light or serious.

A Derangement of

Prana results in hiccoughs, bronchitis, or asthma.
Udana results in dysentery, diarrhea, etc.
Samana results in headaches and intestinal illness.
Vyana results in paralysis in the whole or in a single part of the body: hemaplegia or total paralysis.
Apana results in diseases of the bladder and the large intestines.
 Vayu Is Especially Aggravated
by storms, cloudy weather, and rain
in the morning and afternoon from the hours of two to six A.M. and P.M.
four hours after a meal
after excessive and after violent exercise
by anxiety
by excessive mental and physical work
by taking pungent, astringent, bitter, cold, and parched foods
by suppression of wind, retention of urine or stools
by vomitting and sneezing
by the use on the skin of electricity—ultra violet lamps, x-rays, radium, cobalt
 As long as Vayu remains in the body, the pulse vibrates and life is present. As soon as Vayu leaves the organism, the body becomes lifeless and the pulse ceases to beat.

Pitha or Fire (Khum in Unani Nomenclature)

Pitha means to tap, to heat, to burn, or to warm up.
Its function is
1. to be concerned with the production of those physical and mental processes which are predominately balancing and transformative in nature: sight, heat production, hunger, thirst, softness and suppleness of the body, lustre, cheerfulness and intelligence, idea, digestion, fear, anger, delight, confusion, and lucidity.
2. to be concerned with the thermogenetic activities of the glandular structure, the enzymes and hormones and the nutritional systems whose functions are of vital importance in digestion, assimilation, tissue building, and metabolism.
3. to be responsible for ensuring proper digestion, absorption, metabolism, production of energy and heat, and the appreciation of colors.
4. to include a concept of the force Pitha which comprehends a large group of biochemical substances (Harivansha) that take part in

vital visual functions—especially the splitting of light into photo and chemo-synthesis and higher mental faculties and emotional states (Here they go beyond the Western interpretation of sight).
5. to be likened to the Western science of enzymology.
6. to discharge the process of suppuration.

The function of Pitha is to maintain and regulate oxidation and supply heat as well as maintain the thermal balance of the body. Pitha as a substance is of the nature of a hot liquid or a strong acid, hot in action to the touch. It is very active and slightly viscid; in color it may be yellow, red, or blue; in odor, it smells like raw meat; in taste, it is bitter and sour. Pitha is pungent when fully digested; bitter when raw; and sour when undigested. Fire maintains itself in the blood and in the perspiration. Some authorities place the seats of fire or locations in the body as follows: 1. duodenum (principal seat); 2. sweat or perspiration; 3. chyle; 4. watery parts of the muscles; 5. blood. Other authorities place the seats of fire as follows: 1. duodenum; 2. liver and spleen; 3. heart; 4. eyes; 5. skin. In addition to supplying enough heat for the body, Pitha helps in the proper functioning of: sight; digestion; hunger; radiance of the body; cheerfulness; intelligence; and pigmentation of the skin.

Pitha, like Vayu and Kapha, has five divisions:
1. **Pachaka** (digestive) is situated in the middle of the body and preserves body heat by its thermal properties and thus helps to preserve life. Pachaka also digests the food into chyle, feces, urine, and sweat and supplements the other four kinds of fire listed below.
2. **Ranjaka** (coloring) resides in the liver and spleen and is bright red in color; its function is to give the red color to chyle.
3. **Bhrajaka** (shining) resides in the skin and is the protector of the skin.
4. **Sadhaka** (fulfilling) resides in the heart and by its special power drives away Tamas or delusion. It is the finest of the five fires and is instrumental in the proper functioning of the intellect and memory and in the fulfillment of one's desires. It is the emotional and psychic fire.
5. **Alochaka** (seeing) is situated in the pupil of the eye and its function is vision.

Here, too, derangement of any one or any combination of the five aspects of Pitha will give rise to disease.

A Derangement of

Pachaka produces indigestion, acidity, burning sensation in the heart, throat or stomach.
Ranjaka produces leprosy and diseases of the liver and spleen.
Bhrajaka produces diseases of the skin.
Sadhaka destroys thinking power and produces stupor, apoplexy, senility and emotional diseases.
Alochaka destroys sight.

Pitha Is Aggravated By
anger, fear, grief, physical exertion
excessive exposure to the sun
unnatural sex habits
ingestion, two hours after a meal or taking food
foods that are bitter, acid, salty, and dry
excessive use of mustard and other condiments
foods that are heating in character like meats, eggs, fish, legumes, wines, curds, and wheys and some of the green leafy vegetables

Pitha is always at its highest after the rains in August and September [in India].

Kapha or Water (Balgam in Unani Nomenclature)

Kapha or water is the equivalent of cold in the body. The element of water contained in the human organism is a prototype of the microscopic cold of all varieties. Kapha or water helps keep Pitha in check, modifies its burning or consuming power because it controls oxidation and fevers and maintains the integrity of the body. Kapha, as Slesma, means to embrace, to whirl, or to keep together. It is similar to protoplasm, if not identical, and is the basic stuff of life although its characteristics may be considerably modified from tissue to tissue depending upon the specialized functions each is called upon to perform.

Kapha functions as follows:
1. to lubricate the body, especially the joints.
2. to give grease (oil) to the skin.
3. to increase the size of the body.
4. to generate new tissue and to add strength and firmness.
5. to impart mildness, stability and heaviness to the body.
6. to be concerned with the productivities of those physical and mental processes which are predominantly conserving and stabilizing in nature—like courage, forbearance, zest, vitality, knowledge, and understanding.
7. to be responsible for the skeletal, reproductive, and immunological systems and with the anabolic processes in metabolism.
8. to promote healing and the repairative processes.
9. to conserve or to store.
10. to act as a soothing agent.
11. to generate resistance to disease and decay.
12. to form pus.

The locations of Kapha or water are the chest, stomach, head, throat, joints and fat.

Kapha, like Vayu and Pitha, has five different kinds of water or manifests its characteristics in five different ways:

1. **Avalambaka** (supporter) protects all the joints and enables the heart to perform its duties with the help of the nutrients that the heart derives from the assimilated food.

2. **Kledaka** (moistener) resides in the stomach and controls the quantity and quality of water in other parts of the body. Its chief function

is to help digestion by supplying the necessary enzymes, vitamins, minerals, etc.

3. **Bodhaka** (feeler) is located in the throat and at the root of the tongue. It gives the power of taste to the tongue.

4. **Tarpaka** (pleasing) is located in the head. It regulates the function of the eyes, ears, and nose.

5. **Slesmaka** (phlegm) as a water force is located in the joints or the synovial fluid and keeps them integrated; with phlegm, one can move the limbs without dislocating or injuring the bones.

A fitting conclusion to this account of the Tridoshas is a statement by the Indian Susruta who served the function of an Aristotle in his culture although he may have appeared long before the Greeks; his remarks clearly revealed the interrelationship of Vayu, Pitha, and Kapha:

> In an inflammatory process, leading to the formation of an abscess, there can be no pain without the agency of Vata (Vayu) no paka (bio-chemical reaction) without Pitha, nor puya (cleansing) without Kapha.
>
> Sutra: 17-7

A Derangement of Kapha May Cause

loss of appetite	sweet taste in the mouth
drowsiness	dryness of the body
heaviness	burning sensation of different
feeling of emptiness in stomach	parts of the body
excessive thirst	insomnia
weakness	indigestion
chilly feeling	goitre
dropsy	obesity
white coating on tongue	urticaria
small boils	whiteness of cornea
excessive sleep	white urine and white stools

Kapha Is Naturally Aggravated:

in winter and spring
in the morning and evening hours from six to ten
two hours after a meal
by daytime sleep and by sedentary habits
by foods that are sweet, saline, and sour
by wine, ghee, curds, ice, milk, sugar, cake, molasses, meat
by a marshy or swampy place

All three elements are of equal importance. If balance is maintained in the body among the three elements and their fifteen forces, then the organism functions smoothly and there is no disease.

Recapitulation

There are basic differences between Eastern and Western science; it follows therefore that Eastern science should be studied with an awareness of Eastern methods, philosophy, and values. It is not easy and indeed, at times, almost impossible to represent their scientific explanations in Western nomenclature, but an effort has here been made with respect to the Indian theory of the Tridoshas.

The Ayurvedic system has been built on the Pancha Bootes conception of the evolution of matter, based, in turn, on Sankhya philosophy from which the Tridosha pathology, physiology, and pharmacology evolved. Thus to the Ayurvedists, mere physical perception is not sufficient for fathoming the mysteries of life and their science therefore deals not only with the physical side of the body but also with the metaphysical: the union of body, mind, and soul. They recognized man as an epitome of the external macrocosm for all is creation, preservation, and destruction (Brahma, Vishnu, and Siva). Therefore to understand the microcosm man, it is imperative to study the macrocosm, the universe. Herein is contained the curriculum of Ayurvedic medicine. Their science of philosophy is the science of creation and the universal spirit. Hence the Ayurvedic doctor when treating the physically and emotionally ill pays obeisance to the deity.

Ayurvedic Bibliography in Two Parts

Ayurvedic Medicine: Introduction and Primary Sources

A comment is in order about the changes taking place in the training of native doctors. The Ayurvedic medical schools in India have shifted from a five and a half year curriculum to a four year curriculum geared to Indian, not to Allopathic, medicine, to "pure" Ayurvedic precepts. No students were admitted in 1963 and 1964 to the first and second years of medical training so that syllabus changes could be effected. Related to their nationalistic purposes is the teaching of the courses in the native language of the particular state and in Hindi; English is abolished: for example, the Ayurvedic Medical School located in Hyderabad teaches courses in Hindi and in Telegu. There is one Ayurvedic medical college in every capital city of India which also has two post-graduate institutes (Varanasi Hindi University and Jamnagar, in Gujarat) and a research institute (Jamnagar) together with a drug research center (Lucknow). In May, 1965, the Government's Third Plan included establishing a national Ayurvedic research unit for post-graduate degree courses in the Trivandrum Ayurvedic College as well as a composite drug research unit and a botanical garden together with conducting a survey of Ayurvedic medicine in the state of Kerala. The three research units would undertake post-graduate degree courses in three subjects: "Panchakarma", "Visha Chikilsa", and "Marma Chikilsa."

Three books are basic to Ayurvedic medicine, but only two of them have been available in English translations. They will be discussed as primary references and all others will be arranged in alphabetical order as secondary.

1. Caraka or Charaka was a Kashmirian physician who flourished under the Indo-scythian King Kanishka who reigned probably c. 120 to 162. He wrote a compendium (Caraka Samhita) which represents Atreya's system of medicine (sixth century B.C.) as handed down by his pupil Agnivesa. The Agnivesa samhita itself is lost.

The Caraka Samhita, Expounded by the Worshipful Atreya Punarvasu, Compiled by the Great Sage Agnivesa, and Redacted by Caraka and Drid Habala, Shree Gulabkunverba Ayurvedic Society, Jamnagar, India, popular edition, 6 vols., 1949. (Translations in Hindi, Gujarati, and English.)

Criticism: A.F. Rudolf Hoernlé: Studies in the Medicine of Ancient India (Part I, Oxford, 1907); "The Authorship of the Charaka Samhita," Archiv. für Geschichte der Medizin (Bd. 1 29-40, 1907. Left incomplete). M. Winternitz: Geschichte der Indischen Litteratur (Bd. 3, 545, 1922).

2. Susruta is the name of a surgeon and Atreya is the name of a physician and Hindu tradition places the earliest Hindu medical schools of Atreya and Susruta at some time in the sixth century B.C., a date supported by the Vedas. It is impossible to date the activity of Atreya and Susruta with any precision so that one recites the Hindu tradition that is preserved in the Buddhist Jatakas. In the age of the Buddha there existed two great universities in India, Kasi (or Benares) in the East and Taksasila (or Taxila on the Jhelam river) in the West. Atreya, the physician, taught in the latter university, and his younger contemporary, Susruta, the surgeon, in the former.

The work of Susruta is one of the greatest of its kind in Sanskrit literature. It is especially important from the surgical point of view; it describes a number of operations (including extraction of cataract, removal of hernia, caesarean section, etc.) and contains the earliest accounts of plastic surgery and of surgical use of the magnet; it lays stress on the elaborate training which is needed to produce surgeons. Other parts deals with anatomy, physiology, pathology, obstetrics, and pediatrics. Stress is laid on careful diagnosis and a few diseases can be readily identified. Some 760 medicinal plants are noted, and full attention is paid to diet and bathing.

Bhishagratna, Kaviraj Kunjalal (M.R.A.S. London), An English Translation of the Sushruta Samhita Based on Original Sanskrit Text with a Full and Comprehensive Introduction, Additional Texts, Different Readings, Notes, Comparative Views, Index, Glossary, and Plates (in Three Volumes). Translated and Edited by Kaviraj Kunjalal Bhishagratna (M.R.A.S. London), The Chowkhamba Sanskrit Studies, Vol. XXX. (Chowkhamba Sanskrit Series Office, Gopal Mandir Lane, Varanasi—P.O. Box 8). Note: A fourth volume was scheduled for translation by June of 1964, but it was not yet available when we left the country in the summer of 1964.

Criticism: E. H. F. Meyer: Geschichte der Botanik (t. 3, 3-18, 1856). Iwan Bloch in Puschmann's Handbuch (t. 1, 1902, 131-133). A. F. R. Hoernlé: Studies in the Medicine of Ancient India (Oxford, 1907).

3. Vagbhata the Elder, one of the three greatest Hindu physicians, was author of a medical treatise called Ashtangasamgraha, Sum or Compendium of the eight parts (of medicine). Another treatise called Ashtangahridaya-samhita (Compendium of the quintessence of the eight parts) is written entirely in verse and is obviously a later work derived from the former. The date of his activity is uncertain, but may be placed tentatively in the seventh century, c. 625, for the Chinese Buddhist I-Ching seems to refer to his Samgraha. It is assumed that the second treatise was written by another author, Vagbhata the Younger. The elder Vagbhata was certainly and the

younger probably, a Buddhist. Later Hindu physicians call the earliest work Vriddha-Vagbhata, the later one Vagbhata.

Text: The first one appears to have been published in Bombay in 1888, and the second one, together with Arunadatta's commentary was edited by A. M. Kunte (Bombay, 1880; again, 1891). But the authors could not obtain English copies. Instead they were informed that the third basic text was not yet translated into English, but would be by the summer of 1964. The Minister of Health is in charge of this task. For any recent information, write to the adviser, Indigenous Systems of Medicine, New Delhi, India. The authors used the Sanskrit edition together with a Telegu translation under the able assistance of the Chief Librarian and the efficient staff at the Ayurvedic Medical College at Hyderabad.

Criticism: Palmyr Cordier: **Vagbhata et l'Ashtangahridayasamhita** (Besançon, 1896). J. Jolly: "Zur Quellenkunde der indischen Medizin (1. Vagbhata)," **Zeit d. deut. mor. Ges.** (t. 54, 260-274, 1900). J. Jolly: **Indische Medizin** (Strasburg, 1901). Iwan Bloch: "Indische Medizin," in Newburger und Pagel (**Handbuch der Geschichte der Medizin**, vol. 1, pp. 119-52, 1902, with bibliography). Max Neuburger: **Geschichte der Medizin** (vol. 1, pp. 66-91). A. F. Rudolf Hoernlé: **Studies in the Medicine of Ancient India. Part I. Osteology** (Oxford, 1907, passim). M. Winternitz: **Indischen Litteratur** (vol. 3, 549, 1922).

Ayurvedic Medicine: Secondary Sources

The material that is alphabetically arranged should be prefaced with this explanation: Three Ayurvedists who have contributed to the medical knowledge in the twelfth and thirteenth centuries will be treated in this section, not in the primary sources above: Sarngadhara, Narahari, and Dallana. Further, the reader should note the significance of the practical compilations and commentaries on the basic texts of Caraka and Susruta being made by the modern writers like Dwarkanath, Nadkarni, and Pathi, for they reflect the changing attitude of India toward its own indigenous medicine. The circles which have in the past sought to suppress this medicine and to advance allopathic medicine have now removed the legal restrictions. The result is that the number of Ayurvedic medical colleges is increasing with its consequent increase in the number of trained physicians, and the centers at Varanasi and at Jamnagar are receiving greater government support so that Ayurvedic indigenous medicine is once again coming into its own.

Bhudeb, Mooker Jee, **Rasa-Jala-Nidhi** or **Ocena of Indian Chemistry and Medicine,** Calcutta, vol. 1, (1926)—vol. 5, (1938), Butterworth; Luzac and Co., London W. C.

Central Institute of Research in Indigenous Systems of Medicine, now become Ayurvedic Studies and Research, Jamnagar, **Jamnagar, India: Annual Report for Years 1956/57/58.**

Chatterjee, Rajvaidya Karivaj Probhakai, M.A., **Jyoterbhusan Vesagacharyya, Indian Science of the Pulse,** Compiled in Sanskrit, Principal, Calcutta College of Ayurvedic, with English Translation by the Author, 1934, Calcutta Printing Works, 1934, vol. 1.

Dallana was a Hindu physician who lived probably in the twelfth century and wrote one of the earliest commentaries on the **Susruta-samhita** entitled **Nibandhasamgraha**. The only earlier one extant is the **Bhanumati**, compiled by the Bengali physician Cakrapanidatta in the previous century.

Text: **Nibandhasamgraha**, edited by Jibananda Vidyasagara (Calcutta, 1891). Criticism: M. Winternitz: **Indischen Litteratur** (vol. 3, 548, 1922).

Dastur, J. F., **Medicinal Plants of India and Pakistan: A Concise work Describing Plants Used for Drugs and Remedies according to Ayurvedic, Unani, Tibbi Systems and Mentioned in British and American Pharmacopaeias**, D. B. Taraporevala Sons, 210 Hornby Road, Bombay, 1, (n.d.).

Dwarkanath, C., Dr., **Introduction to Kayachikitsa**, Popular Book Depot, Lamington Road, Bombay 1, 1959. **Fundamental Principles of Ayurveda, Part I, Introduction and Outlines of Nyaya-Viaseshika System of Natural Philosophy**, Bangalore Press, Mysore, 1962. **Part II, Outlines of Samkya Patanjala System**, Hindusthan Press, Mysore, 1953.

Gana Nath Sen, **Pratyyaksha-Shariram (Treatment of the Marmars)**, Kariraj S. K. Sen, Kalpataru Palace, 223 Chittaranjan Ave., Calcutta, Sept. 1940, vols. 2. (Book done first in English and then in Hindi; first edition, 1911).

Girindranath Mukhopadhyaya, Bhisaga-Caraya, **History of Indian Medicine Containing Notices, Biographical and Bibliographical, of the Ayurvedic Physicians and Their Works on Medicine from the Earliest Ages to the Present Time**, (Griffith Prize Essay for 1911), vols. III, Calcutta, 1923, Bhupendralal, Banerjee, Calcutta Univ. Press, Senate House, Calcutta.

Government of the United Provinces: **Report of the Ayurvedic and Unani Systems Reorganization Committee**, vol. I, 1948, Allahabad, Superintendent, United Provinces, India; vol. II, 1949.

Jolly, Julius, Dr., **Indian Medicine, Translated from German and Supplemented with Notes by C. G. Kashikar**, Mandala, Poona, 1951, C. G. Kashikar. (Translation of Jolly's original work published in 1901 in **Encyclopaedia of Indo-Aryan Research**.)

Kanada, Nadi Vignana, see Introduction. His **Science of Sphygmica or Sage Kanada on the Pulse, an English Translation with Sanskrit Passages by Kaveraj Russick Lalla Gupa**, Caicutta: S. C. Addy (1891) has been cited, but the authors have been unable to locate this book in India or in the U.S.

Mooker Jee, Bhudet, see Bhudet, Mooker, Jee.

Nadkarni, K. M., **Indian Materia Medica**, third edition, Popular Book Depot, Bombay 7, 2 vols., (n.d.).

Narahari was a Kashmirian physician and grammarian who composed between 1235 and 1250 a dictionary of material called **Rajanighantu** (or **Nighanturaja** or **Abhidhanacudamani**).

Text: Published in Benares, 1883, also in the Anandasrama Sanskrit Series (Vol. 33, Poona). Edition of the chapter dealing with minerals and translation by Richard von Garbe: **Die indische Mineralien** (Leipzig, 1882).

Criticism: According to Theodore Zachariae: **Die indische Wörterbücher**, Kósa (39, Strassburg, 1897), the **Rajanighantu** is a much later work, later than 1374. M. Winternitz: **Indische Litteratur** (vol. 3, 554, 1922). A. Berriedale Keith: **History of Sanskrit Literature** (512, Oxford, 1928).

Office of the Committee of the Indigenous Systems of Medicine: Dated July 1, 1924: Hakim Munzil's Popham's Broadway, signed, Muhzmmad Osman, Chairman of Committee on the Indigenous Systems of Medicine. **Written Evidence in English, Urdu, Telegu, Tamil, and Malayalam.** Madras, July 1, 1924. (An important document presenting views on behalf of indigenous medicine. It is difficult to obtain a copy.)

Pathi, A. Lakshmi, **A Textbook of Ayurveda (Ayurveda Siksha); Principles of Diagnosis, Ayurveda Sikshaa,** vol. IV, sections 1; **The Principles of Pathology (Roga Samprasapti)** vol. IV, sections II-VII, Ayurvedic Research Institute, 45 Harris Road, Mount Road, Madras. For copies apply to Dr. Pathi, editor, Circus Maiden Governorpet, Bezweda. (Note: Dr. Pathi died in 1963 so that one may encounter difficulties in obtaining his publications, especially the fourth.) He has sixteen other books and pamphlets all published by 1947 of which the next two only will be cited: **The Principles of Treatment,** vol. V, section I, **Ayurveda Chikitsha,** 1947 and **One Hundred Useful Drugs,** vol. III, April, 1946.

Sarngadhara was a Hindu physician who lived at an unknown time after the Muslim conquest, but not later than the thirteenth century. His work **Sarngadharasamhita** is one of the oldest Sanskrit works of its kind dealing with calcination of mercury and other metallic preparations and their therapeutic use. It is divided into three parts: (1) weights and measures, properties of drugs, influence of the seasons, diagnosis and prognosis (in the section on diagnosis there is an elaborate analysis of the pulse — nadipariksha), action of drugs, anatomy, embryology, and varieties of diseases; (2) decoctions, infusions, pastes, powders, pills and mercurial preparations, etc.; (3) ordinary therapeutic methods. His classification of diseases is far more detailed than those of his predecessors.

The popularity of this samhita is attested to by the existence of many manuscripts and of many native editions and translations.

The main quality of his work was its emphasis upon the chemical side of materia medica. In this respect it may be considered an anticipation of the iatro-chemical reforms which were heralded in Europe by Paracelsus centuries later. (He should not be confused with the poet bearing the same name who compiled in 1363 one of the best known anthologies of Sanskrit poetry.)

Text: Critical edition by Prabhuram Jivanram (Bombay, 1891).

Criticism: J. Jolly, "Medizin," **Grundriss der indo-arabischen Philologie,** vol. 3, Part 10, p. 4, 7, 1901). Praphulla Chandra Ray: **History of Hindu Chemistry** (2 vols., Calcutta; vol. 1, 2d. ed., 1903; vol. 2, 1909; new edition, 2 vols., Calcutta, 1925; Isis, vol. 3, 68-73; vol. 9, 555.). M. Winternitz: **Indischen Litteratur** (vol. 3, 157, 551, 1922).

Seal, Sir Brajendra Nath, M.A., Ph.D., **The Positive Sciences of the Ancient Hindus,** Moti Lal Banarsi Dass, Delhi, Varanasi, Patna, 1958.

Wilson, Johan, **India Three Thousand Years Ago** or **The Social State of the Aryans on the Banks of the Indus in the Time of the Vedas: Being the Expansion of a Lecture Delivered in the Town Hall of Bombay before the Mechanics' Institution,** 1858, Vidya-Bhushan Press, Varanasi.

Chapter IV

ARABIAN MEDICINE: THE LINK BETWEEN EAST AND WEST

The role played by the Arabs in advancing the study of medicine or in preserving medical classics is significant and needs to be related to an understanding of pulse lore. During the early Middle Ages of Europe (c. 500-1050) when learning became almost extinct, it was the Arab world which served as the cultural and intellectual center of the West[1]. Their learning at that time preserved the traditions of the past with its translations into Arabic, then the universal language of scholars, of the classics by Hippocrates, Plato, Aristotle, Dioscorides, Galen, and Paul of Aegina, to mention the frequently repeated names. By the eleventh century, these works were also translated into Latin and thus these classics were reintroduced into Europe. These facts are familiar to the Western student who tends to believe that the term Arabian Medicine means a body of scientific or medical doctrines which were written in the Arabic language but which were for the most part Greek in origin and were only to a very small extent the product of the Arabian mind. As a matter of record, however, the Arabian scholars did not restrict their horizons to the Greeks; instead they also translated Oriental philosophical and medical writings and made their own original contributions. They were familiar with basic Indian and Chinese texts. The theories and practices of all these peoples—the Greeks, the Indians, the Chinese, and the Persians—were intermingled by the Arabs with their own observations so that the resultant fusion introduced to Europe became the corpus of Western medicine. One might comment, in passing, that today, among the many views about the origins of Western medicine, two are pertinent to this study: Some schools of Indian thought affirm that allopathic medicine is an offshoot of Indian, chiefly Ayurvedic or indigenous, which came through Arabic sources. Other Western scholars who have specialized in Oriental studies state that it is derived from the Greeks who in turn obtained their ideas from the Indians.

Which country influenced the other's culture and which nation came first—India, China, or Persia—are of no immediate concern to this recounting of medical history. Pertinent is the fact that these civilizations maintained and taught the readings of the pulse as the chief method for the diagnosis of illness and health. All other procedures were ancillary to it. Indeed the reading of the pulse for the diagnosis and the prevention of disease has constituted a part of the art of healing

---

[1] At that time intellectual freedom prevailed in the Arab world. There were no persecutions of minorities and no inquisitions. In such an atmosphere scholars could flourish as was seen later with the appearance of Maimonides (1135-1204).

in these cultures even in mythical times as folk stories and legends reveal when they are correctly interpreted. Arabic practices and translations will be cited to illustrate their continuation of this tradition and philosophical groundwork as well as their enrichment of the field of medicine in the interpretation of the pulse.

Arabic medical literature assigned to the teacher particular responsibility in training the student accurately to read the pulse. Part of their medical curricula was devoted to the study of music so that the physician might appreciate the subtleties of the various tones of the pulse beats. In India the daily utilization of the Aum principle illustrates the recognition of the relation of sound and vibration to man's total being. Thus the training emphasized by the teacher was for the student to listen, to hear, correctly to interpret, and competently to diagnose. This aspect of medical training prevailed in all cultures.

The hundreds of books written on the pulse cannot begin to sensitize the finger-ear-mind in its awareness of the vibration which the informed physician brings to his own reading of the body. Stacked in the library are volumes incorporating all medical lore on the pulse, but these precepts and observations inevitably rest on the teachers' guidance of the students in developing a perceptive alertness. One does not have to be a philosopher or a mathematician to be a good musician; the same applies to the doctor who reads the pulse. In the dark ages of superstition and magic of all cultures when illiterates were medical practitioners, the knowledge which was orally communicated from teacher to pupil aways included diagnosis by reading the pulse. But the training of the student by his teacher cannot be as readily explicated, clarified, or recounted as the recorded facts of medical history like the translations from one language into another about the study of the pulse. In the Arab world, the translations of Hippocrates, Aristotle, Galen and the Indian writers on Ayurvedic medicine preserved the traditions of the past, but they were measured and equated with daily practice, as one concludes from a study of the original contributions made by the great Arabian authorities Rhazes, Al Majusi, Avicenna, and Maimonides.

"Rhazes", as he was named by the medieval Latinists, lived between the ninth and tenth centuries. He was an Arabian authority on the pulse who is ranked with Avicenna as one of the foremost Arabian physicians and he is also regarded as probably the greatest and most original of all Muslim physicians as well as one of the most prolific as an author. His name is spelled out Abu Bakr Muhammad ibn Zakariyya of Ray, but he is also known as ar-Razi. The chronology of his life is uncertain and the dates assigned to his death vary from A.D. 903 to 923. His **Hawi** or **Continens,** which contains books on the pulse, was one of the nine volumes constituting the whole library of the medical faculty of Paris in 1395. It was translated into Latin and published at Brescia in 1486 and again at Venice in 1542.

Another great physician was Haly Abbas or Ali ibn Abbas Al-Majusi, a Zoroastrian or a Magian from southwestern Persia. The exact date of his birth is not known, but he lived during the second half of the tenth century. He is famous for his **al-Kitab al-Sinaah al Tibbiyah (The**

Comprehensive in the Medical Art) which is certainly one of the most complete and concise medical books in the Arabic language. In it the author collected all the medical knowledge of his time and it was the textbook of the Arabic speaking world until the advent of Avicenna's **Quanun.** The arrangement of Al Majusi's subject matter is regarded as the best in Arabic medical literature. His observations about the pulse will be touched upon in this account.

Avicenna (979 or 980-1037) is considered the greatest of the Arabian philosophers in the East and a physician in whom Arabian medicine reached its culmination. He has been called the Leonardo da Vinci of the Arabic period. His philosophical ability was such that he had memorized the **Metaphysics** of Aristotle though its meaning remained obscure until he by chance bought the commentary by Al Farabi who wrote on anatomy and on the pulse and was the first Oriental scholar to comment on Aristotle's logic. At the age of eighteen when Avicenna cured the ruler of a dangerous illness, his reward was access to the royal library. Most of his works were written in Arabic, but among the two in Persian, his native language, was a small treatise on the pulse. His **Canon of Medicine** also revealed his knowledge and use of the pulse, as had been mentioned early in this study when the story was recounted of how he had devised a lie-detector test by reading the pulse to cure the sultan's wife of her love-sickness for a butcher from her home town. Avicenna's **Canon** improved upon and made obsolete, except for historical purposes, the works of Yuhanna ibn Masswayh (777-857) known as Mesue Senior; of Janus Damascenus, whose book on the pulse and fever has not yet been translated into English; of Rhazes; and of Al-Majusi. It has been remarked that with the composition of the **Quanun** or **Canon of Medicine,** Avicenna placed the coping-stone to the arch that bridges between the medical system of Hippocrates and Galen and that of Harvey and modern medicine; it became by means of its translation from Arabic into Latin the text book of all the universities of Europe. The **Quanun** is the largest, most famous and most important of Avicenna's medical works and most accessible. Its encyclopaedic character, its systematic arrangement, its philosophic plan, perhaps even its dogmatism raised it to a unique position in the medical literature of the Muslim world; and it is still regarded in the East as the last appeal on all matters connected with the healing art[2].

Pertinent to a comparison of Eastern and Western views on the pulse is an explication of the role played by the Arabs in preserving the Greek classics, the Indian, and the Chinese.

Hippocrates, known as Ibukrat or Bukrat, was one of the many whose works were made available to the physicians and scholars first through Arabic translations and then through Hebrew, Latin, and Greek. Maimonides (1135-1204) translated the **Canon** of Avicenna into Hebrew and then collected the aphorisms of Hippocrates and Galen in his **Aphorismes Moses,** written in Arabic between 1187 and 1190. This study

---

[2] E. G. Browne, **Arabian Medicine, the Fitzpatrick Lectures Delivered at the College of Physicians in November 1919 and November 1920,** Cambridge, At the University Press, 1962, p. 62.

contained extracts from the sixteen books of Galen on the pulse and is important to this inquiry. Marcus of Toledo (c. 1200) translated Galen's **De Tactus Pulsus** from Arabic into Latin.

An account of the translations from Indian medical literature must be related to the University of Jundi Shapur in South Persia, a medical school which was called the cradle of the Arab system of medicine. Since the town of Jundi Shapur was also the home of the Nestorian bishop where exiles of Edessa were welcomed, Nestorian missionaries for India left from this university center. Among others, Burzuya went to the Orient on a scientific mission to examine the state of medicine, and he brought back from India the game of chess together with the basic scientific writings of the Indian Ayurvedists Susruta and Caraka (see the bibliography of Ayurvedic medicine). The works of these two Indian sages were available in Arabic as early as the seventh century under the title **Kitabi-i-Shaushura-al-Hindi.** One of the earliest Islamic writers, Ali ibn Rabban Tabari, devoted a section of his **Firdaus-ul-Hikmat (Paradise of Wisdom)** to a discussion of the influences of Indian science on Persian medicine. A chronicler speaking of the University of Jundi Shapur wrote that the school followed chiefly the Greek and Indian systems. "They took what was good of each and to the ancient observations added their own."[3]

An interesting slant into how the Hindu doctors and teachings were both esteemed and utilized is told about Harun al-Raschid's sick uncle Ibrahim. The vizier recommended the Hindu doctor Sahleh, son of Bahleh. The patient died and the physician was disgraced, and the doctor, insisting that the uncle was not dead, inserted a needle under his fingernail and proved his claim. Thus even the great Harun al-Raschid confessed that "the Hindus were ever better physicians than the Greeks."[4] Whether or not this incident occurred as some authorities claim, there is no dispute that the Arabs borrowed from the Hindus the drugs aconite and mercury and that they were indebted to the chief Hindu medical works which were translated into Arabic as early as the seventh century. Hindu physicians were to be found in the ninth century both at Baghdad and at Gondisapor and tradition circulated stories similar to the one about Harun al Raschid's uncle.

The rendering of the Chinese medical classics into Arabic is also of consequence. In 1313 Rashiel al Din al Hamdani (1247-1318), a Persian physician and patron of learning, had an encyclopaedia of Chinese medicine prepared which included the **Nei Ching,** the principal manual on the pulse, prepared by Wang Shu Ho; in addition to the pulse lore, the encyclopaedia included material on anatomy, embryology, gynecology, and pharmacology.[5] Needham's historical survey discussed Filliozat's

3 Cyril Elgood, "Medicine in Persia," Clio Medica, A Series of Primers on the History of Medicine, editor: E. B. Krumbhaar, M.D., Paul B. Hoeber, Inc., N. Y., 1934, p. 15. Elgood, M.D. and M.R.C.P., was physician to the British Legation at Teheran in Iran. See also his A Medical History of Persia and the Eastern Caliphate, Cambridge, At the University Press, 1951.

4 See Edward Theodore Withington, Medical History from the Earliest Times; A Popular History of the Healing Art, London, Scientific Press, 1894, p. 174.

5 This history of Chinese thought in Persian literature has been fully described by Adnan Adivar and by Suhi I Uner with Turkish illustrations: Adnan Adivar, Isis, 1940, appeared 1947, vol. 32, p. 44.

La Doctrine Classique de la Médicine Indienne (Paris, 1949) and showed the resemblance of Greek pneumatic medicine to ancient Indian medicine which had close parallels to the ancient Chinese physiological concepts of **Chhi** and **Feng**[6] so that all might find a Mesopotamian origin.

Whether the interpretation of the pulse was the outcome of personal observation or the response to an investigation suggested by translation, the pulse was stressed in Arabic medicine as it was in Indian and in Chinese. Al-Majusi's **Kamil al Sinaah al-Tibbiyah (The Comprehensive in the Medical Art)** sums up the directional drift of the Arabic teachings and writings on the pulse and indirectly reveals how they borrowed and enriched these precepts. In directing the student about the examination of the pulse, Al-Majusi wrote:

> The pulse is a messenger that does not lie and a mute announcer that tells of secret things by its movement. . . . The heart and the arteries move in one motion, in one style, and at one time, which means that the movement of each is equal to that of the other and does not differ from it. Therefore, we can have the condition of the heart and its movements from the conditions of the arteries and the pulse.

> The condition of the pulse differs a great deal according to the differences in the moving power, the difference in the instinctive heat and the difference in the condition of the arteries and what they contain of blood and spirit. . . . Early physicians classified these differences in ten categories:
> 1. Indications taken from the amount of relaxation.
> 2. Indications taken from the time of movement.
> 3. Indications taken from the amount of power.
> 4. Indications taken from the consistency of the artery.
> 5. Indications taken from the contents of the artery.
> 6. Indications taken from the volume of the artery.
> 7. Indications taken from the time of diastole.
> 8. Indications taken from the time of movements and intervals.
> 9. Indications taken from the special amount.
> 10. Indications taken from the number of beats.[7]

Al Majusi, as the second of the great Moslem physicians, intended his volume to form a complete cyclopaedia of medicine for his time (date assigned is generally 994): ten of his books are theoretic and ten practical.[8] Though founded on Galen, his account makes signal observations that reveal originality and in this dual combination, he is symtomatic of the combined uses of the past and the present that enriched Arabian medicine, upon which the medical men of the West drew. A specific listing of the indebtedness of the West to Arabian medicine from the eleventh to the fourteenth centuries will be cited, but the broader

---

6 See Joseph Needham, **op. cit.**, vol. 1, p. 239.

7 Al-Majusi, "Kamel al Sinaah," vol. I, pp. 254-255 as quoted in Amin A. Khairallah, **Outline of Arabic Contributions to Medicine,** American Press, Beirut, Lebanon, 1946, p. 87.

8 E. G. Browne in his account of **Arabian Medicine** (p. 54) remarks that his **Liber Regius** or **Maliki,** another title for the same work, makes Majusi's study the most accessible and the most readable of the great Arabic systems of medicine since an excellent edition in two volumes was printed at Cairo in 1294/1877 and the Latin version, though rare, was fortunately not included amongst the incunabula and could therefore be borrowed from libraries which possess it.

generalizations about the significance of the pulse as a medical diagnostic aid extend up to the present. Occidental medicine until the dawn of the eighteenth century was influenced by Arabian medicine which is, in reality, the bridge between the medical beliefs and practices of East and West. The lore of the pulse was established in the teachings of the East and of the West, but it was lost by the West, rediscovered by the West and again lost by the West when it came to rely very heavily on instruments.

Among the Europeans who between the eleventh and fourteenth centuries were influenced by Arabic medicine were Roger Bacon, Constantine Africanus, Bernard the Provincial, and John St. Paul. When Roger Bacon wrote his medical study **Epistola de Accientibus Senectutis,** he drew from the writings of Avicenna, Rhazes, Issac Judius and Janus Damascenus. Constantine Africanus (c. 1020-87) in his **De Pulsibus Orientes et Occidentis** was the first to make Arabian medicine known to the West through the medium of Latin. Bernard De Gordon, author of **Lilium Medicinae,** was a Scottish professor who taught at Montpellier from 1285 to 1297. His **Lilium Medicinae** was completed in 1307, and thereafter it was translated into French and Hebrew. His other works included **De Pulsibus, De Urinus, De Phlebotomea,** and **De Regimine Sanitatis.** Fabrius (1578-1657), who was a teacher of Harvey, regarded the four volumes by Bernard de Gordon as addenda to the **Lilium Medicinae.** About the year 1155, Bernard the Provincial wrote a commentary on therapeutics which drew on Arabic sources. John St. Paul, one of the teachers of Gilbert the Englishman, was a contemporary of Urso, the authority on the pulse and the urine, the principal diagnostic weapons of the middle ages in the Western world.[9]

It would be useful here to take a page from the Chinese practices of correlative thinking to comprehend how the principle of pulsation and vibration is being used in other areas of study. One example, familiar to all of us, is the recent development of sonar, related to bioacoustics, as used by the United States Navy during World War II for picking up enemy submarines or ships. Any strange sounds would send men to their battle stations but at that time, the scientists had not yet analyzed the sounds in the sea so there were no data for comparing them. Hence depth charges and torpedoes would be fired at a school of snapping shrimp or at courting whales. By 1966, however, the sounds of over 300 different fish and over 20 different sea mammals were analyzed and recorded for the trained sonar expert. Dr. Marie Fish (no pun intended) has made a contribution to the science in her post as research oceanographer at the marine laboratory of the University of Rhode Island. She remarked, "One day we hope to have daily underwater sound forecasts like weather charts for all ships, navy or merchant. So they can tell what sea animals are in a given area at a given time. Unmanned electrical devices may be able to broadcast the location of big schools of fish to fishing fleets and even tell them what kind of fish they are."

---

9 See Charles Joseph Singer, editor, **Studies in the History and Method of Science,** Oxford, Clarendon Press, 1917-21, vols. 1, 2. His volume on **Medieval Contribution to Modern Civilization** is also useful.

Just as the oceanographers are charting the pulse of the sea so did the Chinese, Egyptians, Indians, Greeks, and Arabs chart the pulse of the body. To these experts, the pulse was a musical discipline that told of the symphony or discord of the body. Herophilos was said to be the first Westerner to call attention to the similarity between arterial pulsation and musical cadences. Pliny stated that Herophilos "reduced the pulse or beating of the arteries into the times and measures in musicke, according to the degree of every age." Al Farabi, who prepared the way for Avicenna, also wrote the most important Oriental treatise on the theory of music, **Kitab al musiqi**. Was his interest in music one of the reasons for his becoming an expert on the pulse?

Valentine used a musical scale with notes to record the pulse and Marquet went a step further in a method of representing the pulse by means of musical notes. He simply employed musical notes—long, breve, semi-breve, etc.—to create a visual impression of the tactile sensation of the pulse. Theophile de Bordeu influenced his generation and those who came after with his theory that diseases always pass through certain definite stages terminating in crises which could be predicted by the pulse. He believed that each organ had its own **special humor** (secretion) and may have anticipated the theory of internal secretion or endocrinology. He devised a pulse system for the production of crises. Solano de Luque influenced Nihell and their books were very popular. Ozanam's study greatly influenced Broadbent; Sir James MacKenzie's account of the pulse influenced T. Bennet, a chiropractor who specialized in a form of reflex therapy which became popular between 1955 and 1962.

This parade of Western practitioners can be briefly contrasted with the Easterners. There is no need here to repeat the Aum principle as a basic to awareness of the self that Indian philosophy, literature, and medical practice project. The Chinese interpretation of the sounds made by cricket is not as well known to the Westerners nor their interest in the cicada which was their emblem of resurrection. This study of the sounds of insects led on the one hand to the cultivation of the silk worm and on the other to strange bypaths. A minister of state in the thirteenth century (Chia Ssu-Tao) was one of the cricket fanciers famous in history. By the time he wrote his famous treatise which contained much information on the subject, the Chinese were already very familiar with crickets and had developed considerable lore on their rearing, training, and medical care. The keeping of crickets in cages to enjoy their chirping goes back at least to the T'ang; and the sport of cricket fights (shades of Twain's "Jumping Frogs of Calaveras County") was developed under the Sung. The Chinese language contains a number of special terms without equivalents in Arabic, Latin, or European vernaculars. Some Chinese were especially adept at distinguishing various kinds of chirping and were able to breed musical crickets. Noteworthy is the fact that two generals wrote treatises on crickets and on mushrooms. (See Amber's book on **Color Therapy** for applications of vibrations in the sacred mushroom, drug addiction, and alcoholism.)

Whether it be sonar, music, crickets, the Aum principle, or the pulse—all are symphonies in the cosmos, separate, yet inter-related, each telling the listener the story of its discipline. All have one fundamental basis in common: Vibration. Therein the physician finds the key through the pulse to diagnosis.

Arabian and Western Bibliography

Abercromby, David, De Variationes, ac Varietate Pulsus Observationis. Accessit eiusdem Authoris Nova Medicinae . . . Clavis Sive Ars Explorandi Medicas Plantarum ac Corporum Quorumcumque Facultater ex Solo Sapore, Londoni, 1685, S. Smith.

Abu Sahl Al-Mashihi, from Jurjan, East of the Caspian Sea, was a, Christian physician writing in Arabic and was the teacher of Avicenna. He died in 999. His encyclopaedic treatise on medicine in a hundred chapters (Al-kutub al-mi'a fi-l-sana'a al-tibbya) is one of the earliest works of its kind and may have been the model of the Quanun. He wrote various smaller treatises: on measles, on the plague, and on the pulse. See also F. Wüstenfeld: Arabische Aerzte (59, 1840). L. Le Clerc: Medicine Arabe (vol. 1, 356-357, 1876). C. Brockelmann: Arabische Litteratur (vol. 1, 238, 1898).

Actuarius, Johannes, Methodi Medendi Libre Sex, Quibus Omnia, Quae ad Medicinam Factitandam Pertinent, Fere Complectitus, Venice, 1554, pp. 8-17.

Adnan Adivar, "On the Tanksuq-namah-i Ilkhan dar Funun-i 'Ulum-i-Khitai,'" Isis, 1940 (appeared 1947), vol. 32, p. 44.

Aegidius Corboliensis, De Urines et Pulsibus. Petrus Leo de Urines . . . Tractatus de Iudiciis Urine Metrice Compositus cum Ipsius Commento . . ., Venetiis, G. Arrivabenus, Imp. Heredum O. Scot, 1414 (1514).

Agathinos, Claudios of Sparta, lived in the second half of the first century and was founder of the Eclectic or Episynthetic school of medicine, a development of the Pneumatic school. He wrote a treatise on the pulse.

Agilinus, Gualterus (or Agulinus, Aquilinus), Walter Agilinus, Gauthier Agilon (?), Salernitian physician who flourished probably about the middle of the thirteenth century and was probably a Frenchman. He was influenced by Giles of Corbeil of the second half of the twelfth. His main works are a Summa Medicinalis, which is a complete special pathology and therapeutics based on uroscopy, and a Compendium Urinarum, which appears to be an elaboration of earlier writings on the subject. He also wrote Liber Pulsum and among his earlier works, two were translated into Hebrew; the one on poisons was translated about 1297-1301.

Text: Paul Diepgen: "Gualteri Agiloni Summa Medicinalis Erstmalig Ediert mit einter Vergleichender Betrachtung alterer Medizinischen Kompendien des Mittelalters" (Studien zur Geschichte der Medizen, Leipsig, 232 p., 1911; excellent edition). Julius Pfeffer: Das Compendium Urinarum des Gualterus Agulinus (Diss., Berlin, 1891). Criticism: Emile Littre: Histoire Litterarie de la France (vol. 21, 411-415, 1847). Salvatore de Renzi: Storia documentata della scuola di Salerno (2 ed., 421-423, 1857). M. Steinschneider: Hebraische Ubersetzungen (800, 1893). F. Hartmann: Die Litteratur von Früh und Hochsalerno (37-38, 1919).

Alexander of Tralles was born c. 525 in Lydia, traveled extensively, and settled in Rome where he died in 605. A Byzantine doctor, he was the first original physician since Galen. He wrote on the pulse and on urine as well as on pathology. His works were very influential and not simply in the Greek speaking world, for they were soon translated in Syriac, Arabic, Hebrew, and Latin.

Texts: Latin edition (Lyon, 1504) often reprinted. First Greek edition (Paris, 1548). Bernhard Nosske: **Alexandri (Tralliani?) Liber de Agnoscendis Febrius et Pulsibus et Urinis** (Diss., 39 p., Borna-Leipzig, 1919; Isis, IV, 578).

Alfanus, I., Archbishop of Salerno, "Tractatibus de Pulsibus," **Trascrizione del Codice 1024 della Biblioteca dell' Arsenale di Parigi** (da carta 16 b. a carta 18 R). **Annatazzioni e Commento** . . . Pietro Capparoni, Roma, Instituto Nazional Medico Farmacologica "Serono", 1936, 51 p.

Al-Farabi, known in Latin as Alpharabius, was born near Farab, Turkestan of a Turkish family, lived chiefly in Aleppo and died in Damascus 950-951 at the age of eighty. He was a Muslim Neo-platonist and encyclopaedist, and his system is a syncretism of Platonism, Aristotelianism, and Sufism. He continued the harmonization of Greek philosophy with Islam begun by Al-kindi, and thus prepared the way for Avicenna. His own writings deal chiefly with psychology and metaphysics. He was conversant with the scientific thought of his day and wrote the most important Oriental treatise on the theory of music **(Kitab al-musiqi).**

Al-Majusi, see Haly Abbas and text.

Anfrum, J. F. A., **De La Valeur Diagnostique et Pronostique de la Température et du Pauls dam quelquea Maladie,** Paris, A. Delahaya, 1868, 95 p.

Archigenes of Apamea, Syria, was a physician who lived in Rome under Trajan and the most famous disciple of Agathinos. His was one of the most elaborate theories of the pulse in ancient times. It is to be noted that he wrote on Hindu therapeutics.

See: Max Wellmann: "Archigenes," (**Paul-Wissowa,** vol. III, 484-486, 1895); "Die pneumatische Schule bis auf Archigenes," **Philol. Untersuch.,** XIV, 1895). E. Gurlt: **Geschichte der Chirurgie** (vol. I, 411-414, 1898).

Avicenna, see Ibn Sina; see text.

Barton, W. M. and Yater, W. M.,**Symptom Diagnosis,** D. Appleton and Co., N. Y. and London, 1928.

Berner, Gottlier Ephraim, "Observatio Medica IV. De Pulsu Coturnizante," in his **Exercitatio Physico-Medica de Efficacia** . . ., Amstelaedamie, 1738, pp. 544-48.

Best, C., and Taylor, N. B., **The Human Body, Its Anatomy and Physiology,** 3rd edition, Henry Holt and Co., N. Y., 1932, 48, 56. **The Living Body, A Text in Human Physiology,** 4th edition, N. Y., 1938, 1958, Henry Holt and Co.

Blakiston's Illustrated Pocket Medical Dictionary, McGraw Hill Book Co., N. Y., 1960.

Bonacursi, Bartolomeo di Pompeo (fl. ca. 1618), **Della Natura de Polsi** (Col. Bologna: per Giacomo Monti, 1647).

Bong, Otto Christianus, **De Pulsu et Signo Fallaci,** Halae ad Salam, Aere Beyeriano (1767).

Bordeu, Theophile, **Inquiries concerning the Variety of the Pulse and the Particular Crises Each More Especially Indicates. Written Originally in French,** London, S. T. Lewis, 1764, 539. **Recherches sur le Pouls, par Rapport aux Crises,** Paris, de Bure l'aine, 1756; 2nd ed., Paris., Didot Jr., 1768.

Brendel, Johann Gottfried (1712-1758), **De Pvlsv Febrili Commentariol,** 18 p.

Broadbent, William Henry, **The Pulse,** Philadelphia, Lee Bros. and Co. 1890.

Browne, E. G., **Arabian Medicine, The Fitzpatrick Lectures Delivered at the College of Physicians in November 1919 and November 1920,** Cambridge, at the University Press, 1962.

Campbell, Donald, **Arabian Medicine and Its Influences on the Middle Ages,** Trubner's Oriental Series, Kagan Paul Trench, Trubner and Co., Ltd., Broadway House, 68-74 Carter Lane, E. C. London, 1926.

Cleyer, Andreas, "Tractatus de Pulsibus ab Erudito Europaeo Collectos," in his **Specimen Medicenae Sinecae . . .,** Francofurti, J. P. Zubrodt, 1682. "Auctori Vani Xo Ho Pulsibus Explanatis Medendi Regula," in his **Specimen Medicenae Sinecae,** Francofurti, 1682.

Coca, Arthur Fernandez, **The Pulse Test,** N. Y., University Books, 1956. See also **New Concept of Diagnosis and Causes of Allergy and Other Diseases.**

Cole, see **Fernelius.**

Collinson, Joannes, **De Pulsu,** Edinburgh, Abernethy and Walker, 1810.

Constantine the African or Constantine Africanus was born in Carthage and after many years of travel in the East, he settled down in Monte Cassino c. 1056 to 1070 and died there in 1087. A monk at Monte Cassino (Leo Ostiensis) called him "magister orientis et occidentis." He was the first great translator from the Arabic into Latin and his visit to Salerno acted as a catalyst upon the Salernitan school. Thus he enabled them to take advantage of Muslim experiences as well as of their own Greek traditions.

Text: Eight of his translations are included in the **Opera Issac** (Lyon, 1515). A collected edition of his works appeared in Basel (2 vol., 1536-1539). Charles Singer: "A Legend of Salerno. How Constantine Brought the Art of Medicine to the Christians," **Johns Hopkins Hospital Bulletin** (vol. 28, 64-69, 1917). Fredrich Hartmann: Die Literatur von Früh und Hochsalerno (9-14, 1919, contains further bibliography).

Cornacchini, Tommaso, **Tabulae Medicae. In Quibus es Fere Omni Quae a Principibus Medicis Graecis, Arabibus et Latines de Curationis Apparatv Capitis, ac Thoracis Morbis, Febribus, Pulsibus, Urinis,** Scripta Sparsim Reperiuntur (c. 1552).

Cox, Daniel, **Observations on the Intermitting Pulse, as Prognosticating in Acute Diseases, According to Dr. Solano, a Critical Diarrhea: or, as Indicating the Use of Purging Remedies,** London, A. Miller, 1751.

Culpeper, see Fernelius.

Deichgraber, Karl, **Galen ah Erforscher des Menschlichen Pulses, ein Beitrag zur Selbst darstellung des Wissenschaftlen** (De Dignotione Pulsuum II), Berlin, Akademie-Verlag, 1957.

Democritos of Abdera was born about 460 B.C. in Thrace and died about 370. He might be called the Aristotle of the fifth century. He investigated the pulse and the physiology of the senses and of reproduction among the many other subjects which interested him.

Albert Goedemeyer: **Epikurs Verhältnis zu Demokrit in der Naturphilosophie** (Strassburg, 1897). Adolf Dyroff: **Demokritstudie** (Leipzig, 1899, with bibliography).

Dorland's Illustrated Medical Dictionary, 23rd ed., Saunders Co., Philadelphia and London, 1957.

Ehrhart, Jodocus, **De Pulsibus,** Jenae, Lit., Fickelscherrianis, 1761.

Elgood, Cyril, **A Medical History of Persia and the Eastern Caliphate,** Cambridge, At the University Press, 1951. "Medicine in Persia," **Clio Medica, A Series of Primers on the History of Medicine,** editor: E. B. Krumbhaar, M.D., Paul B. Hoeber, Inc., N. Y., 1934, p. 15.

Emerich, Franz (1490-1560), "An Urinarum vel Pulsuum Observatio Certiores Notas Salutis vel Mortis Medico Praebeat, Utilis Enarratio," in **Montanus, Joanne Baptista, Summaria Declaratio Eorum, Quae ad Urinarum Cognitionem Maxime Faciunt,** Viennae, 1552.

Erasistratos, born c. 304 B.C., flourished in Alexandria c. 258-57. He was a younger contemporary of Herophilos and a pupil in Athens of Aristotle's son-in-law. He may be called the founder of physiology as a separate subject and the founder of comparative and pathological anatomy. He recognized the heart as the motive power in circulation and experimentally demonstrated that the arteries contained blood; he described the chordae tendinea and the valves of the heart.

Rob. Fuchs: **Erasistratea quae in Librorum Memoria Latent Congesta Enarrantur.** (Diss., 32 p, Leipzig, 1892). Hermann Diels: **Anonymous Londinensis** (Berlin, 1893). M. Wellmann, in **Pauly-Wissowa** (1909). C. Singer: **Evolution of Anatomy** (1925).

Ewart, William, **How to Feel the Pulse and What to Feel in It. Practical Hints for Beginners,** N. Y., W. Wood and Co., 1892.

Falconer, W., **Observations Respecting the Pulse; Intended to Point Out with Greater Certainty, the Indications Which It Signifies; Especially in Feverish Complaints,** London, T. Cadell, 1799.

Faraj Ben Selem, see Moses Farachi.

Fernelius Ambianus Joannes, Cole, Abdiah and Culpeper, Nicholas, **Two Treatises: The First of Pulses, the Second of Urines,** London, P. Cole, 1662.

Fields, Albert, "The Pulse in Ancient Chinese Medicine," reprinted in **California Medicine,** 1947, vol. 66, no. 6.

Floyer, Sir John, **The Physician's Pulse-Watch; or An Essay to Explain the Old Art of Feeling the Pulse and to Improve It by the Help of Pulse Watch,**

London, Sam Smith, 1707. He built up a pulse rate under varying circumstances and a special pulse for each disease based on the combined Galenic-Chinese foundation.

Fludel, Robert, **Pulsus, Seu Nova et Arcana Pulsum Historia, e Sacro Fonte Radicali ter Extracta, Nec Non Medicorum Ethnicorum Dictis et Authoritate Comprobata . . .,** Francofurti, W. Hoftmanni, 1630.

Fouquet, Henri, **Essai sur le Pouls, par Rapport aux Affections des Principaux Organes Traduite du Latin de M. Fleming . . .,** Montpellier, A. Seguin, 1818.

Frey, Walter, "Der Arterielle und Capillare Puls," in **Handbuch der Normalen und Pathologischen Physiologie . . .,** Berthe von Bergmann et al, 1927.

Galen is the anatomist, physician and philosopher termed the greatest physician of antiquity after Hippocrates. He was born in Pergamum 129 B.C. and died at the age of 70. He discovered a large number of facts in the field of anatomy, physiology, embryology, pathology, therapeutics, and pharmacology; conducted numerous experiments to determine the mechanism of respiration and pulsation, the function of the kidneys, of the cerebrum, and of the spinal cord at different levels; proved experimentally that the arteries carry blood and that the right auricle outlives the rest of the heart. It is astounding to realize how close he came to the discovery of the circulation of the blood, at least as far as some of the main facts are concerned. He gave a rational interpretation of dreams (physiological), and his chief merit consists in having systematized and unified Greek anatomical medical knowledge and practice. He strove to establish medicine on an experimental and rational basis, but failed to realize the narrow limitations of the deductive method in the field of biology. This great medical philosopher was bent upon teleological explanations and sought to establish more strongly the vitalistic ideas of Aristotelian philosophy.

A bibliography of Galen's works and commentaries would require a book over 500 pages. There is abundant Galenic literature on the pulse including five long treaties and three short ones, the greatest part of which was available in Arabic before the ninth century: in all there are eighteen separate essays concerning the pulse which are briefly listed: 1. **Concerning the pulse; 2. A Little Book Concerning the Pulse for Beginners; 3. Concerning the Differences of the Pulse**—First Essay; 4. Ibid., Second Essay; 5. Ibid., Third Essay; 6. Ibid., Fourth Essay; 7. Concerning the Diagnosis from the Pulse, First Essay; 8. Ibid., Second Essay; 9. Ibid., Third Essay; 10. Ibid., Fourth Essay; 11. **Concerning the Course of the Pulse, First Essay; 12. Ibid., Second Essay; 13. Ibid., Third Essay; 14. Ibid., Fourth Essay; 15. Concerning Prognosis from the Pulse; 16. Ibid., Second Essay; 17. Ibid., Third Essay; 18. Ibid., Fourth Essay.**

The following are included in Kuhn's edition: (1) **Galeni de Pulsuum Usu Liber** (vol. 5, 149-180, 1823); (2) **De Pulsibus Libellus ad Tirones** (vol. 8, 453-492, 1824); (3) **De Pulsuum Differentiis, Libri IV** (vol. 8, 493-765); (4) **De Dignoscendis Pulsibus, Libri IV** (vol. 8, 766-961); (5) **De Causis Pulsuum Libri V** (vol. 9, 1-204, 1825); (6) **De Praesagitione ex Pulsibus, Libri IV** (vol. 9, 205-430); (7) **Synopsis Librorum Suorum de Pulsibus** (vol. 9, 431-549); (8) **De Pulsibus ad Antonium Disciplinae Studiosum ac Philosophum** (vol. 19, 629-642, 1830). All of these writings, but the last one, are included in the Arabic canon established by Humain ibn Ishaq. See G. Bergstraesser's edition of it (Leipzig, 1925) or M. Meyerhof's analysis of it (Isis, vol. 8, 685-724) under the numbers 41, 5, 16 (four treatises) and 66. See also Joh. Gossen: "Synopsis de Pulsibus," **De Galeni Libro qui . . . Inscribitur** (Berlin, 1907).

Gandini, Carlo, **Gli Elementi dell' Arte Sfiygmica . . .**, Napoli, G. Castellano, 1776.

Gerard of Cremona was perhaps the greatest of Italian translators from Arabic into Latin and is perhaps the greatest of all translators. Born about 1114 in Cremona, Lombardy, he died in 1187 in Toledo. Seventy-one works, some of them of immense size, are credited to him and practically all the main Greek and Arabian authors were translated by him. His medical translations were of extreme importance, and they introduced into the European languages a number of new technical terms—such as vena, retina, saphena, cephalica, clavicle, true and false ribs from Avicenna's **Quanun**. No attempt is made here to list his medical translations.

Gesner, Conrad, **Enchiridon Rei Medicae Triplicis. Illius Primum Quae Signa ex Pulsi et Urinis Dijudicat Deinde Therapeuticae, Tertio Diaeteticae,** Tiguri, A. and J. Gesner, 1555.

Giles of Corbeil was a French physician and humanist who studied in Salerno in the middle of the twelfth century. He became canon of Notre Dame in Paris and died between 1220 and 1224. He wrote medical poems in leonine verse, which are very important as being the main channel through which Salernitan lore reached the Parisian doctors. These poems also contain interesting information on the medical customs of that time. Among his books was a very popular textbook entitled **De Pulsibus** (380 lines), first edition, Padua, 1483; reprinted in Venice in 1494; in Lyon, in 1505, 1515, etc.

Gotfredsen, Edvard, **Oldtidens Laere om Hjerte, Kar og Puls; en Medicinsk-Historisch Studie**, Kabenhavn, E. Munksgaaard, 1942.

Gormek, Mirko D., **Les Reflets de la Sphygmologie Chinois dans la Medicine Occidentale**, Paris, Feb. 1962, vol. 51.

Haddad, Sami, see Khairallah.

Haly Abbas, see text: other name for Al-Majusi. He composed for the king Abudu'd-Dawla Fanákhusraw the Buwayhid (949-982), his System of Medicine entitled **al-Maliki ("The Royal") Liber Regius** which was superceded by Avicenna's **Quanun. The Royal** excels on the scientific side while the **Quanun** excels on the practical side. Al-Majusi discusses Hippocrates, Galen, Paul of Aegina, and Razi.

Herophilos lived in the last third of the fourth century and flourished in Alexandria. He is known as the founder of anatomy as a scientific discipline and after Hippocrates and Galen, he is the greatest physician of antiquity. He is said (by Galen) to have been the first to undertake human dissections. As a pupil of Praxagoras, he improved upon his teacher's theory of the pulse and used a clepsydra to measure its frequency and to diagnose fever. The strength of the pulse indicates that of the heart.

Text: K. F. J. Marx: **Herophilus** (Karlsruhe, 1838, Göttingen, 1842). Hermann Schone: "Markellinos Pulslehre," **Aus der Festschrift zur 49 Ver-**

sammlung Deutscher Philologen, 448-472, Basel, 1907. This edition of Marcellinos's Study of the Pulse is a little treatise of no earlier date than the second century, but it is a very important study because of the detailed information it contains on Herophilos's quantitative theory of the pulse.

Hippocrates of Cos was born about 460 B.C. and died at a very old age in Larissa, Thessaly. Known as the "Father of Medicine," he was one of the great clinical physicians of all times. He dissociated medicine from superstition; systematized the empirical knowledge which had accumulated in Egypt and in the schools of Cnidos and Cos; and founded inductive and positive medicine. He did for medicine what Socrates did for philosophy.

Texts: The Hippocratic canon is very large, but the greater part of it is certainly not genuine; yet very much is the direct or indirect fruit of Hippocrates's teaching. The number of Hippocratic writings varies greatly according to the selection made in the complete corpus by each author. References will be made here to three treatises which belong to the Hippocratic corpus because they bear upon the pulse. Here see Julius Hirschberg: "Arztliche Bemerkungen über die in der Hippodratischen Sammlung uberlieferte Schrit," Archiv. f. Gesh. d. Naturw., (VI, pp. 163-173, 1913). In the treatise on nutriment, chapter 48 contains what is probably the earliest mention of the pulse in Greek literature, but the great importance of the pulse is not and was not realized until about 340 B.C. The almost complete disregard of the pulse in Hippocratic literature is the more surprising in that allusions to it are found in the Ebers Papyrus. Probably the Greeks were not aware of the Egyptian views. This fact supports the claim that the Greeks took their ideas from the Indian and the Chinese.

Horine, Emmet Field, "An Epitome of Ancient Pulse Lore," Bulletin of the History of Medicine, Baltimore, 1941, vol. 10, pp. 209-249.

Ibn Sina Husain abd Allah, see Avicenna in the text. He is frequently called the Galen of Arabian medicine. He was born about 980 and died in 1037. He wrote twenty-one major works on philosophy, medicine, theology, geometry, astronomy, and philology, and a small treatise on the pulse, of which he was a master (see text). Omar Khayyam's famous poem is believed by some authorities to have been written by Avicenna. The Quanun is his largest and most famous work. See O. Cameron Gruner, A Treatise on the Canon of Medicine of Avicenna . . ., London, Luzac and Co., 1930.

John of Alexandria flourished in Alexandria c. 627-640. A Jacobite bishop, he endeared himself to the Arabs by his repudiation of trinitarianism. He wrote commentaries on Hippocrates and Galen; an epitome of Sixteen Books of Galen is ascribed to him and this is the name given to the Byzantine canon of Galenic writing edited at about the beginning of the seventh century. The treatment of the pulse is found in sections III, De Pulsibus ad Tirones and XI, Four Books on the Pulse. Another Byzantine canon of Hippocratic writings is divided into twelve parts and these two canons formed the core of Syro-Arabic medicine. On the Muslim tradition of the Sixteen Books, see L. Leclerc: Médecine Arabe (vol. 1, 38-60, 1876). Leclerc wrongly identifies him with John Philoponos. The Arabic translation of the Sixteen Books is to be found in the British Museum, M. S. Arundel, Or. 17.

John of Seville, John of Spain, or John of Toledo was an Hispano-Jewish translator from Arabic into Latin. He was converted to Christianity and his original Jewish name is unknown. He flourished in Toledo about 1135-1153. Among the many Arabic treatises, he translated one on medicine which was popular and of great interest as a prototype of the famous Salernitan regimen sanitatis: **Epistola Aristotelis ad Alexandrum de Conservatione Corporis Humani,** which was translated from the **Sirr alasrar, Secretum Secretorum.** The translation of a treatise on pulse and urine is ascribed to him and to Plato of Tivoli.

Khairallah, Amim A., **Outline of Arabic Contributions To Medicine,** American Press, Beirut, Lebanon, 1946 (excellent bibliography). and Haddad, Sami I., "A Forgotten Chapter in the History of the Circulation of the Blood," **Annals of Surgery,** 1936, vol. 104, p. 1.

MacKenzie, Sir James, **The Study of the Pulse, Arterial, Venous, and Hepatic and the Movement of the Heart,** N. Y., MacMillan and Co., 1902.

The MacMillan Medical Cyclopedia, N. Y., MacMillan Co., 1955.

Marc or Marcus of Toledo was a Spanish physician and translator from Arabic into Latin. The exact time of his activity is unknown; it was probably towards the end of the twelfth century. Among the Canon of Toledo which he translated from the Arabic was Galen's **De Tactu Pulsus** (3) and **De Utilitate Pulsus** (4).

F. Wüstenfeld: **Ubersetzungen Arabischer Werke** (116, Göttingen, 1877). M. Steinschneider: **Europaische Ubersetzungen** (54, Wien, 1904).

Marden, Orison Swett, **Every Man a King or Might in Mind Mastery,** N. Y., Thomas Y. Crowell, 1906.

Marquet, Francois, Nicols, **Nouvelle Méthode Facile et Curieuse, Pour Connoitre le Pouls par les Notes de la Musique, 2 ed., Augmenteé de Plusieuss Observations et Réflexions Critiques** . . . pas M. Pierre Joseph Buchoz, Amsterdam, 1769.

Menuret de Chambaud, Jean J., **Nouveau Traité du Pouls,** Amsterdam, Paris, Chez Vincent, 1768.

Moses Farachi or Faragut or Faraj Ben Salim was a Sicilian-Jewish physician and translator from Arabic into Latin. He was employed by Charles of Anjou to translate medical works and became one of the greatest translators of his time. His main translation was that of **Kitab al-Hawi (Continens)** of Al-Razi (second half of ninth century). He completed it in 1279 together with a glossary. The **Hawi** was the largest encyclopaedia of Greco-Arabic medicine and much larger than the more famous **Quanun** of Avicenna. The importance of this translation can hardly be exaggerated.

Text: **Continens,** first edition, Brescia, 1486. (This was the largest and heaviest of all incunabula—22 pounds.) Later editions: Venice, 1500, 1506, 1509, 1542. Criticism: L. Leclerc: **Médicine Arabe** (vol. 2, 464-467, 1876). F. Wüstenfeld: **Ubersetzungen Arabischer Werke** (107-110, 1877). M. Steinschneider: **Hebraeische Ubersetzungen** (1893, 974); **Europaeische Uberset-**

zungen (14, 1904). I. Broyde, **Jewish Encyclopedia** (vol. 5, 342, 1903). E. Wickersheimer: "A Note on the Liber de Medicinis Expertis," (**Annals of Medical History**, vol. 4, 323-27, 1922; Isis, vol. 5, 537).

Moses ibn Rabban, see Rabban.

Nihell, James, **New and Extraordinary Observations Concerning the Predictions of Various Crises by the Pulse . . . Made, First by Francisco Solano de Luque . . . Illustrated with Many New Cases and Remarks, to Which are Added Some General Hints on Crises**, London, Society of Booksellers for Promotion of Learning, 1741.

Opus . . . Recens Vero in Lucem, Editum a Marco et Horatio, 1605.

Ozanam, Charles, **La Circulation et le Pouls Histoire, Physiologie, Séméiotique, Indications Therapeutiques**, Paris, J. B. Bailliers, 1885.

Philaretus, Theophilus, "De Pulsibus," in **Articella Thesaurus Operum Medicorum Antiquorum**, Venice, Aug., 1487.

Pinder, Ulrich, "De Pulsibus," in his **Epiphanie Medicorum**, Nuremberg, 1506.

Pottenger, Frances Marion, **Symptoms of Visceral Disease, A Study of the Vegetative Nervous System in Its Relationship to Clinical Medicine**, 6th ed., C. V. Mosby Co., 1944.

Praxagoras of Cos flourished about 340-320 B.C. A physician and anatomist, he was a follower of Diocles and his successor as head of the Dogmatic School. He was the first to draw clearly the distinction between veins and arteries, holding that the former carry blood while the others are filled with air. He made a deeper study of the pulse, but little attention was paid to it in Hippocratic writing, and he improved diagnosis and topical pathology.

Rabban al-Tabari, Ali al-Tabari, or Mali ibn Rabban flourished under the caliphate of al-Mutawakkil (847-861) as a Muslim physician and son of a Persian Jew. He was a teacher of Rhazes, and his main work is the **Firdaus—al hikma** (see text) or **Paradise of Wisdom**, which deals chiefly with medicine and which contains about 550 pages divided into seven parts, 30 discourses, and 360 chapters. It is based on Greek and Hindu sources; Part IV, discourse 12 has a dissertation on the pulse; and the last discourse, the seventh part, contains 36 chapters which summarize Indian medicine. E. G. Browne's **Arabian Medicine** (1921, 37-44) has a short analysis of the **Paradise of Wisdom**.

Rashiel-al-Din, see text.

Razes, ar-Razi, Rhazes, or ibu Bakr Muhammad ibn Takariyya of Ray was probably the greatest and most original of all the Muslim physicians. In early life, music was his chief interest. His **Hawi** or **Continens** was a posthumous work. He was an authority on the pulse. See text and see **supra** Moses Farachi for his translation of the **Hawi** or **Continens**.

Rudio, Eustachio, **De Pulsibus Libri Duo**, Francofurti, J. Spiessii, 1602.

Rufus of Ephesus was a Greek anatomist and physician and was called the greatest Greek physician of the Roman Empire after Galen. He flourished under Trajan in Rome and in Egypt; his work was based upon the writings of Herophilos and Erasistratos, but he made elaborate anatomical researches upon monkeys and pigs. He improved the description of the eye and made the first description of the optic chiasmia; understood the difference between motor and sensory nerves; saw the functional importance of the nervous system; wrote a treatise of anatomy which is important and is one of the earliest on anatomical nomenclature. For the purposes of this study, his treatise on the pulse is very important because it contains a good definition of the pulse and the wonderful remark that the pulse and heart-beat correspond to the systole, not to the diastole. This fact was forgotten, however, and had to be rediscovered in the seventeenth century by Harvey and it was the first step toward his great discovery. This treatise represents the earliest attempt to base pathology upon anatomy and physiology.

Texts and Translations: The best edition is that by Charles Daremberg, completed by Ch. Emile Ruelle, with French translation (Paris, 1879). It contains all the Greek works extant and fragments collected from Greek and Arabic authors. German translation was made by Robert von Töply. Criticism: M. Menestrier: "A Propos du Traité du Pouls Attribué à Rufus et de la Sphygmologie des Anciens," (Bull. Soc. Franc. Hist. Méd., 18, 97-98, 1924. In praise of this treatise: Isis, vol. VII, p. 180).

Shem-Tob Ben Issac, also called Babi ha-Tortosi, was born at Tortosa in 1196. An Hispano-Jewish physician and philosopher and translator from Arabic to Hebrew, his main title to fame rests on his translations of two of the greatest medical works of Islam. In 1254 he began and completed in 1258 his translation of the **Kitab al-tasrif** and in 1264 he translated Al-Razi's **Kitab al Mansuri.** Thus Muslim medicine became available to the growing number of Jewish physicians who did not know Arabic.

Singer, Charles Joseph, editor, **Studies in the History and Method of Science,** Oxford, Clarendon Press, 1917-1921, 2 vols. See also his study on **Medieval Contribution to Western Civilization,** which is extremely useful.

Solano de Luque (of Antequera, Spain), Francisco, **Observaciones sobre el Pulso, Obra Póstuma . . .,** Madrid, Imprenta Real, 1787. See also **supra** Daniel Cox, Nihell, and others who followed since they used his study.

Streiff, Johannes Melchior, **De Tactu Pulsus, Certo in Morbis Criterio Tuningae,** Erhardianis, (1753).

Strutheus, Josephus (1510-1568), **Sphygmicae Artis Jam Mille Ducentos Annos Perditae & Desiderate Libre V,** Basil: I Oporenum (1555). **Ibid.,** Venetiis: Jacobi Anelli de Maria, 1573.

Taber, Clarence Wilbur and associates, **Taber's Cyclopedic Medical Dictionary Including A Digest of Medical Subjects . . .,** Philadelphia, F. A. Davis Co., 1950.

Taylor, N. B., see Best, C.

Theophilos Protospartharios, meaning head of the imperial body guard, flourished in Constantinople under Heraclios, Emperor from 610 to 641. Author of various medical and physiological writings, his works on the pulse and on urine are based largely on Galen. His book on urine was one of the most influential writings of its kind in medieval times.

Text: William Alexander Greenhill, edition with Latin translation and notes: **Theophili de Corporis Humani Fabrica, Libri V** (Oxford, 441 p., 1842).

Valentine, (Michael Bernhardus) (1657-1729), **Medicinae Novantiqua Tradens Universae Medicinae Cursum,** Edition Secunda, **Disertatio Mellico Medica de Pulsu,** Francofurte ad Moenun: Ivan, Maximilliani à Sande, 1713.

Valla, Georgius, **De Corporis Commodis et Incommodis, Eiusdem de Differentis Pulsuum, Problematic Aristotelis de Re Medica, Dialogue Parthenif de Sectione Humani Corporis,** Argenenae, H. Sybold, 1529.

Valles, Corarrubias Francisco, **De Uriniis Pulsibus, ac Febricus Compendiariae Tractationes,** A.D. . . . Carolum Emanuelsenm . . ., 2nd ed., Augustae Taurinorum, N. Beuilaquae, 1588.

Withington, Edward Theodore, **Medical History from the Earliest Times; A Popular History of the Healing Art,** London, Scientific Press, 1894, p. 174.

Yater, W. M., see Barton, W. M.

Zumbag de Koesfelt, Conrad, **De Pulsibus ac Urines Fasciculus Indicatorius, Omni Perutilis qui se Medicinae decat** . . . Lugd, Batav, G. Potucliet, 1741.

Chapter V

DEFINITION, EXAMINATION, AND TECHNIQUE OF TAKING THE PULSE IN FOUR CULTURES

The technique used to examine the pulse varies both in East and West and also among the many practitioners themselves. The explanation of the different techniques used is simple, can be readily narrated, and should present no problem in comprehension when the fact is stressed that each school and each individual look to the pulse-reading for something specific. Thus the different methods used by both Easterner and Westerner provide invaluable information for diagnosis, treatment, prognosis, and prevention of disease. The Chinese, for example, look for twelve pulses; the Indians, for three Doshas and their derangements; the Westerner, for circulation. This stage is an art combined with scientific knowledge and usually requires years of practice and experience. All book knowledge is useless without experience in this stage. But the reading of the pulse, what may be called "doing the story", is quite different from narrating the technique. Yet still a third aspect is to interpret the readings of the pulse. This explanation requires pragmatic practice in reading many different pulses as well as a philosophic elasticity and cultural cross-fertilization in stretching the mental reference to include the many contributions made in the past by both East and West for twentieth century space-age medicine. These last two phases of reading and interpreting the pulse, elusively simple yet frustratingly difficult, endlessly challenge the doctor who must learn how to become the artist of healing. He is not the mechanic; not the writer of prescription; not the slave to diagnostic tests and machines; not the inferior doctor who simply corrects symptoms without removing causes and who has allowed a diseased condition to arise. He is the superior doctor who prevents disease and who keeps the patient well.

What follows is a manual on the various ways of reading the pulse: Western or allopathic; Ayurvedic or Indian; Unani or Iranian; and Chinese. The techniques of the general examinations will be explained together with the definitions of the pulse respectively made by the different systems of medicine which have evolved in various parts of the world out of their cultural matrices. Since the diagnosis of the pulse cannot be made in a vacuum, the analysis of the palpation will then lead into the examination of the pulse and its use in diagnosis. The last two sections will provide a practical **vade mecum** wherein the normal pulse and the abnormal will be interpreted by all four groups in the hope that twentieth century medicine can profit by this comparative study in order to heal the individual.

Definition of Pulse: Western Interpretation

The pulse is composed of a rhythmical throbbing caused by the regular contraction and alternate expansion of an artery; the periodic thrust felt over arteries in time with the heart beat. It is actually a wave set up in the wall of the vessel, and the blood contained within is controlled partly by the systole of the left ventricle of the heart and partly by the contractability of the arterial wall.

Owing to the elasticity and distensibility of the arterial wall, the rhythmic rise of pressure corresponding to each heart beat causes an expansion which can be felt by the finger placed on any exposed artery. Just as the blood pressure diminishes from heart to periphery, so the amplitude of the pulse decreases as one goes farther away from the heart.

If the arterial system were perfectly rigid, the increased pressure due to the forcing of the blood into the arterial system at each ventricular systole would occur practically simultaneously at every point or all along the line. The arteries, however, are elastic and distensible so that the first effect of the flow of blood into the aorta is to distend the section of the aorta nearest to the heart. This elastic reaction forces a portion of the blood into the nearest section so that the increased pressure is transmitted from segment to segment of the arteries in the form of a wave at the velocity of about seven meters per second.

It is important not to confuse the velocity of the pulse wave with that of the blood flow; the blood flow is never greater than 0.5 meters per second and is much less than that in the smaller arteries. The cause of the pulsation is due to the fact that at each heart beat, eighty to ninety milliliters of blood are drawn into the aorta and a fluid wave distends the vessels as it passes along the aorta, the great arterial trunk and then to the arteries all over the body. The pulsation gets less marked as the arteries grow smaller and smaller and it is finally lost in the minute capillaries where a steady pressure is maintained. (Capillary pulse is 70 to 74 beats per minute.) For this reason, the blood in the veins flows, as a general rule, steadily or without any pulsation. Immediately after the wave has passed, the artery, by virtue of its great elasticity, regains its former size. The speed of the pulse wave is independent of the speed of the blood itself.

The strength of the pulse is determined by the degree of compression it will bear before it ceases to be felt by the fingers farthest from the heart. It is regular when its beats are uniform in force, frequency, fullness, rhythm, etc. and is irregular when it lacks force, frequency, fullness, rhythm, etc.

Rhythmical throbbing is caused by the regular contraction and alternate expansion of an artery; it is the periodic thrust that is felt over the arteries in time with the heart beat. It is important to point out the role of the carotid artery without going into too much detail about the anatomy. The common carotid artery in the neck bifurcates into the internal and external carotid. The internal carotid supplies the brain and its membranes; the external carotid, the face and all other arteries of the body; in the latter, the circulation is and remains synchronous with the heart; that is, normally heaving or throbbing at the rate of sixty to ninety times a minute.

The motion of the blood in the vessels of the brain itself is **not** synchronous with the heart beat or pulsation, but with the respiration where it throbs at the rate of eleven to eighteen times a minute. This fact may have for its object the limiting or the control of the blood supply to the brain. The brain is a highly exacting organ. Its demands in the resting body are one-quarter of the oxygen of the body although it is one-fiftieth of the body in size. The consumption of oxygen in the brain involves the oxidation of glucose which is brought there by the bloodstream. The brain is very sensitive to any shortage of either oxygen or glucose and is damaged sooner by that shortage than is any other tissue. Therefore the flow of the blood through the brain is carefully controlled by the body and is less subject to fluctuation than is the flow to any other part of the body. While it is easy to cause the blood vessels in any part of the body to dilate by the use of drugs, it is impossible to make them constrict in the brain and thus cut down on its blood supply. The blood enters the skull by the internal carotid and vertebral arteries and leaves by the jugular veins. The liver, kidneys, and other parts of the body may hold more blood at one time than another, a fact which depends on their functioning and rhythm—for these organs can swell and accommodate to the extra supply or constrict whenever needed. The blood supply in the brain changes very slightly because too much blood or too little causes damage.

The instruments in use by the Western physician are the sphygmotonometer and the sphygmotonograph, which measure the blood and pulse pressure, and the polysphygmograph, which takes simultaneous tracings of both the arterial and venous pulse. The electrocardiograph photographs the vibrations of a delicate string galvanometer, which is activated by the current set up by the electrical contractions of the cardiac musculature. This enables the doctor to study the direct action of the heart in contrast to the other instruments which measure the blood vessels.

To the Western physicians these machines have made possible material advances in cardiovascular physiology both normal and pathological. The sphygmotonometer is standard operating procedure (S.O.P.) with practically all Western healers in order to ascertain simply and easily the arterial blood pressure. With the other instruments, it is a different story. Comparatively few medical men own and can use and interpret a polysphygmograph. For the most part, expensive, complex, and delicate machines are installed in hospitals and laboratories and require experts to administer and interpret them. For perplexing cardiovascular cases, patients are sent to the most accessible special laboratories and hospitals for further study. This is a time-consuming and expensive proposition and the element of error is increased. Most doctors instead of relying on the simple, clinical examination of the pulse and their findings shift the diagnostic procedure to the machines.

Before the indigenous techniques are recounted, the Westerners' preferences for machines must be related to the Easterners' preferences for palpation. The twentieth century physician, who seems to be unaware of the history of pulse lore, considers the taking of the pulse by palpation a waste of time and energy since machines can do the job. Further, he asks why it is necessary to know the pulse when there are so many instruments available for correct diagnosis of disease. The Easterner replies that the knowledge of the pulse saves time and money since it enables the physician to foretell the appearance of a disease with its prognosis long before the disease takes possession of the patient's system.

Definition of Pulse: Ayurvedic and Unani Interpretation

To the Ayurvedist, the pulse beating at the root of the thumb is the "Witness to the Soul" contained in the body, and the physician studying its throbbing knows whether the soul is happy or miserable. The pulse is not considered, as it is in the West, the volume of blood passing through an artery; it is regarded as the main diagnostic aid to tell the doctor the physical, emotional, and spiritual condition of the body both in health or ease and in disharmony or dis-ease.

In addition to determining the condition of the three doshas, the Ayurvedic and Unani physician takes into account the pulse in relation to the physiology of circulation, which is what the Western physician is primarily concerned with. His three educated fingers tell him: the pumping action of the heart; the elasticity of the arteries; and the capillary pressure.

Definition of Pulse: Chinese Interpretation

Many centuries earlier than the Ptolemaic School of Anatomy at Alexandria, the Chinese physician Pien Ch'iao, the Chinese Galen, practiced dissection on a cadaver and elaborated a "Science of the Pulse" which is still studied and practiced to-day. According to the Chinese **Nei Ching,** in the chapter entitled the "Mei Chen" or diagnosis of the pulse, this ruling applies:

> Nothing surpasses the examination of the pulse, for with it errors cannot be committed; therefore it is said the disease can be brought to a decline. For, although a disease may be local, it can nevertheless spread; and although a disease may be grave, it can nevertheless be improved; and by the time the disease has disappeared completely, it has also become well-known.

Palpation or Examination of the Pulse: The Views of Four Different Cultures

The Oriental physician depends on touch or palpation to diagnose the individual's illness. He relies not on any instruments, but only on the use of his hand and his touch. The stories told of the physicians' competence because of touch arouse incredulity in the Western mind. If a picture is worth a thousand words, then two stories can be cited to illustrate their phenomenal mastery of the art in reading the pulse. Whether the doctor be Chinese, Unani, or Ayurvedic, whether he be a specialist or a general practitioner, a "superior" or an "inferior" physician, all without exception utilized the palpation method for diagnosis. The Chinese doctor, it should be noted, takes the twelve pulses that from their classic viewpoint relate to every organ of the body and can in that way also follow the flow of energy throughout the organism as it affects the patient's person, mind, emotions, and even his dreams. Two stories will briefly be told: one by Avicenna, also known as Ibn Sina, who was the greatest of all Islamic physicians (980 A.D.) and who was ranked as a second Aristotle; the other, a narrative repeated in all the medical schools of the East.

Avicenna averred and demonstrated that ". . . it is possible to arrive at the identity, appearance, and occupation of the beloved person if the patient will not reveal it" entirely through the pulse. The principle of the lie-detector was used to note the pulse responses to various questions. Avicenna than gave a set of directives that were to be used in guiding the physician as he read the pulse in order to determine the exact cause of the patient's distress: ". . . mention the names of the streets, dwellings, the families and the countries and join each with the name of the beloved and all the time feeling the pulse so that when it alters on the mention of any one thing several times, you will . . . infer about the beloved as regards name, appearance and occupation." In that way he was able to discover that the Sultan's wife was secretly in love with a home-town butcher; his cure—to disillusion her. He brought the butcher to court, fed him drugs that transformed his character and thus reconciled the Queen with the Sultan.

The second story was mentioned in the opening chapter of this book and it dealt with the Unani physician who read the pulse of an unseen object by the vibrations of a piece of twine. The pulse was that of "a creature who eats grass."

A comparison could be made at this point with the Western and Eastern viewpoint. The Westerner uses the pulse as a minor diagnostic aid for the heart and the circulation. The Easterner uses the pulse as a very significant and direct diagnostic tool for the whole man: physical, emotional, and spiritual. Every other procedure is ancillary to it. No attempt is made here to account for the reasons underlying this type of evolution of medical theory and practice. Instead, the pragmatic approach is to note the differences prevailing and hint of the different approach that may, in the future, accommodate to a successful utilization of Eastern techniques in Western methodology. The views as voiced by Western physicians of two different schools of thought will be briefly enunciated: those who trust their machines, but not the senses and those who trust the senses, but disbelieve the machine.

Butler, an authority whose text is used in the West, writes of the pulse since he trusts the machine but not the touch: "The measurement of blood pressure (arterial tension) by simple palpation is now admitted to be notoriously uncertain and usually incorrect. It should always be made by the sphygmotonometer." Other sceptics claim that the six hundred odd shades and conditions of the pulse are too delicate to be appreciated by the touch.

It may be observed that the readings made by the interpreter of the sphygmotonometer are not always accurate because of the individual's reaction or the hearing impediments, if any, of the observer. Tests with the heartometer, which records the pulse and blood pressure electrically, reveal a difference as large as forty points over the sphygmotonometer. It could be added, incidentally with respect to Ayurvedic and Chinese medical premises, that these instruments do not record Vayu, Kapha, Pitha, or the twelve classical Chinese pulses. Furthermore, the machine does not tell whether the pulse is fast, slow, soft, hard, small, large, etc.

Solomon, a recognized authority on the pulse, observed that in the absence of instruments and other aids for diagnosis, the ancient healer had to rely on the pulse for the interpretation of disease. The sense of touch, which should be a necessity for all practitioners of the healing arts, was almost perfected by the ancients who became experts in examining the pulse and interpreting it correctly. Without danger of repetition, it may be remarked that the Ayurvedic and Unani physicians can distinguish the finest shades of differences among the five kinds of pulses that Vayu, Pitha, and Kapha dictate so that from the pulse alone, they can diagnose cases affecting tissues, organs, and systems.

B. H. Hume, a Johns Hopkins professor of medicine whose account reflected Western historical interest in Chinese medical practices, confessed amazement and surprise at the performance of the Chinese doctors' reading of the pulse. His twentieth century praise could be contrasted with Sir William Henry Broadbent's view, who died in 1907. He was physician to Queen Victoria and the Prince of Wales and a Western expert on the Ayurvedic and Unani pulse who may here be placed in the late nineteenth and early twentieth centuries. He stated that every important variety of the pulse revealed by the sphygmotonograph was recognized, described, and named before the Christian era. "I also say that the Sphygmotonograph is rare by necessity for diagnosis and scarcely to be trusted in diagnosis."

Other comments by medical historians may be of some interest to the reader. The critical pulses as described by two European authorities of their day—Francisco Solano de Luque (1685-1738) in his **Observaciones Sobre el Pulso** and James Nihell in his **New and Extraordinary Observations Concerning the Predictions of Various Crises by the Pulse,** published in 1741—reveal their agreement with the Persian and Ayurvedic "ancients" who could diagnose epistaxis and purgation etc. by the pulse. Bordeu and Foguet described a special variety of pulse for the diseases of each organ. Bordeu's study, **Inquiries Concerning the Pulse,** became a text and was translated from the French into English in 1764. This outstanding authority praised the Chinese for their expert knowledge of the pulse. The description of the different kinds of pulse by Rufus of Epheses leaves little to be added.

Western Technique of Palpation

In the West, the radial artery is preferred for examination purposes because of its location and accessibility. Any palpable artery, however, can be used. If the radial and other accessible arteries are found to be thickened or calcified, the condition indicates a general arteriosclerosis. This form of vascular disease (cardiac hypertrophy, intercranial hemorrhage, or aneurism) has a widespread relation to diseases of other organs, but such a relationship is not generally realized by the Western physician who notes the calcification.

The palpator should take care in feeling the pulse not to excite the action of the heart, a movement which would defeat the purpose in view. Tight clothing should be loosened; proper posture observed; emotional factors considered. The pulse may be examined in any part of the body where an artery is so close to the surface that its throb can be plainly felt. While examining the pulse, one must be sure to exert no pressure upon the artery in any part of its course. The patient should be either lying or sitting down in an easy, relaxed, and comfortable position. If he is in the sitting position, the back should be straight, the head on eye level.

The patient's forearm should be semi-pronated as the artery is then more readily palpated and the arm supported. The examiner should place three fingers—the second, third or middle, and fourth—on the radial artery, just above the root of the thumb and the joint of the wrist. It is good practice to examine both radial (for the first time at any rate) arteries in order to detect inequality of the pulses, some of which are listed below:

1. Aneuryism of the Arch of the Aorta; Cause for Unequal Pulse

If the sac involves the great vessels given off from the transverse portion of the arch, the radial and carotid pulses on one side may differ from those on the opposite side. If, for instance, the innominate artery is compressed or its opening is partially blocked by a clot, the right radial pulse will be smaller than the left. In the same way, the opening of the left subclavian may be involved, thus giving rise to a smaller pulse in the left radial. There may be a history of syphilis; pain, mild to angenoid; hoarseness or aphonia; slight hemoptysis; dyspnea, often paroxysmal.

2. Cervical Rib; Cause for Unequal Pulse

If the condition is unilateral, there may be pressure upon and consequent stenosis of one subclavian artery producing an inequality of the pulses on two sides; or if bilateral, it usually predominates on one side and the more prominent rib may press upon the artery of that side with the same results. The condition may be due to motor, sensory, and vasomotor disturbances in the arm.

3. Other Common Causes for Unequal Pulse

Embolism of the brachial artery; atheroma of the brachial or subclavian artery; aneurisms of the subclavian, axilliary, brachial, and innominate arteries; mediastinal tumor; fracture of the arm; cicatrices of the arm; tumor or enlarged gland of axilla; pneumothorax; pleural effusion.

Besides comparing the radial pulses, one is advised to compare both femorals and tibial arteries. It may be found that the pulse wave which should reach symmetrical arteries at the same time is delayed in one, obliterated, or else presents differences in amplitude and strength on the two sides.

In peripheral vascular diseases—especially arteriosclerosis, thrombo-angetis obliteran, Reynauld's disease and acrocyanosis—the pulses of the lower extremities are taken to arrive at a diagnosis.

The pulses of the lower extremities—the femoral, popliteal, anterior tibial, posterior tibial, and dorsalis pedis arteries—are palpated and their condition recorded. In the upper extremities, the axillary, brachial, radial, and ulna arteries are examined.

To feel the posterior tibial artery, the palm of the hand should be placed over the dorsum of the foot and the fingers bent over the ankle joint so that the tips of the fingers are situated behind the internal malleolus. The vessel lies between the medial malleolus and the tendon Achilles. In the obese, firmer pressure must be exercised to feel this pulsation. This vessel sometimes is smaller than normal, although an atypical position is rare. On the anterior aspect of the foot, about one to two inches, above the external malleolus and displaced somewhat laterally from the midline, lies the anterior tibial artery. Complete relaxation of the extensor muscles, with maximum relaxation of the foot aids in quickly detecting this vessel. Of greater importance is the examination of its continuation, the dorsalis pedis artery. Usually this vessel is directed straight down over the dorsum of the foot towards the toes lying between the first and second metatarsal bones. Sometimes it pursues a diagonal course laterally. It is found by placing the palmar surface of the index and middle fingers over the dorsum of the foot and after the general location of the pulsation is detected, palpate carefully until the artery is located with the finger tips. Should there be no normal pulsation in the foot, a careful search for atypically situated vessels should be made about the malleolus usually in the anterior aspect. The popliteal pulse is best found by having the patient in the prone position, the extremity flexed at the knee and supported by the examiner; the popliteal artery is felt deep in the popliteal fossa. About midway between the symphysis pubis and the anterior iliac crest, the large femoral pulse can easily be found.

Difficulties in Examination of the Pulse (Western)

The pulse is the symphony of the body and the only way it can be played and understood (heard) is by practice and more practice. The best instructions, however elaborate, cannot teach the student much. The way to learn the pulse is to examine as many patients as possible and observe the peculiarities and characteristics of each one for himself. The help of a teacher who understands his subject is almost a necessity. In the West, the beat of the pulse is counted and ingenious instruments have been constructed graphically to note the arteriole tension and the cardiac musculature, all measurements of the circulatory system. Broadbent has aptly pointed out that the indications to be obtained from the pulse are, in great measure, independent of the knowledge of circulation.

Ayurvedic and Unani Technique of Palpation

To the Ayurvedic, Unani, and Chinese physicians, the minute knowledge registered in the pulse can never be acquired by reference to a watch or to a cardiograph. At present there is no mechanical device that can ascertain what Doshas are at fault; how precisely to measure that excitement, the imbalances between Yin and Yang or even the relationship of the organs to the meridians. The Oriental healer can estimate with ease and accuracy the diagnostic significance furnished by the pulse to make remarkable predictions of the outcome.

The pulse as a vital diagnostic aid of great prophetic significance was recognized in the Orient, and this lesson has now spread to England, France, Russia, and Germany. True, the pulse changes often with every treatment and prescription. But whether the state of health has changed for better or worse can always be determined by the pulse reading. This art has been lost to the West because the information buried in books is very difficult to transmit through the writings of the past since experience here is absolutely vital, an indispensable handmaid, to put book learning and observation into daily practice. The triad to spell success in pulse examination is theory, observation, and daily practice. (The reply given a stranger stopping a New Yorker for information about how to get to Carnegie Hall was "Practice, Practice, and more Practice" applies to one who seeks to master the readings of the pulse.)

The Ayurvedic and Unani physician knows that the knowledge of the pulse can be gained only by practice and experience. The practitioner should examine the pulses of many healthy individuals and always bear in mind that the pulse of a diseased person is not the same as that of a healthy one **although the pulse count may be the same** in both healthy and diseased individuals. An example may be cited: A pulse rate of 65 will react to a certain medicine or treatment for one patient but not for another although the symptoms remain the same. Why? **Treatment and cure are not in the totality of the symptoms but in the character of the pulse and its various movements.** The Indian would prescribe treatment for the various Doshas that are deranged; the Chinese, for the twelve organs or for the Yin-Yang derangement; the Westerner would not use the pulse at all for symptoms except for circulatory diseases. The pulse takes many forms, affirms the Eastern physician, in accordance with age, sex, seasons of the year, time of the day, food, and the peculiar character of the disease.

The Ayurvedic, Unani and Chinese physician can make his diagnosis whether or not the artery is calcified. Their texts recommend the following arteries: 1) The radial artery; 2) the posterior tibial artery at the ankle; 3) the external carotid artery at the neck; 4) the exterior temporal artery at the temple.

According to Ayurvedic, which translated means science of life,

1. All diseases can be determined by the pulse beating at the root of the thumb (radial).

2. Doctor and patient should sit down comfortably in the morning before breakfast when the pulse is taken.

3. The doctor who is attentive, disease-less, and clear in mind is the only one competent to take the pulse.

4. The pulse should not be taken after a bath; after a meal; after crying; after coitus; after exercise; during an epileptic fit or asthmatic attack;

of one who is hungry and thirsty; who is fatigued or overheated; who is drunk or has used intoxicating drugs.

5. Three precautions should be observed on taking the pulse:
a) The application of moderate pressure on the artery by the palpating fingers.
b) The superficial position of the artery so that the minimum amount of tissue intervenes between the artery and the palpating finger.
c) The location of the artery which must lie against a bone where it can be pressed by the feeling finger.[1]

6. A set procedure is followed when the physician takes the pulse.

First, the pulse at the wrist or the radial pulse is the one that is usually preferred and is examined with three fingers.

The male patient extends his right hand for his pulse to be taken, but the female[2] extends her left hand. This practice is reversed in the Chinese technique.

The examiner uses the three fingers of his right hand: the index, the middle, and the ring finger or otherwise described as the second, third, and fourth fingers, and he places these three in a position two fingers in **width** below the root of the thumb. The physician uses his left hand to press the artery of the elbow and holds the patient's hand in a slanting manner while **he places his right hand**[3] in the manner described above: namely, three fingers over the radial pulse of the patient just above the root of the thumb with the patient's fingers pointing upward.

The throbbing or pulsations of the artery should be felt without haste and should not be pressed too firmly lest it disappear nor too lightly lest the fingers lose contact with the artery. Allow the artery free play. The pulse has its own movements—fast, jumpy, slow, etc.—which are felt under the three fingers. A heavy pulse to the index finger shows air; to the middle finger shows fire; and to the ring finger shows water. These movements should be noted and the questioning of the patient or of the attendants (should the patient be unconscious, senile, or infant) will verify the correct information of the inner body that the pulse reveals. The following rule should be memorized: "The pulse becomes fast with air, jumpy with fire, and slow with water."

Chinese Technique of Palpation

The Chinese physician uses the radial artery, but in a way different from the Western physician's and from the Ayurvedic-Unani physician's. He distinguishes between the pulse of the right hand and that of the left, between the pulse of men and women, and among the three superficial and the three deep pulses on each wrist.

---

[1] Western medicine does not give any reason for using three fingers. But the reason is obvious to the Ayurvedic and Unani physician; the entire wave length of the radial artery can be detected by the three fingers because the artery is superficially near the wrist.

[2] The right wrist was presented to the Unani physician, for the right hand was used for all honorable purposes. The left for all actions, though necessary, was unclean (the washing of the genitals and anus). Cyril Elgood, **A Medical History of Persia and the Eastern Caliphate,** Cambridge, At the University Press, 1951.

[3] According to Ayurvedic and Unani theory, only a woman can take her own pulse. No man can take his own pulse reading.

The procedure of taking the pulse differs according to the sex of the patient. In the man, the left pulse is taken first; in the woman, the right. Here the procedure is the reverse of the Ayurvedic and Unani practice.

According to the "Classic of Difficulties", the length of the pulse is one and nine-tenths of an inch and is divided into three parts called Ch'ih or cubit (forearm), Kuan or bar (Styloid), and Ts'un or inch (thumb).

1. The Kuan, the bar, or styloid, is found at the level of the radial styloid in line with the pesiform bone and is taken to be the key or central position.

2. Above the Kuan, one fingertip in length of the patient's finger, is the Ch'ih or cubit. (To the Chinese every part of the body is in a definite relationship to another, like the diameter and radius to a circle. By using the patient's fingertip measurement, the physician accounts for the size, shape, and form of different individuals.)

3. Below the Kuan, one fingertip in length of the patient's finger, is the Ts'un or inch.

Each of these divisions has two different and distinct pulses—internal or deep and external or superficial—making twelve pulses in all: six on the right and six on the left hand. Each of these twelve pulses represents one definite functioning internal organ or system and the pulse therefore reveals that particular organ's condition—normal or abnormal.

According to Wang Shu Ho, a great authority on the twelve pulses writing about 280 A.D., these readings are to be noted:

1. The Ts'un or inch pulse of the right hand reveals the condition of the lungs and the large intestines.

2. The Ts'un or inch pulse of the left hand reveals the condition of the heart and the small intestines.

3. The Kuan or bar pulse on the right hand reveals the condition of the spleen and stomach.

4. The Kuan or bar pulse on the left hand reveals the condition of the liver and the gall bladder.

5. The Ch'ih or cubit pulse in the right hand reveals the condition of the gate of life (heart constrictors) and san chico (the tri-heaters).

6. The Ch'ih or cubit pulse in the left hand reveals the condition of the kidney and the bladder.

The twentieth century Dr. Soulie de Morant in **The Chinese Pulses** identifies six pulses at the left and eight pulses on the right wrist. If Wang Shu-Ho is correct about the twelve pulses or if de Morant is correct about the fourteen pulses is not of consequence at this stage of the game. What is of significance is to realize that the pulse is controlled by the **brain and not by the heart** and that the reflexes from the visceral organs are revealed in the pulse. Sir William Henry Broadbent, the eminent Western authority of the pulse and physician to Queen Victoria, stated that, "The pulse is in immediate and direct control of the nervous system." Dr. F. M. Pottenger in his excellent book **Symptoms of Visceral Disease** proves conclusively that the viscera are directly under the control of the nervous system.

Here the author Dr. R. B. Amber departs from the Western viewpoint and voices his opinion about pulse, brain and the nervous system. The Chinese intimated but never directly concluded that the pulse is controlled by the brain. It is the author's opinion, based on his own observations supported by many years of clinical practice, that what affects the nervous system affects the pulse. He further maintains that the polarity of the body—its plus and minus factors—is also revealed by the pulse again through the brain, which is the electrical power house, and through the liver, which is the chemical factory of the body. Here are two different energy systems working independently of each other and yet paradoxically closely inter-related. Western physiology and anatomy must shortly begin to take into cognizance these various facts in revising its interpretations, prognosis, and diagnosis. (See author's book **Nu Reflex Therapy.**)

The doctor uses his right hand for taking the left pulse and his left hand for taking the right pulse. (This is different from the Ayurvedic physician who uses his right hand.) He places the middle or third finger on the Kuan or bar pulse. the fourth or ring finger on the Cubit pulse, and the index or second finger on the Ts'un or inch pulse.

At each of these positions, the artery is palpated superficially or lightly at first and then the examiner with a slight movement to the right with his palpating finger exerts deep pressure. In this manner, the twelve classical pulses are obtained. One must note in passing both with respect to technique and philosophy, that the superficial pulse is a dictation from the Yang organs and the deep pulse is a dictation from the Yin organs, as are reflected in the two tables herein. The skin on the surface of the body, the back, and the hollow organs—heart and liver—are Yang. The interior parts of the skin, the abdomen, and the solid organs—spleen, lungs and kidney—are Yin.

Readings of the Pulse as Expressed by Four Authorities in China

Table 3. Pulse of the Right Hand

Pulse	Wang Shu Ho	Nei Ching	Golden Chamber	Li-Shih-chen	Position of Fingers
Ku'an (Bar)					
Deep	Spleen	Stomach	Stomach	Stomach	Middle finger on head of Radium
Superficial	Stomach	Spleen	Spleen	Spleen	
Ch'ih (Cubit)					
Deep	Gate of Life[1]	Kidney	Large Intestines	Kidney	Ring or fourth finger above head of Radium.
Superficial	San Chico[2]	Belly*	Kidney	Large Intestines	
Ts'un (Inch)					
Deep	Lungs	Lungs	Thoracic Organs	Lungs	Index finger below Radium while the thumb rests on the dorsum of Carpus.
Superficial	Large Intestines	Thoracic organs	Lungs	Thoracic organs	

[1] Gate of Life or Heart Constrictor; the latter is the term used in the West.
[2] San Chico or Tri-Heater; also called the three burning spaces.
The deep are Yin organs and the superficial are Yang organs.

Readings of the Pulse as Expressed by Four Authorities in China

Table 4. Pulse of the Left Hand

Pulse	Wang Shu Ho	Nei Ching	Golden Chamber	Li-Shih-chen	Position of Fingers
Ku'an (Bar)					
Deep	Liver	Liver	Diaphragm and Gall Bladder	Liver	Middle finger on head of Radium
Superficial	Gall Bladder	Diaphragm	Liver	Gall Bladder	
Ch'ih (Cubit)					
Deep	Kidney	Kidney	Small Intestines & Urinary Bladder	Kidney	Ring or fourth finger above head of Radium
Superficial	Urinary Bladder	Belly	Kidney	Small Intestines	
Ts'un (Inch)					
Deep	Heart	Heart	Mediastinal Viscera	Heart	Index finger below Radium while the thumb rests on the dorsum of Carpus
Superficial	Small Intestines	Mediastinal Viscera	Heart	Mediastinal Viscera	

In the foregoing tables, the Chinese physicians use the pulse according to Wang Shu-Ho. The reader should note that Wang Shu-Ho accounts not only for the important viscera of the body but also for the energy potential. This is an important fact. The references to the belly, starred in the table, must be interpreted to mean more than the large intestines. It includes the diaphragmatic movements and the regulation of the flow of blood to the head as well as control of the various energy forces of the body. A number of philosophic schools — like Yoga and Zen Buddhism — concentrate on the importance of both belly and diaphragm in health and disease. Unfortunately this is not the time nor the place for treating this fascinating subject. Judo, Karati, Ai Lai, all utilize this concept. What is relevant is to indicate that the French School of Acupuncture uses the concept of the thoracic organs, the diaphragm and the mediastinal viscera as found in the **Nei Ching, the Golden Chamber,** and the **Thousand Golden Remedies.** The location of the specific organs may vary in these four versions, but the over-all picture for practical purposes is the same. The reader is reminded that in Ayurvedic medicine too there is a controversy about the position of the pulse; the important thing to remember is that it is not the position but its movement that is the key to the pulse and on that there is no disagreement among the Ayurvedists.

The Chinese as well as the Ayurvedists break up the time of the day into four hour intervals to correspond with the seasons of the year; a typical classification would go along these lines: Spring is in the morning (spring pulse); Summer is at mid-day (summer pulse); Rainy season is the afternoon; Autumn is the evening; Dewy or Misty season is at midnight; and Winter is the later part of the night. Thus no matter when the doctor takes the pulse, he always includes time in his reckoning.

The Chinese further dictate the pulse should be examined at the place of the Bar, Cubit, and Inch, to see
1. Whether the pulse is superficial or deep.
2. Whether the pulse is regular or irregular.
3. What is the origin of the disease.
4. Whether the disease can be cured, be arrested, or prove to be fatal.

In Kampo, a Japanese Oriental medicine which is derived from Chinese Acupuncture, the physician sits facing the patient. He then takes the twelve pulses, six on each hand, simultaneously making his comparisons as to rhythm, size, beat, time, etc. and in this way arrives at his diagnosis.

Chapter VI

THE NORMAL PULSE

What the Pulse Reveals; Factors Influencing the Pulse;
How Four Cultures Use the Pulse for Diagnosis

The Normal Pulse as Viewed by Four Cultures

The West regards the pulse as normal if:
1. the frequency varies from a low normal of 60 to a high normal of 90;
2. the beat is regular;
3. the artery can be felt with slight pressure;
4. the pulse wave is of medium amplitude; that is to say, it neither rises nor falls abruptly and is neither fast nor slow;
5. the tension is moderate;
6. the pressure is sustained.

The pulse is normal when it is uniform, equal, moderately full, and swells slowly under the finger. It is smaller and quicker in women and in children; it resists moderate pressure and yet yields readily to severe pressure.

Ayurvedic and Unani physicians regard the pulse as normal when the three—Vayu, Pitha, and Kapha—are all in harmony. When none of these three elements is deranged, the pulse is then described as being slow, light, and forceful; if moderate pressure is applied, the pulse continues, is not obliterated. (The Unani also consider the circulation of the blood.)

The Chinese regard the pulse as normal when the Yin and Yang forces are in balance and in harmony with the five elements, the four seasons, the five tastes, and the ten celestial stems. To them, the pulse is the storehouse of the blood. The normal pulse beats are long and the strokes markedly prolonged.

According to the Chinese, the normal pulse of the
1. heart flows and connects;
2. spleen flows softly;
3. kidney flows as though it were panting and weary or as though it were alternately repressed and connected and very firm;
4. liver beats softly and weakly;
5. lungs is calm and peaceful.

Table 5.

Twenty-Six Factors Influencing Pulse Readings—Comparison Chart

A Tabulation of Factors Influencing the Pulse Readings as Practiced
by Physicians in the West, India, Iran, and China

Legend: A blank would indicate that this aspect of palpation and
diagnosis is not used by that respective culture.

Number of Factor	Western (Allopathic) Physician	Ayurvedic and Unani Physician	Chinese Physician
1. Pulse rate or frequency	yes	yes	yes
2. Pulse rhythm	yes	yes	yes
3. Conditions of vessel walls and size of vessels	yes	yes	yes
4. Amplitude of volume of independent pulse waves	yes	yes	yes
5. Blood pressure	yes	yes	yes
6. Nervous agencies or what the Ayurvedists term Vayu	———	yes	yes
7. Chemical agencies or what Ayurvedists term Pitha and Kapha	———	yes	yes
8. Exercises of all kinds—passive or active; includes breathing	active aspects	yes	yes
9. Excitement — physical or emotional	sometimes the emotional	yes	yes
10. Food and Tastes	———	yes	yes
11. Sleep	———	yes	yes
12. Exposure to heat or cold	———	yes	yes
13. Variations at different times	———	yes	yes
14. Variations of different seasons	———	yes	yes
15. Variations of different climate	———	yes	yes
16. Altitude	sometimes	yes	yes

Note: Items 12 to 16 are very important to the Eastern physicians

Number of Factor	Western (Allopathic) Physician	Ayurvedic and Unani Physician	Chinese Physician
17. Posture of the patient	aware of in theory, but not in practice	partially	partially
18. Temperament	———	yes	yes
19. Suggestion; hypnotism	———	yes	yes
20. Temperature	yes	yes	yes
21. Age	yes	yes	yes
22. Sex and sexual intercourse	———	yes	yes
23. Thought	———	yes	yes
24. Psychological aspects	by specialists only	yes	yes
25. Color	———	yes	yes
26. Sound	———	yes	yes

Restatement of findings in table 5 listed above:

1. All twenty-six rules are observed by the Oriental physician, but one rule is only partially observed—number 17.
2. Of the twenty-six rules, the Western allopathic physician follows:
   seven of them completely;
   four of them partially;
   one of them in theory, but not in practice;
   fourteen of them are not taken into consideration.

Has the Western physician missed in his training a highly desirable diagnostic aid?

Seriatim Consideration of the Twenty-Six Factors (Table 5)

1. Pulse Rate or Frequency

   Its frequency may be measured by the second-hand of a watch and by counting; but its peculiar characteristics, as indicative of various disease phases, can be appreciated only by the educated hand, in terms of sensitivity, of the examiner. Count the pulse for fifteen seconds and multiply by four. If the pulse is irregular, count for a full minute.

   In diseases that are not complicated, the pulse rate in an adult will not exceed 120. If higher, the disease must be taken as growing in intensity. A rate as high as 150 indicates very grave danger. If the pulse becomes slower than usual, the patient is getting weaker.

2. Pulse Rhythm

   Are the successive beats equidistant in point of time?
   Are they regular?
   Is the pulse full or soft?
   Can compression render it less perceptible?
   Is it strong and bounding, forcing the palpating fingers almost to jump from the pulse?
   Is it hard?
   Is it small or wiry, like the vibration of a string?
   Is it intermittent, striking a few beats, and then missing a beat or two?
   Is the pulsation flowing one into another in an almost imperceptible motion or a small slight motion?
   Is there an even rhythm? If there is no even rhythm, grave functional disturbances or organic defects are present.

3. Conditions of the Vessel Walls and Size of Vessels

   Empty the vessel by pressure and roll it under the fingers, slipping the skin over the vessel. A normal radial artery is scarcely to be felt except in a very thin wrist, but one that is sclerosed is firm, cord-like and perhaps tortuous. While it is empty, measure its size by running the finger along the vessel in order to detect calcareous beading or plates of lime salts. As a high tension artery may feel very much like one which is sclerosed, cut off the direct flow by firm pressure with the finger nearest the heart, and the recurrent flow, from palmar arch, by firm pressure with the finger nearest the hand. This procedure eliminates the element of the blood pressure and the middle finger is in position to determine the condition of the arterial wall.

The condition of the arterial walls depends upon the degree of elasticity or hardening. Arteriosclerosis is manifested in the peripheral arteries, especially the brachial, by simply stiffening without calcification, by tortuosity, or by calcification with beading of the surface. A contracted artery of high vascular tension is difficult to distinguish from simple stiffening due to scleroses.

4. The Amplitude or Volume of the Individual Wave Is Measured by:
   a) The quantity and velocity of the left ventricle discharge.
   b) The peripheral resistance.
   c) The elasticity of the arterial system. The volume of the pulse wave will vary from large to medium to small. The pulse may be found to be irregular in volume, in strength, as well as in rhythm.

The pulse wave refers to the manner of its ascent, summit and descent: i.e., the rise of blood pressure, its maintenance, and its fall. The following observation will be of clinical and diagnostic significance:
   a) Whether the ascent or increase of pressure is sudden, moderately rapid, or slow?
   b) Whether the pressure is well-sustained?
   c) Whether, having reached its height, it falls off abruptly?
   d) Whether the descent or fall of pressure is rapid, gradual, or slow?

During the descent, there may be felt a second impulse or secondary wave. If this dicrotic pulse is felt with very light pressure, it may be verified by cutting off the recurrent wave from the palmar arch.

Increase of the pulse volume (pulsus magnus) commonly attends conditions provocative of subnormal arterial tension and is recognized by the palpating fingers as an unnatural expansion of the vessels at the time of the pulse beat. The full bounding pulse of fevers, the large pulse of cardiac overaction or hypertrophy and the momentarily voluminous pulse of aortic regurgitation typify the pulsus magnus. Overfullness of the artery during the interval between beats indicates a large volume of blood within the vessel irrespective of its size; but a small, tense, contracted artery may be just as full, relatively, as one which is large, soft, and relaxed.

Pulsus parvus is attended by slight stretching of the vessel walls during the beat and is not infrequently combined with arrhythmia and with increased arterial tension.

The pulse wave will be small when the artery is constricted; then the cardiac output is small because of ventricular weakness, because of diminished venous return or because the speed of discharge is slow, as in aortic stenosis. The pulse wave will be small when peripheral resistance is increased and arterial elasticity is diminished, as in long-standing arterial hypertension. A small pulse may depend upon deficient cardiac force or upon lesions that diminish the volume of blood in the peripheral vessels. A deficient cardiac force accounts for the subnormal pulse volume in conditions of malnutrition and exhaustion and the various functional and structural weaknesses of the heart. The lesions that diminish the volume of blood also account for the small pulse of aortic and mitral stenosis, aneurism, and profound anemia.

Conversely the pulse wave will be large when the cardiac stroke volume is increased, as in brachycardia, or when peripheral resistance is diminished, as in thyrotoxicosis and high fevers.

Palpation between the successive pulse waves will reveal that the vessel remains full or that it empties out more or less completely. When full, the tension may be high, as in chronic renal disease; or low, as in febrile pulse with relaxed arterioles. A full artery does not necessarily imply a large pulse wave. In aortic incompetence, the pulse wave is extraordinarily large while the artery is quite empty in the intervals. For all practical purposes, the strength and the tension of the pulse wave are the same.

5. Blood Pressure by Palpation

Blood pressure by palpation is rarely used by the Occidental physician. He prefers to rely on instruments; but this fact does not apply to his Oriental counterpart.

The blood pressure, arterial, maintained within the blood vessels is dependent upon four factors:

a) The energy of the heart
b) The elasticity and tonus of the arterial wall
c) The volume of the circulatory blood
d) The peripheral resistance

Under normal circumstances each factor is more or less variable within a limited range, and these variations result in normal fluctuations in the intravascular pressure due to the compensating elements possessed by the four factors mentioned above. The force of the pulse corresponds to the systolic pressure and may be obtained by noting the degree of digital pressure necessary to obliterate the pulse wave. Press the artery against the underlying bone with the more proximal of the palpating finger until the pulse wave is no longer felt with the distal finger.

Diastolic pressure can be noted by the degree of **hardness, high tension,** or **softness, low tension,** of the pulse between beats so that nothing is felt at that time. The pulse of high tension is perceptible between beats as a cord that can be rolled beneath the fingers. The elasticity of the vessel walls prevents the pressure from falling too low between the beats of the heart: that is to say, it is responsible for the diastolic pressure and for converting the pulsable or throbbing flow in the arteries into a continuous flow in the veins and capillaries.

6. Nervous Agencies or What Ayurvedists Term Vayu

The pulse is under the direct control of the nervous system. The heart action and the action of the other organs are directly influenced by the vagus nerve. The contraction and dilation of arteries, veins and capillaries are under nervous stimulation. Doctors Henle and Stilling have shown that the diameter of the arteries is influenced by nervous stimulation, and they introduced the term vasomotor (vaso-dilation and vaso-constriction).

Ayurvedic and Chinese beliefs do not use Western concepts for nervous agencies since their terminology and philosophy describe processes. They have a concept of nervous agencies, but their terms of Vayu and Yin-Yang forces with the five elements explain the principles of these organismic relations.

7. Chemical Agencies or What Ayurvedists Term Pitha and Kapha

Drugs are chemical agents that stimulate or inhibit the pulse. They act upon the heart, lungs, stomach, liver, spleen, gallbladder, etc. Amylnitrate, for example, will accelerate the pulse by acting on arteries and capillaries, deflating them, reducing tension inside, and diminishing resistance to the flow of blood. Almost any drug that acts upon the endocrines will affect the pulse. To the Chinese, drugs have this distinction: stimulants, resolvents, expectorants, pungent substances, hot decoctions are Yang drugs. Astringents, purgatives, haematics, bitter substances and cold effusions are Yin drugs. According to the Chinese theory, each drug possesses certain features as to taste and action which produce different effects on the system through the five tastes and four vapors. The four vapors are heating, cooling, warm, and cold. By vapor, the Chinese mean action of the drug.

Chang Tzu-ho taught that disease is due to foreign substances in the system which should be attacked and driven out by drastic drugs such as diaphoretics, emetics and purgatives. Li Tung-Yuan emphasized the importance of the spleen and stomach and ascribed all ailments to the derangements of the digestive tract. Tan-Chi taught that malnutrition was the root of all troubles and extolled tonics.

Eastern drugs, herbs, and pharmacopia have a long history for their effects on what the West calls the nervous and chemical agencies of the body; the Occident has borrowed from their storehouse (Wolfsbane and quinine). It is manifestly impossible to view these aspects in detail except to say that in their explanations of Pitha and Kapha, Yin and Yang, and the Five Elements are revealed the Easterners' approach to these influences on the pulse.

8. Exercise

Action of any kind will increase the pulse, and the action of the heart becomes more forceful and frequent. At first the tension in the artery is elevated, but shortly thereafter, the artery is no longer felt between the beats.

According to Ayurveda, there is stimulation of Vayu and Pitha and gradually the force subsides and the tension is lost. In massage and passive exercise, only Pitha is stimulated. In the massaged parts, the blood is stimulated and there are a greater flow of blood to the affected parts and no fatigue, as results from violent exercise.

In breathing exercises, two of the five breaths—Prana and Udana—are involved according to Ayurvedic. Vayu and Pitha are stimulated alternately, a fact which in turn stimulates the appropriate hormone secretion. The pulse will be alternately increased or decreased.

The Chinese, like the Ayurvedists, are aware that exercise, both passive and physical, affect Yin and Yang.

9. Excitement—Physical or Emotional

The Western physician knows that emotions can quicken or slow down the pulse.

The Eastern cultures believe that each emotion has its own reaction on the heart and, in Western terminology, they know the action of the adrenals and the sympathetic nervous system. They have a set procedure for taking the pulse to eliminate emotion or to accommodate to it as a fact and these rules prevail:

a) During sexual excitement, the pulse is quick, but not frequent.
b) During anxiety, the pulse is feeble and of low tension.
c) During sorrow, the pulse is feeble and of low tension and very slow; later, it becomes quick and vigorous.
d) In fear, the pulse becomes feeble and frequent.
e) In anger, the pulse becomes violent and frequent.
f) In happiness, the pulse is at first slow and has good tension and then later, it becomes quick and vigorous.

10. Food and Tastes[1]

The partaking of food will increase the pulse about four beats on the average. If, however, a food or a combination of foods is bad for the body, the pulse will increase from 10 upwards depending on the severity of the case. Ayurvedic states that the pulse should not be examined during hunger, thirst, or eating.

The Chinese, Hindus, and Iraneans stress the fact that the pulse is affected by the type of foods eaten during the various seasons of the year. The five tastes of the Chinese and the six of the Hindus and the Unanis are described in their literature where the do's and dont's are all itemized.

Ayurvedic View on Tastes

According to Ayurvedic medicine, there are six tastes, and each one of them affects the pulse. In other words, the proper nutrition keeps the body healthy; improper diet upsets the balance of the body and causes disease. The effect of the food—whether healthy or not—is reflected in the pulse.

All of these six tastes react favorably or adversely on the Tridoshas, depending on the condition of the organism. The following tables show the relationship of the tastes to the doshas:

Table 6.

Sweet, sour, saline are anti-Vayu.

Astringent, bitter, sweet are anti-Pitha.

Bitter, sour, saline are anti-Kapha

Table 7.

Bitter, pungent, astringent will promote or increase Vayu.

Sour, pungent, and saline will promote or increase Pitha.

Sweet, pungent, astringent will increase Kapha.

---

1 See R. B. Amber's **Color Therapy** and **Nu-Reflex Therapy** for further explanations.

The Physiology of the Six Tastes

The molecules and ions in the solution tasted will set up vibrations which in turn stimulate the nerves of the taste buds. The impulses are collected, differentiated, and then transmitted through the related cranial nerves to the brain.[2] The glosso-pharyngeal, the lingual branch of the trigeminal nerve, the chodra-tympani of the facial nerve, and the hypoglossal are the motor nerves to the tongue.

Sweet

Is the main, readily available fuel substance.
Is beneficial to the skin, hair, voice.
Is an indispensable component of blood when digested.
Is stored in the liver as glycogen and in the muscles.
Acts as a healer of the thoracic lesions.
Enters into the constituency of protoplasm, especially the nucleus.
Proper functioning of the body, including the various organs and the special senses, is almost exclusively dependent on it.
Overindulgence leads to fat, impairment of digestive processes, coma, convulsions, glycosuria, and malignant tumors.
Promotes strength, cheerfulness, vitality, and satisfaction; secretion of milk in the mother.

Sour

Has the properties of the acids.
Has a powerful influence on the nervous system.
Stimulates and supports the heart.
Promotes digestion and relish for food.
Gives strength to the supporting tissue.
Restores health to the body.
Stimulates reflexly an abundant secretion of saliva, as though to clean the mouth.
Causes loose skin and chilly sensation in the teeth as well as shrinking sensation in the eyebrows and the contraction of the pupils.
Produces different types of Vayu diseases.
Relieves constipation.
Is a good tonic in small amounts.
Is good respiratory stimulant.
Is mild stimulant of higher brain center.
Is carminative in action and viscous in quality.

Pungent[3]

Destroys ulcers.
Dries up oily, fatty, and other such exudates.
Is valuable in diseases of the throat, dermatitis, gastric stasis.
Is light, hot, and dry.
Is a carminative and imparts relish to food.
Will excite the heart to move rapidly.

---

[2] The molecular and ionic contents possessing different tastes set up vibrations; their frequencies and lengths are specific to each taste bud and this fact results in the stimulation of gustatory hairs of the taste buds (R. B. A.).
[3] This taste has been added by the Hindus to the basic five tastes which the Chinese also list. In this regard, Ayurvedic and Unani medicine differs from the Chinese.

Helps remove toxic substances from the body.

Overindulgence leads to excessive thirst; inhibition of the production of the reproductive elements; causes asthenia; coma; constriction of the organs of the body; pain in the back and waist; delusion; wasting of the body; suffocation; exhaustion; vertigo; burning sensation of the throat; and heat and thirst in the body.

Astringent

Reduces disturbances caused by Pitha and Kapha.

Purifies the blood.

Heals ulcers.

Dries up tissues.

Increases auto-intoxication.

Promotes retention of specially injured parts and fractured bones.

Heals injuries.

Dries up moisture.

In the intestines, its effect is antagonistic to purgatives.

Is good for diseases of alimentary canal.

As a haemostatic, it precipitates a hard coagulum which blocks the vessels.

Excess leads to incoordination of the parts and functions of the body; itching sensation all over the body; pallor; boils; thirst; pyrexin; vertigo; distention of the abdomen; increase of Vayu diseases; produces periodic pain, hemiplegia, facial paralysis, asthenia, impotency, obliteration of channels of biological fluids, and the retention of feces.

Saline or Salt (NACL)

Is essential for the proper functioning of the body (Na, Ca, and K).

Lack of calcium results in increased irritation and twitching of skeletal muscles; considerable lowering of calcium in the blood leads to convulsions and death.

Proper balance of Na, Ca, and K ions is indispensable for the normal actions of the heart's muscle cells.

In a pure solution of sodium, the heart stops beating in a relaxed state.

In a pure solution of sodium and calcium but without potassium, the heart stops beating in a contracted state.

In a solution with an excess of potassium, the heart stops beating in a relaxed state.

Is responsible for the osmotic exchanges which are constantly going on in the human body.

Is the great conserver of energy, respiratory interchange, and metabolism.

Brings about shrinkage of the organs and tissues of the body.

Produces dryness.

Relieves constipation.

Improves digestion.

Promotes viscosity and diaphoric action.

Possesses carminative properties.

Is a laxative.

Will accelerate the pulse slightly.

Lack of salts results in muscular and mental weakness, vomitting, and diarrhea; psychologically, in loss of cheerfulness, delusions, and dryness of the mouth.

Overindulgence leads to neuritis, alopacia, greying of hair, wrinkling of the skin, thirst, skin disease, toxic state, erysepelas and depletion of body strength.

Bitter

Has the properties of the alkoloids.

Sweetish taste in many organic compounds gradually yields to bitter taste with the increase of the molecular weight.

Possesses antihelminitic and bacteriocidal properties and is anti-toxic.

Is good for obstinate skin diseases, loss of consciousness, pyrexias, salivation, inflammatory reaction, biliousness, bile, and phlegmatic (Kapha) disorders.

Reduces the accumulation of fat in the body.

Is light and dry in quality.

Promotes intellect and clearness of the throat.

Cleans the breast of milk.

Cures fainting and coma.

Alleviates burning sensation in the body, itching sensation in the skin, dermatitis, and thirst.

Tones up skin and muscles and possesses anti-pyretic action.

Chinese View on Tastes

According to the Chinese medical belief, there are five flavors or tastes and each of them affects the twelve pulses. The flavors have their basic tendencies in connection only with their related viscera as follows:

a) Sweet is related to the liver: its color is green; and the proper foods that contain sweet are dates, beef, meats, non-glutenous rice, etc.

b) Sour is related to the heart; its color is red; and the proper foods are plums, small peas, etc.

c) Bitter is related to the lungs; its color is white; and the proper foods are apricots, almonds, scallions, wheat, mutton, etc.

d) Salty is related to the spleen; its color is yellow; and the proper foods are chestnuts, coarse green vegetables, large beans, pork, etc.

e) Pungent is related to the kidneys; its color is black; and the proper foods are peaches, onions, chicken, meat, etc.

In connection with other viscera, their characteristics change. The **Nei Ching** gives numerous examples, some of which will be cited here:

If acidity exceeds the other flavors, then the liver will be caused to produce an excess of saliva (bile) and the forces of the spleen will be cut short.

If salt exceeds among the flavors, the great bones become weary, the muscles and the flesh become deficient, and the mind becomes despondent.

If sweetness exceeds among the other flavors, the breath of the heart will be asthmatic and full, the appearance will be black, and the force of the kidneys will be unbalanced.

If bitterness exceeds among the other flavors, then the atmosphere of the spleen becomes dry and of the stomach becomes dense.

If pungent exceeds among the other flavors, then the muscles and the pulse become slack and the spirit will be injured.

The Chinese **Nei Ching** then remarks that if people pay attention to the five flavors and mix them well, their bones will remain straight, their muscles will remain tender and younger, their breath and blood will circulate freely, their pores will be fine in texture and consequently, their breath and bones will be filled with the essence of life.

The five flavors are effective not only upon the five viscera but also upon all parts of the body that are connected to or that ramify from these viscera. These additional comments reveal their extraordinary skill in observation.

The pungent and the sweet flavors have a dispersing quality, like Yang. The sour and the salty flavors have a circulating quality and flow like Yin.

Excess of salty flavor hardens the pulse, changes the complexion, and has a softening effect.

Excess of bitter flavor withers the skin and makes the hairs of the body fall out; has a strengthening effect.

Excess of pungent flavor knots the muscles, affects the fingers and toe nails which wither and decay.

Excess of sour toughens the flesh, causes wrinkles, and slackens the lips.

Excess of sweet flavor makes the bones ache and the hair on the head fall out.

RULES

Pungent flavor counteracts sour; the lungs crave sour.

Salty flavor counteracts bitter; the kidneys crave salty.

Sour flavor counteracts sweet; the liver craves sour.

Bitter flavor counteracts pungent; the heart craves bitter.

Sweet flavor counteracts salty; the spleen craves sweet.

These rules may be rephrased with stress on the organs:

The lungs crave sour flavor; the kidneys, salty; the liver, sour; the heart, bitter; the spleen, sweet.

These rules may also be phrased with reference to the law of complementarity about flavors or with regard to the tastes:

Pungent flavor counteracts sour.

Salty flavor counteracts bitter.

Sour flavor counteracts sweet.

Bitter flavor counteracts pungent.

Sweet flavor counteracts salty.

(See R. B. Amber's **Color Therapy** for the color equivalents of these tastes.)

11. Sleep

To the Western physician, the pulse has nothing to do with sleep and dreams and no Western doctor would interpret the pulse rate for an insight into the content of dreams that may elude the sleeper on awakening. To certain schools of Western psychology and psychiatry, the interpretation of dreams is a method of determining the emotional state of the patients. The physical causes and interpretations are here fertile fields that have not been explored in the West and that yet remain to be discovered.

The Ayurvedic and Unani physicians are aware that sleep and dreams affect the pulse, but their interpretations are elementary when compared with the Chinese insights. The Chinese do not compartmentalize the physical and emotional; instead they are treated as a whole unit, as one interrelated field force. They use physical methods; namely, the pulse, to ascertain the emotional level and they use the emotional methods to ascertain the physical level and thus the physician obtains a complete picture or as complete a picture as is possible of the individual.

According to Ayurvedic, the pulse should not be examined during sleep. Sleep is a temporary anemia of the brain and very little stimuli are transmitted from the brain to excite the heart. In dreams and nightmares, however, respiration is increased and the heart is stimulated. During sleep the circulation runs down in vigor as well as in frequency, and the Ayurvedist considers the brain as an organ where Kapha predominates and keeps the pulse neither vigorous nor frequent. Stressors during sleep, like nightmares, act as Pitha or Vayu to the brain and accelerate the pulse. It is believed that airy persons will dream of flying through the air. Fiery persons will dream of long journeys by land, moving through jungles, catching or missing trains etc. Watery persons will dream of aquatic animals, sea voyages, etc.

According to the **Nei Ching,** dreams are caused by an imbalance of Yin and Yang:

Thus one can know that when Yin is flourishing, then there occur dreams, as if one had to wade through great waters, which cause bad fears; when Yang is flourishing, there occur dreams of great fires which burn and cauterize. When Yin and Yang both are flourishing, there occur dreams in which both forces destroy and kill or wound each other. When the upper pulse flourishes, then there are dreams as though one were flying; and when the lower pulse flourishes, then there are dreams as though one were falling down. When one is replete with food, then one dreams that one gave up one's inner surplus; when one is hungry or starved, then one dreams that one obtained enough to satisfy one's interior. Fullness of the lungs produces dreams of sorrow and weeping. When there is a multitude of small insects, then the dreams picture that one has collected all of them. When there is a multitude of large insects, then the dream pictures them as clashing together so that they will be injured and destroyed. (Shades of Kafka!)

12. Exposure to Heat or Cold

According to Ayurveda, the pulse should not be examined after exposure to heat or cold. External warmth excites Pitha, a fact which accelerates the pulse. Too much heat is relieved by nature's device of copious perspiration. Cold excites Kapha, and the tension of the pulse produces just the contrary effect: chills.

To the Chinese, one of the major causes of disease is attributed to the winds which help to disturb the balance of Yin and Yang. The east wind arises in the spring and is responsible for ailments of the liver, throat and neck. The south wind arises in the summer and causes ailments of the heart, chest, and ribs. The west wind arises in the fall and is responsible for ailments of the lungs, shoulders, and back. The north wind arises in the winter and is the culprit of kidney diseases, ailments of the loins and thighs.

Cold injures the body while heat injures the spirit. When the spirit is hurt, severe pain ensues. When the body is hurt, there will be swelling. Thus in cases where severe pains are felt first and swelling appears later, one can say that the spirit has injured the body and in the cases where swelling appears first and severe pains are felt later, one can say that the body has injured the spirit.

The Chinese were aware of and practiced psychosomatic medicine from the very beginnings or from their earliest experiences in healing.

13. Variations of the Pulse at Different Times of the Day and Night

Ayurvedic and Unani medicine teaches that the best time to examine the pulse is in the morning when the pulse indicates the true state of the body. During noon and the afternoon, slight variations take place: e.g., hot at noon and quick in the afternoon. Further, the pulse varies in tropical, temperate, and cold climate.

According to the **Nei Ching,**

The pulse should be taken at dawn when the breath of Yin (which is negative or the female principle in nature) has not yet begun to stir and when the breath of Yang (positive, the male principle of life and light) has not yet begun to diffuse itself; when food and drink have not yet been taken, when the twelve main vessels are not yet abundant and when the lo vessels are stirred up thoroughly; when vigor and energy are not yet disturbed—at that particular time one should examine what has happened to the pulse.

All those pulses of the nine subdivisions that beat deeply and thinly, that are suspended and interrupted are caused by Yin, the principle of darkness, which rules over winter. Hence a number of deaths occur at midnight.

All those pulse beats that are abundant, hasty, panting and accelerated are caused by Yang, the principle of light, which rules over Summer. Hence a number of deaths occur at noon.

For these reasons diseases brought about by heat and cold finally find their death at dawn or early morning. Those who burn within from a disease caused by heat find their death at noon. Those who suffer from a disease that is caused by the wind die at the time of dusk. Those who suffer from a disease of water find their death at midnight. Those whose pulse beats are suddenly interrupted or suddenly accelerated or suddenly retarded or of sudden haste and urgency, find their death during the four seasons at the time the sun rises.

With this knowledge of the pulse, the superior physician can take the necessary steps to help the patient as he is well aware of the critical periods and what is wrong with the patient. Here the body tells its own story accurately and reliably. The song of the pulse can be a dirge or a dance depending on whether the inferior or superior physician is conducting.

The atmospheric conditions vary at different times of the day and night. As the environment changes, the sympathetic and endocrine systems react so that these moods, the workings of the organs together with the viscera are all reflected in the pulse.

Ayurvedic medicine maintains that Kapha is excited during the early hours both of the day and the night; Pitha is excited both at about midday and midnight; and Vayu is excited in the late parts of the day and the night. These interrupted sequences seem to act in twelve hour intervals and have a rhythmic cycle of their own: morning and night are Kapha; noon and midnight are Pitha; afternoon and the late part of the night are Vayu.

The rhythm of these three Indian elements can be compared with the Chinese view wherein each organ has a rhythm of its own and where the energy Chi-hua passes from one meridian to another.[4] But here it must be stressed that the Chinese see the movement of energy as a cycle taking twenty-four hours in its flow from one organ and its tissues to the next organ and tissues, a ramification in the following order: from the lungs to the large intestine, to the stomach and on to the spleen, thence to the heart, to the small intestines and on to the bladder, to the kidneys, to the heart constrictor, to the tri-heaters, to the gall bladder, to the liver and then to the lungs. Furthermore, the Chinese maintain that each meridian has its tide of energy with its maximum and minimum points of energy flow. Should a strainer act on a particular organ at its minimum point of energy supply or at its nadir, serious injury or death would follow. The organs have their highest energy level or potential reflected in the meridians for a two hour period out of the twenty-four. The following table will illustrate the maximum and nadir points to be watched for best healing effectiveness.

---

[4] This energy is primarily the life force or cosmic energy. It is not thermal energy, not nervous energy, not electrical energy, not chemical energy! The Indians call this Prana.

Table 8

Chinese Zenith and Nadir Hours for Energy Flow of Organs

Organs and Cycle Flow of Energy	Hour in Chinese Terminology	Zenith or Maximum Energy Potential	Nadir or Time of Lowest Energy Ebb: Danger Zone[5]	
Lungs	Yin	0300-0500	*	1500
Large Intestines	Mao	0500-0700	*	1700
Stomach	Ch'en	0700-0900	*	1900
Spleen	Ssu	0900-1100	*	2100
Heart	Wu	1100-1300	*	2300
Small Intestines	Wei	1300-1500	*	0100
Bladder	Shen	1500-1700	*	0300
Kidneys	Yu	1700-1900	*	0500
Heart Constrictor	Hsü	1900-2100	*	0700
Tri-Heaters	Hai	2100-2300	*	0900
Gall Bladder	Tzu	2300-0100	*	1100
Liver	Ch'u	0100-0300	*	1300

According to Ayurvedic, there are three different types of time, and each plays a part in the drama of the pulse:

a) Ayoga or inaction: e.g., when the season does not manifest itself at the scheduled time, the body may be thrown out of rhythm with the result that there will be an imbalance of three elements in Ayurvedic belief, of four elements in Unani belief.

b) Atiyoga or overaction: e.g., when there is excessive heat in summer or excessive cold in winter; or when the weather is hotter or colder than is usually the case.

c) Mithyayoga or improper action: e.g., when it is cold in summer and hot in winter or when it rains in the dry season and fails to rain in the rainy season.

Basically, the Chinese are in agreement with the observations above.

One must pause and think of the implications of pulse and time, for in this interrelationship is the possible key to the different cultural frameworks of reference. Why do the Indians phrase three doshas and why do the Unani add a fourth element—the circulation of the blood? Why do the Chinese base all on the five elements and the two forces: Yin and Yang? Yet all three cultures recognize that the pulse is fundamental to the diagnosis and prognosis of disease.

---

5 The nadir hour leads into the "death point" which is the time when the organ is at its lowest declining point just before it starts to mount upward on its cycle of replenishing its energy. The symbol of a star (*) is used here rather than at the two-hour time span that is indicated for the zenith point in order to caution the observer to use the pulse readings and the reflex points to determine the lowest ebb of energy flow. This aspect is extremely important for surgeons and doctors because the nadir is the critical period for the patient. See R. B. Amber's account of the Marmars in his **Nu Reflex Therapy.**

14. and 15. Variations of Different Seasons and Climates

Seasons are caused by the rotation of the earth, and consequently the effects are well marked because the three elements or forces—Vayu, Pitha, and Kapha—in Ayurvedic, and the five elements in Chinese are accounted for in reading the pulse. The climate of the locality varies with the nature of the country and this fact also affects the pulse: for example, in hilly and jungle country, Pitha and Vayu are excited; in marshy country, Kapha is excited; on the plains where it is not too hilly or wet, the pulse is normal.

Ayurvedic and Unani physicians send patients with dry bronchitis to the sea shore so that the Vayu and Pitha subside and the patient is relieved. Patients with moist bronchitis, with too much secretion, are sent to the mountains so that the dosha Kapha subsides and thus gives relief to the patient. According to Ayurveda, when the climate changes, the three doshas are affected and consequently the pulse. It must be remembered that the seasons in India are well-marked though they do not include a long winter, as the Western climate does.

Table 9

Ayurvedic Pulse—Season Interrelationship

Season	Kapha (Water)	Pitha (Fire)	Vayu (Air)
Early winter	slowly excited	normal	slowly excited
Spring	excited to excess; spring is season of Kapha	————	————
Summer	normal	slowly excited	slowly excited
Rains	normal	slowly excited	slowly excited
Autumn	irritation subsides	excitement continues; autumn is season of Pitha	irritation subsides

Air accumulates in the summer, is aggravated in the rainy season, and is ameliorated in the autumn.

Fire accumulates in the rainy reason, is aggravated in the autumn, and is ameliorated in the winter.

Water accumulates in the winter, is aggravated in the spring, and is ameliorated in the summer.

Those who are sick or weak and already have certain elements in excess will be increasingly ill in a season that aggravates those very elements and will come down with diseases peculiar to that element. If the imbalance is too great, they will die.

According to the **Nei Ching,** these generalizations apply to the seasons:

Spring: The pulse of the stomach should be fine and delicate, like the strings of a musical instrument. If the strings are touched too frequently, the stomach functions intermittently and the resulting illness affects the liver [detoxifying organ]. If the strings give only one tone, the stomach ceases to function and death results. When the stomach has a defect, an illness will make its appearance in harvest time. When the defect is great, the illness will strike at once.

Summer: The pulse beats should be like the beats of a fine hammer. When the beats are too heavy, the stomach works insufficiently and an illness of the heart results. When there is only one single hammer beat, the stomach has ceased to function and death ensues. When the stomach contains stones, a disease will make its appearance in winter. When the stones are large, the disease will break out presently.

During the long summer, the pulse should be soft and feeble. If it is too feeble, the stomach functions insufficiently and an illness of the spleen results [blood dyscrasia]. When the pulse is soft and feeble and there are also stones, a disease will make its appearance in winter. When the pulse is of great weakness, the disease breaks out suddenly.

Autumn: The pulse is small and rough. If it is too rough, the stomach functions insufficiently and a disease of the lungs results. When it is merely rough, death ensues. When it is rough but also taut, like the strings of a lute, disease will make its appearance in the spring. When the pulse beats too closely, like the tautness of a musical string, disease breaks out presently.

Winter: The pulse is small and hard, like a stone. Then it is healthy and well-balanced. If the pulse is too much like a stone, malfunctions of the stomach and diseases of the kidney result. If it sounds like a single stone, the stomach ceases to function and death ensues.

In Spring, the pulse is like the string of a lute; the pulse is that of the liver; earth is the element; the direction is east.

In Summer, the pulse is like the beat of a hammer; the pulse is that of the heart; fire is the element; the direction is south.

In the Fall, the pulse is superficial and flowing; the pulse is that of the lungs; metal is the element; the direction is west.

In Winter, the pulse is well-regulated; the pulse is that of the kidney; water is the element; the direction is north.

The pulse has ways of telling whether the patient follows or disobeys the laws of the four seasons and whether there are not hidden symptoms: for instance, when in Spring and Summer, the pulse is thin and when in Fall and Winter, the pulse is superficial and large, it is clearly indicated that the patient is in discord with the four seasons.

16. Altitude

All cultures are aware of the fact that altitude increases the red blood corpuscles; the higher the altitude, the more blood corpuscles, the slower the pulse; altitude, pressure and oxygen affect the pulse.

17. Posture of the Patient

The position of the patient influences the frequency of the beat on an average of eight per minute between the standing and recumbent positions. The higher frequency in the upright position is not due to the muscular functioning required. It beats ten to twelve times faster when one is standing than it does when one is sitting and beats faster when one is sitting than when one is lying down. As a general rule, the better the posture, the lower the pulse.

18. Temperament

Naturally, the pulse will vary in different types of individuals with different temperaments. The Oriental physicians are well aware of these facts and have classified individuals according to their temperaments and then treated them. Some Western theoreticians have classified individuals according to temperament, but make no reference to the pulse with respect to temperament.

19. Suggestion and Hypnotism

These aspects can lower or quicken the pulse depending on the circumstances. (The reader is referred to items 24, on psychological aspects, and 11, on sleep.

In Arabian folklore, the story is told of the rivalry between two court physicians who challenged each other to a duel by poison. It was agreed that each should take a poison supplied by his antagonist, of which he should then endeavor to counteract the effect by a suitable antidote.

The first prepared a poisonous draught, "the fierceness of which would have melted black stone." His antagonist drained the cup and at once took an antidote which rendered it innocuous. The second physician then picked a rose from the garden, breathed an incantation over it and bade his rival smell it; thereupon the first one fell dead.

Oriental literature and philosophy—Chinese, Indian, and Persian— are replete with stories which illustrate the effects of suggestion on the body. Even in detailing directions to the physician, mythology voices medical aphorisms.

The Unani physician has accepted as his doctrine the ruling that "Science is twofold: it must embrace theology and medicine." In other words, prayer is as powerful as or more potent than drugs; suggestion can be used to cure or to destroy. (Here parenthetically is the basis of New Thought healing in the West as spearheaded by Christian Scientists and by other New Thought developments.) The folklore endlessly narrates stories that reveal how the emotions of anger and shame are successfully used in the treatment of rheumatic afflictions of the joints, a disease that plagues allopathic physicians in the West and for which they have no cures at the present time.

Two stories can be briefly recapitulated about a king and a queen, both suffering from rheumatism.

The king told the physician that if he failed in the cure, he would forfeit his life. The physician then took the king to the baths, but left a fast horse and a donkey outside. In the baths, he approached the nude king with a knife, an insult which incensed his majesty. The physician then fled on his horse to the border and informed the emperor by note that the cure had been effected through the anger aroused by the incident in the baths. And so it was!

The queen was advised to undress in order to alleviate her pain and as she followed the directions, she realized that she was undressing before the court and shame effected the cure.

In both incidents, the Unani physicians understood that the body secretes a hormone, known to us in the West as ACTH (cortisone), which can cure rheumatism. They understood, further, that for it to be effective, the ACTH (cortisone) would have to be manufactured by the body. The West has met with setbacks in its use of synthetically manufactured cortisone in the treatment of rheumatism; folk wisdom of the past still narrates its message of truth.

20. Temperature

There is a three-way correlation — pulse beat, temperature, and respiration — which must be considered in most diseases. As a general rule, an increase of fever one degree raises the pulse beat ten points. (This fact does not hold true in some heart cases.) The pulse in fever quickens in proportion to the rise of temperature.

If the pulse beat is above the normal theoretical limit, then it should be taken for granted that some altered function or "abnormal"[5] condition is taking place or that some obstruction exists within the organism. This means that the defense mechanisms are trying to absorb the blockage and carry it, as waste, to the excretory organs for elimination by increasing the rate and volume of the blood supply. Thus this increase gives the body more power to remove the stressor. A certain degree of fever is always present if not on the outside of the body or on the surface, then in the centers of one or more of the vital organs. Lowering the pulse is not the answer—whether by drugs, acupuncture, massage, reflex therapy, etc. Treating and removing the cause of the disturbed pulse must be the concern of the doctor. If the pulse decreases,

---

[5] Abnormal or pathological in our terminology, but a normal process for the body.

it is an indication that the curing process is going on. All cultures are aware of this fact.

21. Age

The pulse varies according to age; all cultures here agree.

Pulse Rate	Age	Pulse Rate	Age
150-160	in embryo	80-85	seven to fourteen
130-140	after birth	85-90	adolescence
115-130	first year	75-80	adulthood
100-115	second year	60-75	old age
90-100	third year	75-80	decrepitude
85-90	three to seven		

The pulse is higher in children and as a rule decreases with age. If there are structural changes in the arterial coat because of improper diet or faulty circulation, the pulse rate will increase. As a general rule, the pulse is slower in tall persons and faster in short ones. A glance at the table shows that the pulse rate by itself is meaningless unless it is correlated with age, sex, posture, temperature, altitude, food, kind of beat, chemical, physical, and electrical agencies, etc.

22. Sex and Sexual Intercourse

The pulse is faster in the female by from six to fourteen beats than it is in the male. But the difference occurs only after about the eighth year. The proper use of the sex act relieves excess tension and helps to normalize the pulse in disease or to keep it balanced in health. The improper use of sex or sexual abuse will drain the body of energy and cause tension and strain which lead to altered function and premature senescence or senility.

The Hindus and the Chinese believe that the seminal essence is in every cell of the body and not confined to only the reproductive organs. When these fluids are used up, the body gallops on towards old age, according to the Hindus.

23. Thought (Blood Follows the Thought)

Thought affects the circulation of the blood and, of course, the pulse. Professor W. G. Anderson of Yale showed by his experiments that when subjects were placed on a tilt board and told to do mental exercises, the board would tilt toward the head. When the same subjects were told to imagine that they were doing leg gymnastics, the board tilted toward the legs (Orison S. Marder, **Every Man A King,** N.Y., Thomas Crowell and Co., 1906).

Western medicine as yet does not consider thought a factor in health and disease. The New Thought Movement, psychosomatic medicine, hypnosis, and the influence of Eastern philosophy on the West— all are making the Occident somewhat aware of the power of thought.

The Ayurvedic, the Unani doctors, and especially the Chinese and Tibetans, all were aware of the influence of thought on the human body. They set aside time for meditation to cleanse the body both spiritually and physically and this became a part of the daily ritual. They stressed right thinking for right physical action; one without the other is useless, they said, and leads to mental and physical chaos and disease.

24. Psychological Factors

The mere taking of the pulse will greatly accelerate its frequency with some people, even those who appear outwardly calm and composed. (See dreams in item 11, Sleep.)

In Ayurvedic and Unani medicine, the physician is well aware first of the significant play or effect on the pulse of psychological factors and then of how the conscious and unconscious levels influence the pulse (they include the deep dreamless state as well as dreams). They have used the pulse as a lie-detector to ferret out the sources of inner emotions, a technique which prevailed centuries before the West devised its methodology. Both cultures have a pulse for each of emotions, but for our purposes, the Chinese methods will be detailed here; in these examples will be explicated as well their principles of masking.

The Chinese believe that strong passions reduce and exhaust the emanation (not quite an aura, but closely similar to the life force since the Chinese do not quite accept the aura as do the Indians). Moderate passions strengthen the emanations and make them fertile. Strong passions reduce, consume, dissipate, or exhaust the emanations whereas moderate passions conserve the emanations and beget life and creativity. (Mens sana in corpore sano.) The Western equivalent for emanations would be electromagnetic force.

Violent anger is hurtful to Yin; violent joy is hurtful to Yang. When emotions rise to heaven, the pulse expires and leaves the body. (Any violent emotion will kill: e.g. apoplexy.)

When joy and anger are without moderation, then cold and heat exceed all measure and life is no longer secure. Yin and Yang should be respected to an equal extent. Any excess of joy or anger is dangerous to health. Any imbalance in the emotions of Yin and Yang brings on disease or death as explained below:

> Anger is injurious to the liver, but sympathy counteracts anger. Extravagant joy is injurious to the heart, but fear counteracts happiness.

> Extreme sympathy is injurious to the stomach, but anger counteracts sympathy.

> Extreme grief is injurious to the lungs, but joy counteracts grief. Extreme fear is injurious to the kidneys, but contemplation counteracts fear.

> Joy is the emotion of the heart which then influences the lungs leaving the heart unprotected; thus the influence of the kidneys is permitted to come to the fore. (Example—Joy makes the heart beat faster; more oxidation is required. Lungs must take in more air; the kidneys carry away the waste products).

Fear is the emotion of the kidneys and it influences the heart and leaves the kidneys unprotected. (Example—Student preparing for an examination runs to the bathroom frequently and heart races).

Sadness is the emotion of the liver and then influences the spleen, leaving the liver unprotected. (Example—Sadness depletes the liver of glucose and strains circulatory system and thereby affects red and white blood corpuscles; spleen overworked).

A word of note: they were thousands of years ahead of Selye with his theory of stressors and G.A.S.—General Adaptation Syndrome.

25. Color

Psychologists in the West are aware that color affects the pulse. A person placed in a red room will have his blood pressure go up; placed in a green room, his blood pressure will go down.

To the Indian, color is the basis of the microscopic and macroscopic world. All living things are nothing but color in certain proportions. The Chinese have a color for every organ of the body, for the five elements, for the five tastes, and for the four seasons. Color is very important in diagnosis and healing to the indigenous Oriental physician. (For a fuller explanation, see Amber's **Color Therapy.**)

26. Sound

Psychologists are aware that sound can have a soothing effect as well as a stimulating effect. A screeching sound can drive certain individuals "out of their minds." Music is used in the West as therapy for the emotionally disturbed. Yet the Western physician pays no attention to the effect sound has on the pulse.

The Oriental physician is well aware of the effect of sound on the human organism and uses it in his diagnosis and treatment and also in his daily life. The sound of the temple bell in India is only a casual daily reflection of the significance of the Aum principle which as a sound is believed to sum up all language, for all combinations and permutations are derived from this sound. The symbology of how the three levels of man are reflected in the Aum- A for logical mind; U for dream state and the apparently logical evolution in the state of dreams; and M for the deep dreamless state of endless creative potential—is only partially grasped or developed in the readings of the West. Some schools of psychological interpretations are opening the Western horizons to this phase; further, the development by teachers of modern languages and linguistics is on a more advanced scale than are the physicians in their awareness of sound.

The Chinese use sounds to describe their pulse findings; e.g., music of the lute; the rustles of the reeds, etc. But time does not permit of an extensive treatment of this glorious symphony of the body to which some people are tragically tone-deaf.

Chapter VII

WESTERN EXAMINATION OF THE PULSE

As Described in Texts and as Honored in the Breach by Physicians

The material in this section is an alphabetical arrangement of the various pulse beats which have been described in the medical texts published in the Western world. Much has been done to acquaint the medical practitioner with these refinements in interpreting the pulse, but in the future, both the schools and the physicians will have to give their attention to enriching the findings of the present-day texts. The West needs to reflect in the medical literature on its readings of the pulse some aspects of the competent insights and techniques which have enriched the Easterners' viewpoints and training methods, especially the frame of reference projected by the indigenous schools of their respective countries.

P., **ABDOMINALIS.** The soft compressible, but usually regular p. occurring in certain abdominal diseases.

P., **ACCELERATED.** A common symptom in all fevers. The pulse of the adult rarely exceeds 150 beats per minute even in acute inflammatory infection; in prostration it runs above.

An accelerated pulse may be due to valvular defects of the heart except in aorta stenosis, in which case the pulse will be slow. It is usually found in instances where compensation fails.

When there is no cardiac condition or fever present, look for early phthisis, Addison's Disease, exophthalmic goiter, locomotor ataxia, pernicious anemia.

The excessive use of coffee, tea, drugs, alcohol or tobacco will give an accelerated pulse. So will sexual excesses, lack of sleep, indigestion, and neurasthenic conditions. Shock and collapse are accompanied by a rapid feeble heart action.

P., **ALLORHYTHMIC.** Irregular in rhythm. Among the arrhythmia beats are:

1) **EXTRA SYSTOLES** — due to a premature contraction where the first or second sounds can be heard at the apex. If the ventricle is contracting twice as fast as the pulse rate, it is due to extra systoles—as a general rule.

2) **AURICULAR FIBRILLATION** — where the pulse is totally irregular in time and strength with a beat of 120 or more per minute and a beat which bears no relation to the phases of respiration. In an elderly person, if

the pulse rate is 30 to 168 per minute over a period of weeks, look for auricular fibrillation.

3) **PAROXYSMAL TACHYCARDIA—PULSUS ALTERNANS** — is a pulse which suddenly jumps to a rate varying from 110 to 200 or over per minute and just as suddenly drops to normal after an uncertain interval, especially in young adults.

4) **HEART BLOCK** — where a regular pulse rate below 35 per minute is generally due to a complete heart block. The auricles and ventricles beat independently. If between 40 to 50 beats, partial heart block should be suspected. When both the ventricle rate and the pulse rate drop abruptly to one half the previous rate, it is due to a heart block. Rarely is a dropped beat due to a heart block. Add four to eight beats to the above in females. (R.B.A.)

When the slow rhythm develops suddenly and is of extreme degree, loss of consciousness and possible convulsions may occur (Adam-Stokes syndrome). If the block is partial, every other beat may be dropped or every third beat and so on. If the impulses reach the ventricles at irregular intervals, there will be irregularly recurring pauses in the pulse beats without alteration of the force or rhythm. If every second impulse from the auricle fails to reach the ventricle, there is no irregularity; if every third auricular impulse is blocked, pulsus bigeminus results, two regular beats being followed by a pause equivalent to one cardiac cycle; while if every fourth impulse is blocked, pulsus trigeminus results. Transition from one form to another is not uncommon, and a considerable increase of pulse rate, as by exercise, usually causes the disappearance of partial blocking and produces regularity of the pulse.

5) **PREMATURE CONTRACTIONS** (extra systoles)—Premature beats may be simple or complex and may recur at regular or irregular intervals. The pulse shows a rhythm which dominates the action as a whole. The premature beat is a small beat and is often followed by a compensatory pause especially in ventricular extra systoles, and the beat next following the pause is often increased in magnitude. If the beat is too feeble to open the aortic valve or to reach the wrist, it will be denoted in the pulse by a pause.

6) **INEQUALITY OF THE PULSES**—This inequality may be a perfectly natural phenomenon. One frequently finds that the radial arteries of the two sides are not of the same caliber, owing to variable degrees of collateral circulation by an enlarged comes nervi mediani. Inequality of the pulses is a much more important sign when it is known to have developed in a patient whose pulses were formerly normal. The inequality may show itself either in a definite delay of one behind the other or in a difference in strength.

7) **SINUS ARRHYTHMIA** — is a pulse rate which accelerates with inspiration and declines during expiration (decelerates). This is a physiological matter and occurs normally in the young. Other types occur, but are rare; they show no correlation with the respiratory phases. The pulse is comparatively slow in these pathological types with irregularly long diastolic pauses. P., ALTERNANS, ALTERNATING. A succession of strong and weak beats. Alternations in amplitude of the pulse wave, large pulsation alternating with small one in cycles of equal length. It occurs in normal hearts with excessive tachycardia and may occur with a slow rate if myocardium is

impaired. Rhythm is normal, but a weak beat occurs alternately. This pulse is a grave sign in cardiovascular diseases because it usually indicates serious left ventricular weakness. The Chinese would say the pulse is not in harmony with the four seasons. This pulse should be differentiated from **pulse bigeminus** which results from a premature beat. In pulse alternans, the beats are equally spaced; in pulse bigeminus, the strong beat and the following weak beat are coupled.

P., **ANACROTIC.** One showing a secondary wave on ascending limb of the main wave.

P., **ANGRY.** Wiry p.

P., **AORTIC VALVE INCOMPETENCY.** Pulse rising very suddenly and collapsing suddenly.

P., **ARDENT.** Artery seems to raise itself to a point in order to strike the finger at a single point.

P., **ARRHYTHMIC.** See allorhythmic p.

P., **ASYMETRICAL RADIAL.** May result from an anomaly of distribution, size and division of the vessels; aortic aneurism; embolism; an atheromatous plate within a vessel; fracture; luxation causing compression of a vessel; or compression of a vessel by tumor within or without the thorax; cervical rib.

P., **AURICULAR FIBRILLATION.** Irregular rhythm in force and beat, except in digitalis. There is absolute irregularity of the heart beat; the beats are rapid, entirely haphazard and vary continually in rate, intensity, and interval. The pulse rate may be considerably slower than the ventricular rate; the weaker beat may not open the aortic valve or may not be sufficiently strong to send a wave to the wrist. See allorhythmia.

P., **BAMBERGER'S BULBAR P.** Observable in the bulbar of the jugular vein and synchronous with the systole; occurs in tricuspidal inadequacy. A pulse may also at times occur in a vein in a vascular organ, as in the case of the liver.

P., **BIGEMINAL.** Two regular beats followed by a longer pause. It has the same significance as an irregular pulse.

P., **BIGEMINUS.** Paired beats. The strong beat and the following weak beat are coupled.

P., **BISFERIOUS.** An arterial pulse with two palpable peaks, the second stronger than the first. Aortic insufficiency with Aortic Stenosis.

P. **BOUNDING OR COLLAPSING.** Due to a shortened ventricular systole and a concomitant diminution of peripheral resistance. Found in febrile states, thyrotoxicosis, emotional disturbances and disorders causing peripheral vasodilation. Pulse feebly strikes the finger, then subsides abruptly and completely. Aortic regurgitation chief sign. Arterial throbbing, tumultous apex beat; galloping radial and visible capillary pulses; left ventricular hypertrophy; diastolic aortic murmur; large pulse pressure. See Corrigan's p. and Waterhammer p.

P., **BREATH.** A peculiar audible pulsation of the breath corresponding to the heart beat. Seen in cases of dry cavities of the lung with thick walls not separated from the heart by permeable lung tissue..

P., **CAPILLARY.** Alternating redness or blanching of capillary region, as in the matrices beneath the nails, occurring chiefly when an excessive cardiac impulse coincides with general arterial narrowing. Can be demonstrated by pressing the finger nail at its distal end so that the base of the nail remains pink and the anterior portion blanched. There is alternating reddening and pallor of the paler portion with each beat of the heart; can be seen by transillumination through the finger pulp with an electric light. The capillary pulse can be observed at any place where there is an area of pallor as, for example, along the margin of an area of skin which has been caused to redden by slight friction and in the lips or gums when gently compressed with a glass slide. See Quincke's p.

P., **CAPRISANS.** An irregular, peculiar weak pulsation succeeded by a stronger one. A bounding leaping p. irregular both in force and rhythm. See goat leap p.

P., **CATACROTIC.** One showing one or more secondary waves on descending limb of the main wave.

P., **CELER.** A pulse beat swift to rise and fall, particularly that associated with high blood pressure in aortic regurgitation.

P., **CELERIMUS.** A water hammer pulse.

P., **CHANGEABLE.** Denotes nervous derangement and sometimes organic heart disease.

P., **COLLAPSING.** See bounding p.

P., **CONTRACTED.** Indicates a capillary obstruction and intense engorgement. Epidemic cholera. Nearly the opposite of the full pulse, pulsation being narrow, deep, and somewhat hard.

P., **CONVULSIVE.** Unequal frequency or unequally hard.

P., **CORDIS.** The apex beat of the heart.

P., **CORRIGAN'S.** See bounding p.

P., **CRITICAL.** The subsidence of irritation results in a more perfect equilibrium in the circulation and a general improvement in the patient's condition. After having been irregular or abnormal in respect to the diseased condition, the pulse returns to normal with the subsidence of the irritation and as it return to normal, the pulse feels free, open, and soft.

P., **DEBILIS.** A weak p.

P., **DEEP.** Pertaining to the situation of the artery. Cannot be felt without difficulty nor without strong pressure.

P., **DEFICIENT** or **FLICKERING.** A feeble beat which seems every instant about to cease. Lack of a beat due to the failure of the heart to contract.

P., **DEFICIT.** The difference between the ausculatory heart rate and the rate of the peripheral pulse determined by palpation.

P., **DEPRESSED.** Weak and contracted; deep.

P., **DICROTIC** or **DOUBLE PULSE.** In which the finger is struck twice at each contraction of the heart; one lightly and one more forcibly.

Organic affliction of the heart or large arteries sometimes found in very nervous dyspeptics especially those who have indulged freely in narcotics and nervenes.

One heart beat for two arterial pulsations. It indicates low arterial tension and is noted in fevers, in low states of the nervous system and sometimes in typhoid fever.

P., **DIFFERENS.** A condition in which the pulses in the two radial arteries differ in strength.

P., **DOUBLE.** See dicrotic p.

P., **DROPPED BEAT.** Rhythm interrupted by a pause, heart actually misses a stroke. Denotes heart block.

P., **DUPLEX.** Dicrotic p.

P., **DURUS.** A hard incompressible pulse, indicating arterial hypertension.

P., **ENTROPTIC.** The subjective illumination of a dark visual field with each heart beat. Sometimes noted after violent exercise; due to the mechanical irritation of the rods by the pulsating retinal arteries.

P., **FEBRILE.** A full, soft, frequent, and bounding pulse at the onset of fevers becoming weak and feeble when fever subsides or on prostration.

P., **FIBRILLATION.** See auricular p.

P., **FILIFORM.** Resembling a thread, slightly vibrating.

P., **FINE.** Scarcely perceptible. Denotes great exhaustion and approaching death. May be caused by wasting disease or hemorrhage.

P., **FIRM.** See resistant p.

P. **FLICKERING.** See deficient p.

P., **FLUENS.** Undulating.

P., **FORMICANS.** A very small, nearly imperceptible p.

P., **FORTIS.** A rapid p.

P., **FREQUENT** or **RAPID.** See also rapid p. Irritation or inflammation and when very frequent, great debility. Beyond 90 per minute, debility is generally proportional to the frequency of the pulse. In complicated affections of the thoracic and abdominal viscera, the frequency of the pulse is an important indication of the locality of the principal morbid condition. In dyspeptic consumption, that commences with a diseased liver and stomach and ends up with tuberculosis or ulcers of the lungs, the pulse will be moderately slow when the abdomen is the principal seat of the disease; it will gradually increase in frequency as the disease extends itself to and occupies the lungs; and be very frequent when the viscera of the chest become the point most dangerously affected.

In most chronic diseases of the abdominal organs, the pulse is preternaturally slow while in all ideopathic afflictions of the chest, the pulse is preternaturally frequent. In these dyspeptic disorders of the liver, attended with a dry husky cough, a tenacious secretion of the throat, or a glutineous mucous expectoration from the lungs, there is always danger of confirmed consumption when the pulse begins to beat with considerable frequency 80 to 100 times.

P., **FULL.** Occurs in general plethora or in the early stages of acute diseases. A good degree of superficial capillary circulation found in apoplexy, hot stages of fever, incipient stages of T.B. Gives to the finger the sensation of repletion or fullness. Sthenic inflammation.

P., **GASEOUS HEMORRHAGIC.** A soft, full and feeble p., readily compressible. Denotes a distended artery that has lost its tone.

P., **GOAT LEAP.** See caprizant p. Imperfect dilation of the artery being succeeded by a fuller and stronger one. Artery seems to leap.

P., **GUTTURAL.** A p. felt in the throat.

P., **HAMMER.** See water hammer p. and steel hammer p.

P., **HARD.** See resistant p. A lesser degree of inflammation than strong pulse or a great degree of irritation without great debility. Found in many forms of acute and subacute inflammation: gout; rheumatism, pneumonia; in that form of continual fever called Synochus; in bilious remittent fever; in the early stages of intermittent fever; during the hot stages of paroxysm and generally in the early stages of exasthema, measles, smallpox, scarlatina, erysipelas, etc. Bleeding renders it softer for a few hours, but unless the cause is removed, the hardness soon returns. Due to changes in the arterial wall or to vascular distortion.

P., **HECTIC.** Weak, feeble, observed in hectic fever.

P., **HEMORRHAGIC.** A soft, full and readily compressible pulse marking a distended artery that has lost its tone.

P., **HEPATIC.** Due to expansion of veins of liver at each ventricular contraction. Slow, soft p.

P., **HETEROCHRONICUS.** An arrhythmic p.

P., **HIGH TENSION.** Force of beat is relatively increased and one which may be roughly estimated by noting the amount of pressure of the fingers that is required to arrest the beat. Observed in cardiac disease, hypertrophy, chronic nephritis, cerebral affections, irritations of the vasomotor centers, as in apoplexy, tumor, and beginning meningitis. In the use of certain drugs — such as digitalis, ergot, and alcoholic stimulants—and chills, angina pectoris, epileptic seizure, lithemia, gout, uremia.

P., **INAEQUALIS.** A pulse irregular in rhythm and force.

P., **INCISURA.** Sharp fall in pulse pressure.

P., **INCOMPETENCY.** See aortic valve.

P., **INFREQUENT.** Observed in organic heart disease, especially fatty degeneration and fibroid induration, jaundice, pressure at base of brain sufficient to irritate the vagus as in the beginning of meningitis, at the close of febrile disease, as in typhoid fever and pneumonia. May follow the use of certain drugs such as digitalis, aconite, and opium.

Physiologic slowness is noted in repose during fasting, in puberty, and in old age; it is habitual in certain people (40-60).

P., **INTERCUSSENT.** Where a superfluous pulsation seems to occur.

P., **INTERMITTENT.** One in which a pulsation is occasionally omitted and is due to some obstruction in the circulation of the heart or lungs, inflammation or softening of the brain, apoplexy, etc.; also in some forms of valvular diseases of the heart. Prolonged over-exertion, want of rest, anxiety, etc. may produce it. In minor degrees, indigestion with flatulence may produce it. It is often a symptom of the gouty constitution without indicating the presence of any organic disease.

A beat is occasionally missed. The intermissions are usually quite irregular, as one in 5, 6, 10, 20. In those subject to constipation and with old people, it may indicate quick viscid blood, capillary obstruction or nervous exhaustion. Overloading a weak stomach almost always produces an intermittent pulse.

Caused by an apparent drop of a heartbeat. It is not inconsistent with health; yet it is commonly an indication of disease frequently derived from gastric, hepatic, uterine and renal causes. Common in lithemic and fatty degeneration of the heart and is habitual in certain people after exercise, eating, excitement, alcohol, tobacco, tea, coffee, cocoa, and other stimulants like digitalis, ergot, etc.

P., INTRICATE. Unequally slow and imperfectly developed.

P., IRREGULAR. Loss of force and frequency. Same significance as intermittent pulse. Common in myocarditis and valvular disease especially mitral regurgitation. Heart trouble may have a long irregular pulse. Excess of tea, tobacco, alcohol or exercise may cause irregular pulse.

P., IRREGULAR PERPETUUS. Permanently irregular p. found in arterial fibrillation of which the pulse is characteristic.

P., JARRING. Jerky and sharp.

P., JERKING. Marked by a quick and rather forcible beat followed by a sudden, abrupt cessation, as if the direction of the wave of blood had been reversed, indicates that structural disease of the valves of the heart may be present. A pulse in which the artery is suddenly and markedly distended. Aortic regurgitation. Artery from a state of emptiness is suddenly filled with blood.

P., JUGULAR VEIN, pulsation in. This is always more marked on the right side along the vessels upward over the clavicular belly of the sternocleidomastoid muscle. Presystolic jugular pulsation represents the physiological negative venous p. The pulsation is generated by the sudden arrest of the venous column during auricular systole and is timed by palpation of the jugular vein with the finger tips of the left hand while applying the tips of the fingers of the opposite hand to the opposite carotid artery or the cardiac impulse.

P., LABORING. Blood seems to be partially emptied at each pulsation.

P., LANGUID. Slow and feeble.

P., LARGE. Open and full beat.

P., LONG. One in which the duration of the systolic wave is comparatively long.

P., LOW. Pulsation scarcely perceptible.

P., LOW TENSION. One with rapid onset, short duration, and rapid decline especially noted in degeneration of the heart, collapse, debility, fevers, and low state of nervous system.

P., MAGNUS. A large full p.

P., MOLLIS. A soft easily compressible p.

P., MONNERETIS. A full slow and soft pulse—jaundice.

P., MONOCROTUS. Grave condition of the circulation and impending death. Sphygmograph shows a simple ascending and descending uninterrupted line and no dicrotism.

P., MYOCARDITIS ADVANCED. There is a feeble impulse associated with a feeble irregular pulse.

P., **MYOCARDITIS, ACUTE.** Enfeeblement of the cardiac impulse is accompanied by a forceless, empty, and often arrhythmic pulse beat.

P., **MYUROUS.** One with gradually weaker beats of diminishing amplitude, marked by the apex which is reached suddenly and which subsides very gradually.

P., **OPPRESSED.** Small, contracted, and slow.

P., **PARADOXES.** One in which p. becomes weaker during inspiration. Thought to be due to compression of the great vessels by inflammatory adhesions which are stretched during act of inspiration. Frequently noted in adherent pericardium, in acute and cardiac compression, and in mediastinal tumor.

P., **PARVUS.** A small pulse.

P., **PISTOL SHOT.** Pulse produced by rapid distention and collapse of an artery as occurs in aortic regurgitation.

P., **PLATEAU.** One slowly rising, but which is maintained. A prolonged p. usually with an anacrotic interruption. Aortic stenosis.

P., **PRESSURE.** The difference betwen the systolic and the diastolic is the pulse pressure. For good health there should be a three to one ratio, as explained below, among the systolic, diastolic, and pulse pressure; it is expressive of the tone of the arterial wall:

$$\frac{\begin{aligned}120 \text{ systolic} \quad ....\text{divide systolic p. by p.p.} \quad .... \text{ gives } 3\\ 80 \text{ diastolic} \quad ....\text{divide diastolic p. by p.p.} \quad .... \text{ gives } 2\end{aligned}}{40 \text{ is pulse pressure} \quad ....\text{divide p.p. by itself} \quad .... \text{ gives } 1}$$

Normal pulse pressure: The systolic must be about 40 points over the diastolic pressure.

Abnormal pulse pressure: Over 50 points and under 30.

P., **QUICK.** One which strikes sharply and suddenly against the finger without reference to the number of pulsations: hence it may be quick and frequent and quick and slow. A quick pulse is never very frequent; seldom over 90. Inflammation or fever of acute inflammatory character.

P., **QUINCKE'S CAPILLARY** p. Pulsation in the capillaries which may be detected by a perceptible nail pulse with its alternate flushing and blanching of the nail due to aortic insufficiency. Aortic regurgitation. Also seen on forehead.

P., **RAPID.** See frequent p. Especially if strong, full, and hard, it indicates inflammation or fever; if small and very rapid, it points to a stage of great debility, such as is often present in the last stage of enteric fever. Irritation will also cause the condition as will debility or inhibition by the cardiac nerve due to disease or other causes: e.g., long suppressed emotion, blood poisoning, organic defects. Undue retention of urine seems to have an appreciable effect on the pulse.

To lower pulse, place patient in bath for about five minutes in temperature of 100° F, no hotter or colder. As the water is very slightly above the body heat, this bath will have the effect of gradually withdrawing the blood from the internal organs, including the heart, to the periphery, without sudden shock or harmful reaction. Patient should be dried rapidly, put to bed and kept warm. Make patient breathe deeply in slow regular inspiration. Relaxation of muscular system and mind is essential. Gentle friction applied to skin for about five minutes will lower the pulse. Drugs can be dangerous; they deplete the vitality of the body.

P., REGULAR. When the force and frequency are the same: that is when the length of beat and number of beats per minute and the strength are the same.

P., RENAL. A hard and full pulse, seen in coma; from kidney disease.

P., RESISTANT; HARD, FIRM. When it resists compression, it is said to be hard, firm, or resistant. Tense. Offers nearly as great a resistance at first as a strong pulse, but yields more easily and completely to strong pressure.

P., RESPIRATORY. Alternate dilation and contraction of the large veins of the neck occurring simultaneously with inspiration and expiration following rapid exercise.

P., RUNNING. A very weak frequent pulse with low tension in the arteries, one pulse wave running into the next with no apparent interval; seen in hemorrhage.

P., REVERSED PARADOXAL. Amplitude of the p. increases with respiration and decreases with expiration as seen in some cases of tricuspid insufficiency.

P., SHARP. Debility with great irritation. Combination of quick and frequent; the artery strikes the finger both abruptly and rapidly.

P., SLOW 40-60. Indicates torpor, inaction, especially in the function ancillary to digestion, compression of the brain from contusion or other means, tumor, etc. or engorgement. Dyspeptics and hypochondriacs frequently have slow pulse, less than the given number of strokes in a given time. A full slow pulse indicates weakness of the nervous system.

Bradycardia pulse may beat from 12 to 40 times a minute. May indicate a cardiac lesion, fatty degeneration, chronic myocarditis, or sclerosis of the coronary arteries. The pulse of aortic stenosis is usually slow. Because of damage to the pulmonary circuit, the pulse is slow during an attack of emphysema and spasmodic asthma. Certain diseases of the nervous system are responsible for a reduced pulse, cerebral hemorrhage, tumor, meningitis, or other lesions which give rise to an increased intracranial pressure, epilepsy, injuries of the spinal cord, mania, melancholia, and myxedema.

Poisonous substances circulating in the blood may slow the pulse by acting on the cardiac centers or ganglia: e.g., bile in jaundice, urea, and other retained excrementitious materials in urea, glucose, lead, opium, alcohol, carbon dioxide, tea, coffee, and tobacco.

The pulse is slow in cancer, in gastric ulcers, in convalescence from acute infectious diseases like diphtheria, erysipelas, pneumonia, typhoid fever, malaria, and acute articular rheumatism. Chronic digestive disorders and mental depression also retard the pulse. A pulse rate of below 50 should arouse a suspicion of heart block.

P., SLUGGISH, FULL. Evinces want of nervous energy, usual slowness, chiefly met with in chronic softening and tuberculosis, infections of the brain. Also common in diseases attended with coma resulting from concussion or compression of the brain.

P., **SMALL.** Debility with more or less local irritation. Unites the character of the weak or feeble with the contracted pulse. Small and rapid as seen in great prostration from wasting diseases or hemorrhage.

P., **SOFT.** Not marked by active inflammation or much debility; one which may be stopped by digital pressure.

P., **STEEL HAMMER.** Abrupt and energetic as the rebound of a blacksmith's hammer; observed in arteries near a joint in rheumatism.

P., **STRONG PRETERNATURALLY.** Characteristic of high fever and active inflammation. It is the kind of pulse which bears bleeding well. Bleeding does not prostrate patient but often relieves pain and lessens sensitivity. When the pulse excites, wet sheets or cold oblations should be freely used. Almost incompressible; a strong pulse is never very frequent, rarely exceeding 80 and never 90.

P., **SUBNORMAL.** Due to lowered vitality.

P., **SUPERDICROTIC.** Where the preceding dicrotic wave falls on the ascending limb of the next pulse wave. Tachycardia.

P., **SYSTOLIC.** The period of the contraction of the heart causing the greatest arterial pressure, which normally is 100. Two or three beats followed by a longer pause. It has the same significance as the irregular pulse.

P., **TACHYCARDIA.** A pulse of 170 or above. In some diseases, it is a common symptom. If such an acceleration does not diminish within a short time, the prognosis is unfavorable. When quick and bounding, it indicates acute fever or inflammation; a toxic goitre; organic heart disease; a pressure at the base of the brain sufficient to paralyze the pneumogastric nerves, as in a clot, tumor, and advanced meningitis; shock; reflex irritation, as in ovarian or uterine disease; rheumatoid arthritis; independent paroxysmal neurosis. May be due to the results of certain drugs, such as belladonna, nitrites, or alcohol. See p. allorhythmic.

P., **TARDUS, PARVUS, ET.** Slow pulse particularly seen in aortic stenosis. Beat slow to rise and fall; plateau p.

P., **TENSE.** When artery resembles a cord fixed at each extremity, a hard full pulse. When it feels still harder and smaller, it is called wiry. Excessive irritation with considerable debility.

P., **THREADY.** A scarcely appreciable one as observed in syncope. Rate is rapid; wave appears quickly, is small, and disappears quickly. Myocardial failure and peripheral circulatory failure.

P., **TRACUUS.** A very weak pulse hardly distending to the arterial wall.

P., **TREMULOUS.** A feeble fluttery pulse, one in which a series of oscillations is felt with each beat. Extreme nervous debility with violent irritation or excessive internal congestion. Tea, snuff, alcohol, tobacco are among its common causes.

P., **TRIGEMINAL.** Three regular beats followed by a pause.

P., **UNDULATORY.** Resembles that of a wave.

P., **UNEQUAL.** Pulsation being unlike or returning at unequal intervals. Varies in strength of its beats.

P., **VAGATONIA.** 66 beats per minute.

P., **VAGINAL.** Arterial pulse perceptible in the vagina in inflammatory disease or in pregnancy.

P., **VAGUS.** A slow pulse due to the inhibitory action of the vagus on the heart. Will increase pulse of stomach. (R.B.A.)

P., **VENOUS.** Pulsation noted in the right sternoclavicular jugular vein just above the junction often noted in tricuspid regurgitation. A venous pulse on dorsum of the hand may be due to forcible propulsion in the blood through the capillaries, as in aortic regurgitation with great hypertrophy of left ventricle, or to extreme relaxation of arterioles and capillaries, permitting the transmission of the pulse waves as in grave cachexia and anemia.

In this case the pulse is due not to pressure transmitted through the capillaries, but to pressure changes of both a positive and a negative nature occurring in the heart or neighboring arteries and transmitted to the great veins. Venous pulse provides a means of determining the rate of the auricles just as the arterial pulse curve permits counting of the contractions of the ventricles

The arterial pulse is not transmitted through the capillaries to the venous system. The peripheral veins, therefore, do not pulsate, but the **jugular vein** is in direct communication with the right auricle, and any change in intra-auricular pressure causes a reflex of blood and volume changes in the blood within this vein, changes which can be recorded clinically.

P., **VENTRICULAR VENOUS PULSE.** Jugular pulsation in which the auricular wave disappears or coincides with the period of ventricular systole. Positive venous pulse or pathological venous pulse.

P., **VERMICULAR.** Resembles the motion of a worm. A small rapid p.

P., **VIBRATORY.** Jarring, like the motion of a musical instrument.

P., **WATER HAMMER.** Characterized by a short, powerful, jerky beat which suddenly collapses. The peculiar pulsation may be distinctly visible not only in the carotids, but throughout the brachial artery. It is diagnostic of aortic regurgitation during the period of compensation and its force is due to excessive ventricular hypertrophy and to the large amount of blood expelled with each systole; its sudden recession is due to the incompetent valves failing to support the column of blood.

P., **WEAK.** Denotes impoverished blood and an enfeebled condition of the system. When pulse is said to be small as well as hard, it is called weak. Debility. Beats lightly against the finger ceasing entirely on very slight compression.

P., **WIRY.** See tense p. A small, rapid, tense pulse which feels like a cord. Seen in acute peritonitis.

Chapter VIII

AYURVEDIC AND UNANI EXAMINATIONS OF THE PULSE

The generalizations that will be made during the course of this study on the Ayurvedic examination of the pulse apply as well to the Unani interpretations because the principles of the three doshas, the forces that manifest themselves when the body is deranged, are the structural supports for both Ayurvedic and Unani medicine. Both are concerned with a process which is a dynamic, not a static, state. Knowing that the pulse will record the changes as the disease runs its course, they have devised a set of readings for these pulse changes — all geared to the three doshas. The Unani, however, have added a fourth, Shonita, for the circulation of the blood, but the Ayurvedists accommodate to this precept of Shonita without creating another principle. These indigenous schools of medicine, like the Chinese, also describe the death pulse which warns the physician of impending death.

Their treatment seeks to keep the elements in harmony and to restore balance to the body, to treat the whole man and to use the pulse according to a principle not stressed by the Western physician. To the Easterner, the disease is a dynamic movement and the pulse reflects the constantly changing body relationship to the disease or to the derangement; to the Westerner, the disease is static and the pulse relates mainly to circulation and to circulatory diseases. Herein resides the difficulty of clarifying the viewpoints of Occident and Orient to each other: they begin with different premises.

The Ayurvedist and Unani physician in using the doshas seeks a harmonious relationship. But the Chinese weave into their interpretation a more subtle refinement which results in an extremely accurate, almost photographic picture of the condition of the body. Their physicians use the twelve classical pulses coupled with the Yin-Yang principles and the Five Elements to provide what may be termed a motion picture reading of the organs of the body through the beatings of the pulse. The Chinese have charted the changes in the organs themselves as the disease progresses by way of the pulse readings so that they know the condition of the body. If the Socratic "Know Thyself" be applied to these three cultures for their interpretation of the pulse, then the West has known the body and the pulse as a static situation not accommodating to change; the Chinese have charted all the unknown wonders of the body through the pulse beat; and the Ayurvedist as well as the Unani physicians have opened the door to the realization that the body is constantly undergoing a dynamic change to which the pulse readings are significant.

Panoramic View of Ayurvedic and Unani Examination of the Pulse
  I. Recapitulation of techniques for taking the pulse
 II. Basic pulses characteristic of doshas; pulses in fevers for all doshas individually or in combination
III. Various pulses manifested in fevers
           before fever   in intermittent fever
           during fever   in relationship to food
 IV. Various pulses manifested in physical illness other than fever:
           alphabetical arrangement
  V. The death pulse
 VI. Two Tables
           Table 10—the Ayurvedic readings of the doshas pulses
           Table 11—the Unani readings of the doshas pulses

Recapitulation of Techniques for Taking the Pulse
If the pulse impinges on:
    the index finger, Vayu or air is deranged;
    the middle finger, Pitha or fire is deranged;
    the ring finger, Kapha or water (phlegm) is deranged.
If the pulse impinges between:
    the index and middle fingers, Vayu and Pitha are deranged;
    the middle and ring fingers, Pitha and Kapha are deranged;
    the middle of all three fingers, all three doshas are deranged.
If slight pressure is felt at two fingers and more pressure is felt on the third, the corresponding dosha — where the most pressure is felt — is deranged.

Basic Pulses Characteristic of Doshas Individually or in Combination
    When the Ayurvedic and Unani physician describes the pulse in disease, he likens its course to the motion of several animals. In any disease due to the excitement of Vayu or air, the pulse assumes a curvilinear motion which is compared with the movements of a snake or a leech. This is called a fast pulse which can be recognized by the number of beats being above normal when there is no fever. The derangement of the dosha Vayu or air indicates indigestion, nervous troubles, fever, etc. If the pulse is inflated, Vayu is in excess.

    When the element of Pitha or fire is deranged, the pulse resembles the movement of a frog, a sparrow, or a crow. A frog jumps forward in a jerky movement and hence the pulse is called jerky or jumpy. A jerky or jumpy pulse indicates excess of fire and its resultant diseases are insomnia, diarrhea, vertigo, high blood pressure, heat of the skin, palms, soles, and burning in the eyes. In asthma, rheumatism, gout, chronic headache, haemoptysis, the pulse is thin, wiry, hard, stiff, jumpy and often fast.

    When the element of water predominates, the movement of the pulse resembles that of the peacock, dove, swan, or cock. The swan is not only slow but also restricted in movement. This is called a slow pulse, for the number of beats per minute is below normal. Slow pulse shows an excess or derangement of the dosha Kapha or water, which is indicated by coughs, melancholia, constipation, etc.

When the pulse moves alternately as a snake and a frog at frequent intervals, excess of air and fire is indicated. This shows mixed symptoms of air and fire and is generally accompanied by great heat, thirst, vertigo, headaches, suppression of urine, pain in the extremities, etc. When Pitha is in excess and Vayu deranged, the pulse is jumpy and hard.

When the pulse moves alternately like a snake and a peacock at frequent intervals, it indicates an excess of the two elements air and water. The pulse shows symptoms of both elements: they include a sense of chill, pain in the extremities, frequent urination, cough, insomnia, drowsiness, etc. The pulse is slow and fast alternately and soft and expanded. The Vayu-Kapha complaint becomes chronic and aggravated from time to time, especially at the new and full moon. When Kapha is in excess and when Vayu is deranged, the pulse is soft and slow, as in gonorrhea and asthma.

When the pulse moves like a frog and a peacock alternately and at frequent intervals, it indicates an excess of the two elements fire and water. Here is an example where fire and water do mix. The patient suffers from the symptoms of both.

When all three elements are in excess or deranged, the pulse moves like a snake, a frog, and a swan. The pulse moves slowly, quickly, jerkily and has to be examined carefully. This is called, in Western thought, the thyroid pulse.

If the three doshas are regular in action; that is, if one kind of motion succeeds another in uniform order, the disease may be regarded as easily curable. On the other hand, if the motion becomes irregular; that is, if no uniformity of succession is present, the disease is serious and difficult to cure.

The treatment of the above is to neutralize the dosha or doshas that are at fault. Here skill is required and great harm can be done with improper treatment: for example, if heat is given — whether in food, drugs, etc. — to a patient already suffering from too much fire, iatrogenic or doctor-induced diseases result and the doctor may unwittingly act as a messenger of death.

Pulse Beat in Fevers for All Doshas, Individually or in Combination
Fever due to Excitement of Vayu or Air

Generally, in fever due to the excitement of air or Vayu, the pulse becomes slow and weak especially if fever sets in during those times when Vayu accumulates[1] — that is, during the periods when digestion is going on: at mid-day, at mid-night, and in summer time. If, on the other hand, fever sets in when Vayu becomes naturally excited:[2] — that is, during the rains (in India), after digestion, in the afternoon, and at the close of the night, the pulse becomes heavy, hard, and quick.

---

[1] The Ayurvedic term signifying the energy required to carry out the automatic functions — like digestion, respiration, circulation, etc.
[2] The Ayurvedic term signifying a stimulus from the environment.

Fever due to Excitement of Pitha or Fire

In fever due to derangement of Pitha, the pulse beats are clearly and distinctly felt by the three fingers and they become quicker. If fever sets in during the time when Pitha begins to accumulate: viz., during the rains, after meals, in the morning and evening, the pulse shows only these characteristics. If, however, fever sets in when Pitha becomes naturally excited: viz., during autumn, during digestion, at mid-day and at mid-night, the pulse becomes hard and quick and strong, as if it would burst. Should the arteries burst, a stroke occurs, as a Westerner would say.

Fever due to Excitement of Kapha or Water

When Kapha begins to accumulate: i.e., in autumn and winter, during meals, in the evening, and at the close of night—or when Kapha is noticeably excited: i.e., after meals, in the morning, after evening, during the spring time, the pulse becomes weak and thin as a thread and slightly cold. The pulse shows no difference when Kapha begins to accumulate or when it becomes fully excited.

Fever due to Derangement of Doshas

If Vayu and Pitha are deranged, the pulse becomes thick and hard and seems to move with an undulating motion.

If Vayu and Kapha are deranged, the pulse is slow and hot. If during these fevers, the measure of Kapha becomes less than that of Vayu, it becomes dry and continually quick.

If Pitha and Kapha are deranged, the pulse becomes slow, thready and weak, and sometimes slightly cool and sometimes colder and slower.

If all three doshas—Vayu, Pitha, and Kapha—are deranged, the fevers manifest the same characteristics as the pulse does when the three individual doshas are excited. In addition, there are other characteristics that should be noted in order to ascertain whether or not the patient will be cured or will die; they are as follows:

a) If the pulse can be felt at the root of the thumb, the fever is curable.

b) If the pulse falls off from the root of the thumb and becomes perceptible only for a second and there is a burning sensation in the heart, life continues only as long as the burning sensation lasts and ends when the burning sensation ceases.

c) If the pulses of Pitha, Vayu and Kapha beat like the quickness of Pitha, the curvilinear motion of Vayu and the slow motion of Kapha in that order, the fever will run its course with no danger to the patient.

d) If the pulse does not beat in rhythm of the doshas in the order of Pitha, Vayu, and Kapha, but is mixed in the order of the doshas—such as Vayu, Pitha, Kapha or Kapha, Pitha, Vayu, etc.—the prognosis is grave and death is lurking in the wings.

e) If the characteristics of the pulse are sometimes slow, sometimes without tension, sometimes irregular, sometimes fast—as a person in fear—sometimes thready and almost imperceptible or if at another interval, the pulse may be felt at the root of the thumb one time and not at all at another time, then the disease is difficult or incurable.

f) If the pulse is very cool though the heat of the body is excessive, death takes place at the end of the third day.

When the pulse is alternately rapid and imperceptible, when it is only sometimes perceptible or when the pulse beats once or twice at the end of the second finger as quickly as a flash of lightning and becomes at times imperceptible and disappears after a beat or two, then death takes place within twenty-four hours.

Various Pulses Manifested in Fevers
Pulse before Fever

The course of the pulse just before an attack of fever resembles the motion of a frog, but only for a short space of time. If the frog-like motion remains unchanged for some time, the fever that will set in will be accompanied by a burning sensation. When the pulse is slow and the temperature is high, all three doshas are deranged. When Vayu is excited, Pitha in excess, and Kapha deranged, the pulse is fast, sometimes jumpy and slow alternately.

Pulse during Fever

After fever sets in, the pulse is hot to the touch and rapid. It should be noted that the pulse would appear hot in the morning if the subject indulged in too much food or in any sexual excesses at night. Though the pulse is hot under such conditions, it is never rapid.

Pulse in Intermittent Fever

Appearing on alternate days, the pulse is sometimes felt at the root of the thumb and sometimes at its side. In fever appearing on every third or fourth day, the pulse generally becomes hot and its course appears to be gyratory and then seems gradually to recede farther and farther away. In incurable diseases, the pulse shows this similar character, but then the heat is not perceptible.

Pulse in Relationship to Food during All Fevers

If the wrong types of foods are eaten during fever, the pulse rate will rise; for example, if curds are eaten, the intensity of the fever increases and the pulse becomes hotter.

If the wrong combinations of food are given during fever, the pulse rate increases and death may even ensue.

If the patient indulges excessively in foods and drinks that are sour, Pitha becomes very hot. In India, the drinking of sour gruel or rice in copious measures will slow the pulse and bring on indigestion. The pulse will then become hard, and the beat slow and indistinct.

The reader is reminded that the Ayurvedists divided the three doshas into fifteen subdivisions, two of which will now be discussed: AMASAYA is that division of the intestines into which the food first finds its place (the stomach in Western language). Its pulse is thick, heavy, and slightly hard.

PAKVASAYA is that into which the food passes in its second stage (the small intestine in Western language); its pulse becomes thin and slow. In indigestion brought about by the excitement of Vayu, the pulse besides presenting the ordinary characteristics, becomes harder.

Various Pulses Manifested in Physical Illness Other Than Fever Diseases:
Alphabetical Arrangement

ABDOMEN. DEEP-SEATED PAIN OF ABDOMEN (Shoola). In Shoola or deep-seated pain in the abdomen and in all diseases whose principle symptom is deep-seated pains in the stomach or abdomen, the course of the pulse is curvilinear since they are caused by the excitement of Vayu. But when the disease is caused by Pitha, the pulse is very hot. In Shoola which affects only the Amasaya or which is due to worms the pulse is heavy.

ABSCESS. Before it becomes ripe as in the case of excess of Pitha — p. is hot and rapid. In fistula and sinus, p. becomes hot and moves as in the case of Vayu. In the thigh, p. is thin, dejected, slippery, crooked, rapid, and hot, but all of these pulsations are not felt at one time. In abscess, a slow and thin p. leads to death.

ACIDITY. P. is crooked, shaken, large, slippery, and slow. The p. carries an excess of Pitha and gives the picture of all symptoms of colic. In acidity, a feeble and thin p. indicates approaching death.

ALCOHOLISM. P. is thin, hard, and cold.

ANEMIA. P. is faintly perceptible and felt at intervals; is weak and beats separately.

ANXIETY. P. is slow.

APPETITE (loss of). P. is strong, slow, hard, and soft.

ASTHMA. P. is full, inflated, beating under all three fingers, is somewhat hollow, seems to be filled with gas, has thick walls, and is not easily compressible. The Pitha p. is hard, inflated, jumpy, hard-walled, and beats heavily on the second finger. It can also be wiry, hard, stiff, jumpy, and fast. If p. is thin, restless and beats very rapidly and if patient suffers from loss of appetite, death is near.

BOILS. P. is Pitha if the boils have yet to suppurate; p. is Vayu for internal boils.

BUBO. P. is porous, thick, crooked, slow, absorbed in the flesh and seems to be attached to the pulse.

CANCER. For p. see Tumor and see Urine suppression.

CEPHALEGIA. P. is filled with air and becomes restless; see headaches.

CHOLERA. P. is like a frog, barely perceptible. If p. does not go away from its place, prognosis is good; if it does, death is on hand.

COLIC. Vayu p. is crooked; Pitha p. is hot; if wind is in the stomach, p. is forceful and slow, separate and expanded; sometimes it goes away from the rest of the wrist.

CONSTIPATION AND STRANGURY. P. is strong and forceful. In vomitting, in wounds, and in suppression of stools, p. moves like an elephant and a goose as it does in excess of Kapha. In obstruction of stools, p. is crooked. In strangury and calculus, a thin and restless p. indicates approaching death.

CONVULSIONS. P. is thick and rapid; in hysterical convulsions, p. is crooked and rapid.

CONSUMPTION. P. is weak and with cough, p. trembles. In lung cavity, p. takes an upward motion.

COUGH. P. is very small, slow, and hot. If the p. is thin and constantly fickle and if the body is emaciated, death is waiting.

DEAFNESS. P. is quick and it spreads. In Otitis, p. is rapid; with patient's description of sounds in ear, p. is also rapid.

DIABETES. P. seems to have knots in its course. If with the diabetes, there be any disease affecting the Amasaya, the p. becomes slightly hot. In **DIABETES MELLITUS.** P. is thin like a hair. When there is blood in the urine, Pitha p. becomes agitated. The Vayu or Kapha pulse becomes thin and a burning sensation develops in the body and the patient becomes emaciated. In **DIABETES INSIPIDUS,** Kapha p. beats slowly and Pitha p. beats quickly; Vayu p. becomes thin and crooked. There are thirst and parching of the mouth; the face becomes yellow; constant burning sensation persists in the eyes. If the p. becomes thin, thready, restless and rises, death is around the corner.

DIARRHEA (VISUCHIKA). The radial p. in chronic cases is like a frog, but very often the p. is so weak that it can scarcely be felt. Vitambika is the term used when there are pain and flatulence and an uneasiness about the abdomen; then the p. resembles a frog. Vayu p. is crooked; Pitha p. is rapid; Kapha p. is mild. In loss of appetite and in diseases characterized by waste of ingredients of the body, the p. becomes thready, cool, and very slow. If the digestive fire be keen, the p. becomes light and strong.

In diarrhea, after evacuation the p. becomes very weak. In that form of disease which affects only the Amasaya, the p. becomes heavy and composed.

In diseases of Grahani (the principal duct by which the food juice passes into the blood) the p. at the root of the thumb resembles the jerking motion of the frog, but the p. at the ankle resembles the motion of a swan.

DROPSY. P. is influenced by the three doshas; after some time, the p. becomes weak, thin, and cold. Sometimes its movement suddenly stops and it feels like a human body filled with water. In **ascites**, the p. is large and moves slowly and crookedly, like a crocodile. In **dropsy** and **edema,** if the p. be steady, thin, and extremely cold and if complications set in, the case is very serious.

DRUGS: Pulse Reactions to 3 Specific Drugs

IPEISE: The Ipeise p. is highly inflated, expanded almost hollow inside, and filled with gas, soft to the touch, with thin walls. In fevers of old persons, this p. is often seen.

STAPHYSAGRIA: The Staphysagria p. is soft, flabby, listless, beats heavily on the third finger. This drug is used for chronic swellings and for tumors; the p. is then soft, slow, easily compressible, languid, and listless with little or no tension. When it is used for asthma, tuberculosis, rheumatism, arthritis, leucoderma, chronic ulcers, and skin disorders, the p. appears to be solid, like soft lymph flowing through a vessel.

THUJA: The Thuja p. is thin, wiry, hard, stiff, jumpy, and often fast. This drug is used for chronic effects from vaccination, where Pitha is out of order; for rheumatism, gout, chronic headaches, chronic swellings and tumors without pus or discharge. When tumors are soft and yield to slight pressure, the p. is soft, flabby, listless, and beats heavily on the third finger to show an excess of fluids and serum.

DYSENTERY. P. moves like a leech in summer. Vayu p. is crooked; Pitha p. is rapid; and Kapha p. is slow. When Vayu and Kapha are involved, p. is like a frog. When due to typhoid, p. is hardly perceptible.

DYSMENORRHEA. P. is steady and quick.

EAR DISEASES. If the p. is weak and there is a concomitant ailment, the signs usually lead to death.

EPILEPSY. If the p. becomes thin and rises and falls slowly, death is indicated.

ERYSIPELAS. P. is restless, jumps up and moves like a serpent. If there be too much inflammation of the flesh, the p. becomes slow, trembling, harsh, and crippled.

EVIL SPIRITS, Pulse due to. P. is quick and hot when the wraith excites the individual; p. is also curvilinear. If these fevers become violent or gain in strength, the p. becomes hot and quick to a more marked degree.

EYE DISEASES. P. is hard and moves slowly; it becomes slippery and crooked.

FEAR. P. is slow.

FEMALE DISEASES. P. becomes weak and after delivery, p. becomes steady and weak.

FEVERS. See preceding section; p. is rapid. In chronic fevers, p. is thin, rapid and weak. In fever with enlarged spleen, p. is extremely heavy, moves swiftly, and is always filled with Kapha and Pitha.

FEVER. Pulse due to Fevers Aroused by Love or Lust — Sexual intercourse indulged in during fever makes the p. become weak and slow. In fevers due to **violent** love or lust, the p. is quick and hot and also curvilinear; the p. becomes hot and quick to a more marked degree when the fever rises.

FISTULA, ANAL. P. becomes shrivelled, thin, and slippery; in fistula, if p. be thin and restless, death is calling.

GOITRE. P. is thick and moves very slowly.

GONORRHEA. P. is hot if there is mucus in the system; p. is full of knots, slippery, and agitated.

HEAD, DISEASES OF. P. is hard and moves slowly, but sometimes it seems to jump and move rapidly.

HEADACHES. If p. is fickle, weak and if patient is losing weight, beware of death.

HEMORRHAGE. P. is hard and slow; if p. is restless and thin and is accompanied by a constant headache and glazed eyes, the cemetery is calling.

HERNIA. P. jumps up. On ring finger, it is thick; on middle finger, it seems to be hiding in the flesh; on the forefinger, it is felt as if having an overgrowth of flesh.

HICCOUGH. P. is rapid and quakes; if p. is very restless and thready, death is present.

HOARSENESS. P. small and thready, rapid.

HYSTERIA. P. weak and rapid.

INDIGESTION. P. is hard and cold; advanced p. is weak and beats slowly. If p. seems to be steady, but crooked inside and the patient is emaciated and weak with complications, he is sure to die.

INSANITY. P. always moves crookedly; p. is very fine, small and rapid as in the case of excess Vayu; p. moves as in fever; p. becomes restless and sometimes seems to have a gyrating motion, like the tumor pulse. In insanity, for a weak patient whose p. sometimes feels as thin as a thread, sometimes restless and sometimes crooked, the prognosis is death.

INTUSSUSCEPTION. P. is almost extinct and trembling.

IPEISE. See drugs.

JAUNDICE. P. is faintly perceptible and hot; if p. is thready and if patient is pale, death is the next visitor.

LEPROSY. P. is mild, crooked, hard, and slow; later it becomes contracted and moves slowly. When the p. becomes restless and vibrating, the patient is finished.

LEUCORRHEA. P. is very rapid and its middle part seems to be void. If p. becomes thin, is steady, feeble and cold, death is in the room.

LOVE. See fever.

MEASLES. P. is same as in chicken and small pox, but differs in that the movement of the p. is not felt by the forefinger.

MENORRHAGIA. P. is hot and rapid.

MOUTH, DISEASES OF. P. is fleshy, crooked, strong, and rapid. If p. becomes weak and thin and there are complications, death ensues.

MUCUS EXCESS. P. is thick and like a serpent; it feels thin on the middle finger and ring finger but crooked on the forefinger.

NOSE, DISEASES OF. P. is agitated and moves slowly; if p. is weak and if there are complications, it leads to death.

OBESITY. P. is mild. When p. is plump and steady, it indicates impending death but before death, it becomes feeble, unsteady, and thready.

PARALYSIS. P. is clear and is attended with all the symptoms of an excess of Vayu. In paralysis of the tongue, the p. is dry and beats regularly.

PARAPLEGIA. If p. is unsteady, feeble, and extremely thin, like a thread, it indicates impending death.

PHTHISIS. P. varies; if p. becomes thin, restless and thready and there is loss of appetite, death is impending.

PILES. P. is sometimes straight, sometimes slow, sometimes crooked, and sometimes mild. Vayu p. is crooked; Pitha is like a frog; Kapha p. is slow; Kapha and Vayu combined p. is strong and rapid; Vayu and Pitha combined p. is slow; Kapha and Pitha combined p. is always like a snake and a goose. If p. becomes thready and slow and if there is swelling in the cheek and if the lungs are affected, death is impending.

POISONS, PULSE FOR. As the poisons begin to permeate the system, p. begins to beat very restlessly. In **poisoning**, the p. takes an upward course. In **blood poisoning**, the p. is agitated, porous, thick, restless, and sluggish in action. It beats slowly on the ring finger and gradually takes an upward motion.

POX. SMALL AND CHICKEN. P. moves rapidly with a little bit of crookedness; p. is fickle and trembling.

PREGNANCY. P. is weak and moves slowly.

PROLAPSUS UTERI. P. moves very slowly.

RHEUMATISM. P. is rapid and sometimes feeble and at other times vehement. If p. is very thin and if patient has indigestion and derangement of the doshas, death is impending.

SCIATICA. P. is thick, slow, and crooked.

SEXUAL INTERCOURSE. P. is weak and rapid.

SINUS. P. is crooked and extremely slippery; it takes a slow and downward motion indicating derangement of all three doshas. Then p. becomes shrivelled, thin, and slippery.

SMALLPOX. See pox. If p. be steady, feeble, accompanied by various ailments, and p. is hollow within, death is impending.

SPASM. P. is rapid, tortuous, and agitated.

STAPHYSAGRIA. See drugs.

STRANGURY. See constipation; see urine, suppression of.

SYPHILIS. P. is torn, tortuous, thin, slippery, and slow in motion. If p. becomes thin and restless, death is impending.

TETANUS. P. is dry and jumpy.

THIRST. P. is like a leech; if p. becomes thin and slow, and cold, death impends.

THUJA. See drugs.

THYROID. P. is rapid if hyperthyroid; p. is slow if hypothyroid.

TUMOR — OF ABDOMEN. P. becomes restless and sometimes seems to have a gyrating motion; p. is rapid and moves like a pigeon; is hard and stiff; also becomes slippery, thin, and beats crookedly from the root of the thumb. If the p. becomes excessively feeble and lean, the patient is in a very serious condition. See urine, suppression for cancer p.

TUMOR — OF THE THROAT. P. is thick,, moves slowly, and trembles.

TYPHOID. P. is rapid. If internally a burning sensation develops and if p. becomes clear and cold, expect death within three days.

URINE — SUPPRESSION OF URINE AND STOOLS. In Strangury, Epistaxis, Dysuria, Calculus, and other diseases in which there is difficulty in passing urine, whether or not accompanied by suppression of stools due to intussuception or obstruction of the bowels, the p. becomes subtle and its course resembles that of a frog. If p. becomes thin and restless, death is near. In Epistaxis and Strangury, the p. generally becomes hard and heavy.

If p. is hard, inflated, expanded with thick walls and, what is more important, non-compressible even with heavy pressure, it denotes cancer and tumors like lipoma, neuroma, fibroma, etc. Person is usually large, flabby, and obese. In contractions of the bowels or in deep-seated tumors in the abdomen, the p. becomes curvilinear. Before the symptoms are fully developed, the p. seems to have a quick upward motion.

URTICARIA. P. is heavy, slippery, and from the root of the thumb, moves rapidly, restlessly, and crookedly; may be slow and hard.

VAGINAL DISEASES. P. is large and slow and is hard under the forefinger.

VOMITTING. P. is almost imperceptible.

WORMS. P. is hard and slow.

WOUNDS. P. is quick, crooked, and shivering. If any limb is fractured, the p. sems to be crippled and imperfectly perceptible.

WRY-NECK. P. is dry, hard, and heavy.

The Death Pulse or Arista Lakshana

Ayurvedic medicine has observed carefully the relation of the pulse beat, its distance from the root of the thumb and the nature of its beat to determine the hour of death. It has also made other observations which reveal acute perception and have embodied these in a body of materia medica to guide the physician in recognizing the death pulse and in determining the time of death.

Specific Observations of the Death Pulse to Guide the Physician

In the following sequences of distance from the root of the thumb, the hour of death can be pinpointed (the width of one finger measures one-half an inch). If the pulse goes away from the root of the thumb and is felt

1. ¼ of a finger, expect death in 48 hours.

2. ¾ of a finger, expect death in 30 hours.

3. 1¼ fingers, expect death in 15 hours.

4. 1½ fingers, expect death in 12 hours.

5. 2 fingers, expect death in 1½ hours.

6. 2½ fingers, expect death in 3 hours.

If the pulse goes away from the root of the thumb

1. ¼ of a finger and the p. beats quickly, expect death in 3 days.

2. ¼ of a finger and p. is hot, expect death in 5 days.

3. ½ of a finger and p. is cold, expect death in 39 hours.

4. ½ of a finger and p. is hot, expect death in 42 hours.

5. ½ of a finger and p. beats quickly, expect death in 15 hours.

6. ¾ of a finger and p. is hot, expect death in 36 hours.

7. ¾ of a finger and p. is cold, expect death in 33 hours.

8. 1¼ fingers and p. is motionless, expect death in 18 hours.

Generalizations to Guide the Physician as Medical Precepts for the Death Pulse

1. If the pulse is sometimes weak, smooth, and curvilinear, and at other times strong, full, and curvilinear, and again very weak and imperceptible, then the end may be expected after one month.

2. If the pulse is thin, thready, and delicate, if the pulse is full and accompanied by marked edema or if the pulse is weak and yet agreeably full, the end may be expected in one month.

3. If the pulse is very thin and very rapid and very cold, the patient will not live long.

4. If the pulse falls off as much as a breadth of half a barley seed from the root of the thumb, death comes within three days.

5. If the pulse is at first slow and thin, it will kill a man; if the pulse beats falteringly, the man is dead in no time.

6. If the pulse beats with moderate force, but is very weak at the root of the thumb and often takes an upward movement, it indicates approaching death.

7. If the pulse beats intermittently, it means death; so also does the pulse that gradually recedes from its place.

8. If the pulse is weak, restless, and hollow inside and if there are burning sensations of the body, death is impending.

9. If the pulse beats very quickly for some time and then beats slowly for some time, death is expected within a week. The exception is inflammation of the limbs.

10. If the pulse is cold and the body warm or if the pulse is warm and the body cold and the pulse irregular, the patient must die.

11. If the pulse beats quickly and the patient has a burning sensation and feels cold but has difficulty in breathing, he will live for 15 days.

12. If the pulse is very thin and crooked, and if the outside pulse is cool but the inside is hot, there is no hope.

13. If pulse is agitated, very soft and slow, if the beats are separated by long gaps, and if the pulse gradually leaves its normal position, it marks death.

14. If the pulse is not felt under the forefinger, the person will die within thirty-six hours.

15. If the pulse is in its own place and beats like lightning, the person will live for only one day.

16. If the pulse is felt in the foot and not in the hand and if the patient's mouth is open, the case is hopeless.

17. If the pulse of the right foot in the man and the left in the woman is specifically felt at the end of the fore toe, the individual will die in four days.

18. If the Vatanadi (Vayu) becomes very rapid for some time and very cold for some time and if the patient perspires freely, death will come within seven days.

19. If the Vatanadi (Vayu) is not felt and if the other pulse is slow, if the patient feels cold inside and is fatigued, death is less than three days away.

20. When Vayu takes the place of Pitha and Pitha replaces Kapha and Kapha goes to the throat, death has arrived.

21. If the pulse moves very rapidly in keeping with the rapid respiration and if the pulse becomes cold, the patient dies within three hours.

22. If the pulse is rapid and if all three doshas are deranged and if there is a high fever at mid-day, patient will die within twenty-four hours.

23. If a strong pulse becomes very weak, it signifies death.

24. If a weak pulse becomes very strong, it signifies death.

25. A very weak and cold pulse means death.

26. If the pulse is absent, there is no hope for life.

27. If the pulse lies cold under the middle finger, the person will die within twenty-seven hours.

28. If the pulse is felt by the middle finger alone and is not felt anywhere else, death will occur within six hours.

29. If the pulse moves crookedly under the middle finger (i.e., between the forefinger and the ring finger) then death will occur within twenty-four hours.

30. If the pulse beats straight, but mildly under the middle finger only, death will occur within twenty-four hours.

31. If the pulse is perceptible only below the second finger and not below the third and the fourth, death comes on the fourth day.

32. If the pulse having coursed quickly for some time suddenly becomes slow or very slow and if there is no dropsical swelling, death may be expected within seven or eight days.

Table 10.

Ayurvedic Readings of Dosha Pulses

How the doshas Vayu, Kapha, and Pitha acting individually or in combination affect the pulses — a partial listing of the chief characteristics to guide the physician.

Vayu or Air Pulse Is	Pitha or Fire Pulse Is	Kapha or Water Pulse Is	Air and Water Pulses Are	Air and Fire Pulses Are	Air, Fire and Water Pulses Are
fast	jumpy	slow	thready	accelerated	faltering
full	harsh	cold	crooked	circular	hairy
hard	hot	excited	feeble	dry	hesitating
inflated	nodular	heavy	fleshy	agitated	non-compressible
lightning-like	rapid	large	forceful	fickle	pinpointing
expanded	wiry	crippled	hollow	high tension	trembling
plump		low tension	irregular	imperceptible	thready
shrivelled		without tension	mild	intermittent	
		very soft	motionless	knotty	
		soft	porous	restless	
		waddling	prostrate	ropy	
		rigid	slippery	thick	
		weak	sluggish	thin	
			splitting		
			straight		
			torn		
			tortuous		
			tremulous		
			vanishing		
			vibrating		

Table 11.

Unani Readings of Dosha Pulses

Note: The Unani use the three doshas as do the Ayurvedists but, as earlier explained, they added a fourth force or element, Shonita, their term for the circulation of the blood. For convenience in remembering the similarity to the Indian and in avoiding confusion, the Indian terms will be used instead of the Unani after this clarification about nomenclature: Vayu for Unani Hawa; Pitha for Khun; Kapha for Balgam; but the Unani term Shonita for the circulation of the blood will be retained.

Single Dosha	Combination of Two Doshas	Combination of Three or Four Doshas
1. Vayu	5. Vayu-Pitha	11. Vayu-Pitha-Shonita
2. Pitha	6. Vayu-Kapha	12. Vayu-Kapha-Shonita
3. Kapha	7. Pitha-Kapha	13. Pitha-Kapha-Shonita
4. Shonita	8. Vayu-Shonita	14. Vayu-Pitha-Kapha
	9. Pitha-Shonita	
	10. Kapha-Shonita	15. Vayu-Pitha-Kapha-Shonita

Chapter IX

CHINESE EXAMINATION OF THE PULSE

The Chinese physician accepts as axiomatic that the actual state of the organ is "reflected" to the pulse and that therefore nothing can be more accurate in diagnosis than reading the pulse. The Chinese were aware of reflexes but did not use this term. To them the "reflection" is more than an image in a mirror and hence more than the automatic process which the word reflex signifies. The term "reflection-reflex" could be coined here to interpret their theory of the "reflection" as a dynamic force that tunes into the organs of the body wherein the pulse registers any minute changes in the organs with great accuracy.

Thus the chief means of diagnosis or examination related in the **Nei Ching** is the examination of the pulse. All other methods of determining diseases are only subsidiary to palpation. The theory of the pulse is based upon various stages of the interaction between Yin and Yang and upon crasis or dyscrasis of the five elements and the four seasons. Health is the correct balance between Yin and Yang and the harmonious mixture of the elements; disease is the lack of balance and disharmony. The system of palpation propounded by the **Nei Ching** and the **Classic of the Pulse** by Wang Shu-ho (circa 280 A. D.) was believed to be effective in the diagnosis of the nature and location of any disease. The basis of this practice is that the pulse is sub-divided into six parts, three sets of pulses in each hand, each connected with a particular point of the body and each able to record even the most minute pathological changes taking place within the body. Wang Shu-Ho is given credit for the discovery (or re-discovery) of the superficial or the external pulse; there are three superficial pulses on each hand (a total of six for the body). In addition there are six deep or internal pulses which together with the superficial make up the twelve classical pulses. The deep correspond to the Tsang or Yin organs and the superficial to the Fu or Yang organs.

ELEVEN FACTORS TO BE CONSIDERED IN TAKING THE PULSE

     I. The healthy pulse
    II. Time
   III. Examination of the pulse
   IV. Procedure in taking and reading the pulses
    V. The seasons, the noxious airs and the winds
   VI. The sounds of the normal pulse
  VII. The state and the results of disease
 VIII. The dreams of the individual

THE HEALTHY PULSE OF THE YIN AND THE YANG AND THE FIVE VISCERA

The healthy pulse is in accord with Yin and Yang and obediently follows the four seasons; the term healthy pulse is used collectively in Chinese medicine to mean the twelve classical pulses. The pulses of the region of the lesser Yin sound near at first but then change abruptly to more distant sounds; they are short at first and then they change suddenly to longer sounds. The pulses of the regions of the "sunlight"— the term for Yang —-are superficial and large and also short and without volume. They strike the finger sharply and leave it quickly.

The healthy pulse beats of the five viscera are as follows:

The liver beats softly and weakly as if one sounded a long thin bamboo rod without a tip. The viscera thoroughly expel into the liver which harbors the force of life of the muscles and the thin membranes.

The spleen is like a wave that softly flows to come together as well as gently to fall apart. The viscera fills the spleen with moisture. Thus the spleen harbors the force of life of the flesh.

The kidney flows as though it were panting and weary, as though it were alternately repressed and connected and very firm; the lowest of the viscera are the kidneys. Through the kidneys, the force of life of the bones and marrow is harbored.

The heart is a normal steady flow: like pearls joined together. The motion of the vessels underneath the breast serves to support the life force and to keep it from leaking out. The viscera are in complete communication with and are bound by the circulation of the heart; the blood that is stored by the heart fills the pulse with the force of life.

The lungs are large slow beats. The lungs are the highest of the five viscera and make the blood and the vital essences circulate freely — guarding and protecting the Yin and Yang (the principles of life and death). "Man has one exhalation to one pulse beat which is then repeated; and he has one inhalation to one pulse beat which is then repeated." Exhalation and inhalation determine the beat of the pulse. When there are five respiration movements to one pulse beat, it means that there is one extra movement inserted — bringing about a deep breath. Such a breather is a healthy and well-balanced person.

TIME

In taking the pulse, the physician has to consider the auspicious moment[1] for his undertaking and to decide which of the ten celestial stems

---

[1] The Hindus also have auspicious days and months as do all Orientals and some Westerners. This poses an interesting question — Did the Chinese anticipate the bio-rhythm curves?

(their term) started the first month of the year. Their constellations determine the day on which the examination was to take place.

EXAMINATION OF THE PULSE

While examining the pulse, the doctor seeks to:

1. Judge the appearance of the body to determine whether it is flourishing or deteriorating.
2. Feel whether the pulse is in motion or still.
3. Observe the patient with attention and skill.
4. Examine the five viscera and the five colors to determine whether or not there is an excess or deficiency of the Yin or the Yang, a fact that causes disease.
5. Examine the six bowels to determine whether they are strong or weak.
6. Determine the time of the day for taking the pulse.

The best time of the day for taking the pulse was considered the early morning from three to nine o'clock, local mean time, when the physician himself was cool and collected and "When the breath of Yin has not yet begun to stir and when the breath of Yang has not yet yet begun to diffuse itself and when food and drink have not yet been taken, when the twelve main vessels are not yet abundant, when vigor and energy are not yet exerted." It is at this time that the meridians[2] are calm and the conjunctive vessels are empty and no energy is transmitted between the coupled meridians. It is at this moment ONLY that the circulation of the blood and the energy channels are calm and that a correct diagnosis can be made. The pulse reveals whether the five Tsang are in excess (Uyu) or deficient (Pu Tsu) and whether the six bowels (Fou) are strong (Ch'iang) or weak (Jo).

It is important that causes of error be taken into consideration and eliminated. This is easy to verify by the pulse which faithfully follows the psysiology of the organ: for example, the pulse will **tell whether the stomach is empty or the bladder full.**

When the pulse is taken in the morning, questioning the patient can easily remove all cause of error with regard to the bladder, the stomach, and the intestines. Since the doctor is called upon at any hour of the day or night, he must remember and use the horary cycle or the tides of energy, all discernible by the pulse. The pulse of the stomach, for example, if taken at three o'clock in the afternoon may indicate an exaggerated condition. The doctor should suspect physiological repletion due to food rather than an excess of energy because the hour of zenith, which is the time for the maximum flow of the energy, is 0800 for the stomach. The Chinese doctor usually schedules a second confirmatory examination to support a formal diagnosis. It is when the physician eliminates the cause of error for the disharmony of energy that he is acting in accordance with the law of the Five Elements to command the energy.

When the examiner has used all these methods and combined their results, only then is he able to decide upon the balance of life and death.

---

2 The meridians are the vessels or paths that carry Chi-Hua, the life force.

Procedure in Taking and Reading the Pulses

The procedure of palpation differs according to the sex of the patient. If a man, his left pulse is taken first and it should be large to correspond with the Yang principle; if a woman, her right pulse is taken first and it should be small to correspond with the Yin principle. The commentator Wang Ping explains this procedure in his fifteenth chapter, by stating that Yang, the male principle, is represented by the left hand and Yin, the female element, represented by the right hand. Thus the left pulse, that of Yang, indicates the diseases of men while the right pulse, that of Yin, the diseases of women. Since, however, both Yin and Yang are representative in both sexes, it is necessary to consult the pulses of both hands in order to make a complete diagnosis. To the Chinese physician, the left side is positive and the right side negative in the male; the right side positive and the left side negative in the female. This view should be compared with E. E. Eeman's experiments which led him to conclude that in right-handed individuals, the right side is positive and the left, negative; in left handed individuals, the left side is positive and right, negative. One may cite here two different views as presented by the Indians: one, that the head is positive and the feet negative; the other, which reverses the Chinese, says that in the male, the right side is positive and the left negative; in the female, the right side is negative and the left side, positive.

The next step in the procedure is to take the inner and outer pulses (deep and superficial) and the inch, bar, and cubit so that all twelve classical pulses may be read for the twelve different organs. The interpretation by the famous pharmaceutical naturalist Li Shih-chen (1518-1593) will be utilized below:

Reading the Inner and Outer Pulses, the Deep and Superficial

Fu is a superficial pulse, is a light flowing pulse like a piece of wood floating on the water.

If Fu is superficial and . . . it indicates

Yang	. . . external disease and the six influences: wind, cold, dampness, heat, dryness, and fire.
strong	. . . wind and heat
weak	. . . deficiency of blood (anemic pulse)
slow	. . . chills
quick	. . . wind and fever
tense	. . . wind and cold
tardy	. . . rheumatism
soft	. . . sunstroke
hollow	. . . hemorrhages
overflowing	. . . weakness and fire
thready	. . . fatigue through overwork
small	. . . seminal weakness or female disorders
scattered	. . . exhaustion and collapse
taut	. . . indigestion
slippery	. . . wind and phlegm

Ch'en is a deep pulse, is deeply impressed, like a stone thrown into the water.

If Ch'en is deep and . . . it indicates

Yin	. . . the external diseases due to the seven passions: joy, anger, anxiety, worry, grief, fear, and shock; this is a psychological pulse.
slow	. . . weakness and cold
quick	. . . latent heat
tense	. . . colic due to chills
tardy	. . . accumulation of water (edema)
slippery	. . . indigestion
hidden	. . . vomitting and diarrhea

Ch'ih is a slow pulse, has three beats to one cycle of respiration and reveals the condition of the internal organs, the five solid organs — heart, liver, spleen, lungs and kidneys — and the Fu's or hollow organs — gall bladder, stomach, small and large intestines, urinary bladder, and the tri-heaters. When **Ch'ih** is strong, it indicates pain; when weak, debility.

Shu is a quick pulse, has six beats to one cycle of respiration, and indicates the diseases of the viscera. If it is strong, it indicates internal heat [fever]; if weak, abscess.

Hua is a slippery pulse, like pebbles rolling in a basin, and denotes diseases due to mucus.

If Hua is slippery and . . . it indicates

on the right bar pulse . . .	there are wind and mucus
on the right inch pulse . . .	there will be vomitting and regurgitation
on the right cubit pulse. . .	there are pus and blood in the stools

Se is a small fine pulse, is slow and short — like scraping bamboo with a knife — and indicates debility and collapse.

If Se is small and . . . it indicates

on the bar -. . .	cessation of secretion [disfunctioning of hormones and enzymes]
on the inch . . .	profuse perspiration
on the cubit . . .	loss of blood and vitality

Hsien is a taut pulse — like a tremulous musical string.

If Hsien is taut and . . . it indicates

on the bar	. . . symptoms of phlegm
on the inch	. . . headaches result
on the cubit	. . . colicky pain occurs
tense	. . . pain due to chills
quick	. . . .pain caused by internal heat or excessive sweating and hemorrhage

Huang is a full overflowing pulse, bounding and forceful with a rising and a gradual decline and it signifies burns and scaldings.

Tung is a tremulous pulse, quick and jerky; its pulsation covering a space no longer than a pea is indicative of pain caused by internal heat or excessive sweating and hemorrhage.

Wei is a thready pulse, very fine and soft, easily obliterated by pressure, and it indicates general debility.

San is a scattered pulse, large and irregular — like willow flowers scattering with the wind — and means extreme exhaustion.

Ke is a hard pulse, tense and hollow — like touching the surface of a drum.

Chin is a hard tense pulse and full — like a cord. It signifies seminal loss in men and uterine hemorrhages in women.

Loa is a wiry pulse, deep, strong and slightly taut; it indicates hernia or heart pain.

Jo is a feeble pulse, very soft and deep, felt on light touch and disappearing on pressure; it signifies the deficiency of the Yin essence.

Ch'ang is a long pulse, neither large nor small and the strokes markedly prolonged.

Sh'h is a full, large, long, and slightly tense pulse felt on both light and heavy pressure.

Hsu is an empty, slow, large, and compressible pulse.

Tuan is a short pulse, no volume; it strikes the fingers sharply and leaves it quickly.

K'uang is a hollow, superficial pulse, soft and hollow — like an onion stalk.

Ju is a soft pulse, superficial and fine — like a thread floating on water; it denotes deficiency of the Yang essence.

Huan is a tardy pulse, four beats to one cycle of respiration and all of equal strength — like willow branches swaying in a light breeze.

Hsi is a slender, smaller than feeble pulse, but always perceptible, and thin — like a silk thread.

Chich is an intermittent pulse, slow with an occasional missing beat.
Tai is an irregular and tremulous pulse and its beats occur at irregular intervals.

T'su is a running rapid pulse with an occasional missing beat.

Fu (not to be confused with Fu the superficial pulse) is a hidden pulse embedded in the muscle and is felt only on strong pressure.
Note: The long pulse, the short pulse, the large pulse, and the small pulse — all denote derangements of the respiratory systm.

Table 12

Location of Pulses and Organ Relationship

Symbols: **D** signifies the deep pulse and **S** signifies the superficial pulse of the classical version; **E** signifies the version of the viscera as accepted by the European school of Acupuncture.

Location	Right Wrist	Left Wrist
Inch or T'sun	D. Lungs S. Large Intestines E. Thoracic Organs	D. Heart S. Small Intestines E. Mediastinal Viscera
Bar or Kuan	D. Spleen S. Stomach	D. Liver S. Gallbladder E. Diaphragm
Cubit or Ch'ih	D. Heart Constrictor S. Triheaters E. Abdomen	D. Kidney S. Bladder E. Abdomen

The norm or the rate of the pulse beat is one expiration and one inspiration of the doctor's own breath; during this time the normal pulse of the patient should pulsate four times. Since the respiration of the patient is important, the doctor counts the number of times the pulse beats to see whether the patient's breathing is smooth or rough, light or heavy (compare this with the Ayurvedic technique).

Table 13

Relationship of Inner or Deep Pulses, Outer or Superficial Pulses to Organs

The Deep or Inner Pulse denotes a state of	The Outer or Superficial Pulse denotes a state of
1. the adjacent regions and the short ribs	1. the kidneys
2. the stomach	2. the liver
3. the right side: the spleen	3. the right side: the thoracic cavity
4. the left side: the diaphragm	4. the right side: the stomach
5. the left side: what goes on within the middle of the thoracic cage	5. the left: condition of the heart

The Pulses and Yin-Yang

A disease is Yang when due to external causes.
A disease is Yin when due to internal causes.

The Yang pulse is strong, bounding and large in volume.
The Yin pulse is weak and of low tension.

When the Yang predominates, one suffers from a Yin disease.
When the Yin predominates, one suffers from a Yang disease.

When the Yang is in excess, the body is hot and feverish and does not
perspire.
When the Yin is in excess, the body perspires heavily and gets cold and
chilled.

When the Yang is deficient, the pulse is soft.
When the Yin is deficient, the pulse is feeble.

A Special Note: Those who treat the patient should themselves be
free from illness.

The Seasons, the Noxious Airs, and the Winds

(The reader is advised to turn to the section on the Celestial Stems
in this chapter to complement this phase.)

The seasons, the airs, the winds, and the celestial stems all are
reckoned in the interpretation of the pulse beat. With regard to the
seasons, four of the five viscera are related to the progression of the
weather; only the spleen is not directly tied in to the activities of
nature which are explained in this quotation: "In spring the pulse is
dominated by the liver, in summer by the lungs, and in winter the
pulse is dominated by the kidneys." The spleen, though not related
to any season, is tied to the earth, for the spleen, a solitary organ,
irrigates the **four** others. (The vital force of the spleen regulates the
blood.)

Another major cause of disease is the winds: east, west, north,
and south—together with the noxious airs, their term for germs, fumes
and any evil that could be attributed to bad habits of living and to
infractions of the rule of Tao: namely, wrong foods, wrong combinations of foods, bad sex habits, faulty sanitation, etc. Their rule is
summed up with the following: "When the force of the pulse is turbid
and the color disturbed like a bubbling well, it is a sign that the disease
has entered the body, the color has become corrupted and the constitution
delicate."

The Sounds of the Normal Pulse

The doctor must know the normal sounds of the pulse beats of
each of the five viscera and their respective changes during the four
seasons and then be able to interpret the slightest aberration from the
normal sound for the pathological changes it represents. Furthermore,
the six pulses on each hand were subdivided into an external and internal pulse (otherwise termed deep and superficial) and by means
of the consequent twelve divisions, all parts of the body could be

interpreted. Then the three different qualities of Yin and Yang were palpable by each of the twelve pulses (see table 12 above).

State and Results of Diseases

The doctor—who had to be able to judge the state of disease, its cause, its incubation, its duration—approached the problem with certain directional slanted inquiries as will be superficially hinted at in the following:

1. Is the disease chronic or acute?
   a) If the pulse is reduced and the complexion not violated or undisturbed, the disease is a recent one or acute.
   b) If the pulse is not discordant and yet the complexion is affected, then the disease is chronic.
   c) If the pulse and the five colors (of the complexion) are all equally disturbed, then the disease is chronic.
   d) If the pulse and the five colors are equally undisturbed, then the disease is of recent date, acute.
2. Will the disease result in recovery or in death?

The answer will be determined by the volume, strength, weakness, regularity or interruption of the four main varieties of the pulse beats. This would therefore require knowing the inner body and the outer body.
   a) To know the inner body and the interior is to know the pulse and the respiration. Here the feeling of the pulse provides the principal diagnostic device.
   b) To know the exterior of the body is to read the complexion and appearance—especially the five colors—used for diagnosis of death and birth.
   c) The pulses, six on each hand, and the five colors provide the means whereby the physician knows the shifting and changing conditions communicated by the pulse recordings: an important medium of diagnosis.
   d) How do appearance and color of the body guide the physician?

The examination of the color of the various parts of the body, what is termed "appearance" by the Chinese, was carried out according to a fixed system of correlations between the color of the body and of the viscera rather than according to the colors externally of observable phenomena, an idea sometimes difficult for the Westerner to grasp. Why? Because the physical appearance is made up of five elements and the pulse is responsive to Yin and Yang.

Chapter ten of the **Nei Ching** provides a number of combinations for certain colors and viscera to denote health, sickness, and death. Chapter seventeen then gives minute descriptions about how to combine the examinations of the pulse beat with the color of the complexion for sound diagnosis:

> When the pulses of the liver and kidney coincide and the related colors are azure and red, the corresponding disease has destructive and injurious power . . . .

> When the ochre color, the color of salt, indigo blue, and the grey color can be seen, it means the ruin of all appearance (disintegration of appearance) and therefore life will not be long . . . the five viscera which are within the body must be guarded. When they are harmonious and similar, then the life-giving forces have a supremacy over the disease.

If the appearance changes from clear to turbid, then the location of the disease is revealed.

If there are coughing and short-windedness, the patient should be carefully watched.

The sounds and the notes should be listened to for then the location of the affliction will become apparent.

The Dreams of the Individual and the Pulse

Dreams and their interpretations played an important part in the complete examination and in treatment. Unlike the Ayurvedic, the Chinese claimed through the pulse reading to be able to fathom the condition of the mind and body in deep dreamless sleep as well as in deep dreams.

This is a study unto itself and time does not permit of an extensive treatment of the subject at this juncture. The reader is referred to section eleven in the chapter on the normal pulse.

The Pulse in Disease

The Chinese regard disease as an imbalance of the Yin and the Yang and as a result of wrong habits in living. To them the pulse is intimately connected with respiration, and the physician is watchful to note whether the breathing is normal or abnormal. The Chinese were aware thousands of years ago that man was subjected to stimuli from within as well as without and that some were more important than others — like the four seasons, the winds, and the five elements: they first classified the disease as a process coming from inside or from outside the body. As time went on, they further classified the pulse reactions into the Yin and Yang, the superficial and deep or the upper and lower, the abnormal and the death pulse, etc. The following is a brief introduction to the various abnormal pulses and their significations in disease:

Abnormal pulse	Fever Pulse
Readings of Inch Pulse	Pregnancy
Readings of Cubit Pulse	Celestial Stems
Pulses of Five Viscera and Stomach	Death Pulse

The last two sections on the **Celestial Stems** and the **Death Pulse** can properly be regarded as matter related to this section on the pulse in disease.

Abnormal Pulse

The physician must distinguish among the three regions of Yang and be aware of the Yang diseases from their beginnings and among the three regions of Yin in order to determine the dates of life and death. He then knows the actual condition of the viscera and the possibility of death for the one who can no longer overcome the disease (what the Westerner may call the patient's lack of resistance).

How to Recognize the Abnormal Pulse

If the pulse is

1. short and without volume, it is always abnormal.
2. quick and contains six beats to one cycle of respiration, it indicates heart trouble.
3. large, the disease becomes grave.
4. the lower one and is abundant, then it indicates flatulence.
5. the upper one and is abundant, then the impulse of life is strong.
6. irregular and tremulous and the beats occur at irregular intervals, then the impulse of life fades.
7. slender (smaller than feeble) but still perceptible, thin like a silk thread, then the impulse of life is small.
8. small and fine, slow and short like the scraping of bamboo with a knife, then the heart is irritated and painful.
9. empty and slow, the disease is within.
10. fine and vigorous, the disease is at the outside.

All the pulses listed above indicate that the illnesses are difficult to cure, for they are known to be caused by opposition to the laws of the four seasons. When the pulse is not reinforced by the stomach, man must die. The pulses which are not reinforced by the stomach merely obtain the support of the viscera, but not the vital force of the stomach. Patients who are deprived of the vital force of the stomach have a pulse of the liver that is not taut like a musical string and a pulse of the kidneys that is not coarse and rough like a stone.

If the pulse is

11. abundant and slippery and vigorous, the disease affects the external body.
12. small, long, and slightly tense and vigorous, it affects the internal body.
13. weak, small, very fine, slow and short, it indicates a chronic disease.
14. inside and yet indicates the outside pulse and vice versa, the outside pulse indicates the inside pulse, there is a harmful accumulation within the heart and the stomach (see items 9 and 10 above).
15. deep and violent, congestion under the ribs and "evil" accumulations within the stomach will cause pain.
16. beating in accord with Yin and Yang, the disease changes for the better and comes to an end.
17. beating in opposition to the Yin and the Yang, the disease becomes worse.
18. obediently following the four seasons, there will be no disease.
19. not beating in consonance with the four seasons, the pulse will not extend to the regions between the five viscera and the resulting disease will be difficult to cure.
20. fine, slow and short, there is an excess of Yang.

21. slippery, like pebbles rolling in a basin, there is an excess of Yin.
22. small and heavy and stem from the Yin region, the result will be aching bones.
23. in the upper region is slow and empty and the pulse in the lower region is full and large and the illness departs very slowly, the condition indicates an evil influence. Thus it is found that Yang suffers evil influences within the body.
24. for the upper is full and large and for the lower pulse is empty and slow and the illness departs very slowly, the symptoms indicate madness.
25. heavy, the region of the lesser Yin is rebellious.
26. **the pulse of Yang** for a stretch of time during which the disease has progressed, the urine and stool which are secreted contain pus and blood.
27. strong and hard, it indicates a hypertonia or a repletion of the organ.
28. feeble and soft, vacuity or hypotonia is indicated.
29. small, fine, and slow, numbness is indicated.
30. is light, floating, scattered, and irregular, dizziness and blurred vision result.
31. drained of blood, then the arms are prone to be of a greenish gray color.
32. accompanied by much coughing and troubled breathing and if the breath is frequently interrupted, then an illness within the stomach will develop causing coagulation and irritation through an accumulation of food; this will never be able to pass through, and death will result.
33. of the neck (carotid) is abundant, then coughing and troubled breathing occur; this is said to be caused "through the vapors of water."
34. felt at the highest point and it does not descend, it means that the loins and the feet are in poor condition (emaciated).
35. felt at the lowest point and it does not ascend, it means there is an ache within the head and the neck.
36. calm and quiet, the disease is indicated by the pulse of the foot.

The pulse has ways of indicating whether the patient follows or disobeys the laws of the four seasons and whether there are not hidden violations: for instance, when in spring and summer, the pulse is thin and when in fall and winter, the pulse is superficial and large. This condition reveals clearly that the patient is in discord or disharmony with the four seasons.

Readings of the Inch Pulse

If the inch pulse is
1. deep and violent, there is congestion under the ribs, and within the stomach there is an evil accumulation located crosswise, which causes pain.
2. deep and there is a shortness of breath, it indicates chills and fever.
3. deep and yet feeble, there will be chills and fever and even rupture of the bowels and pain of the small intestines.
4. short and without volume, a headache will result.

5. too much prolonged, extreme pains on shinbones and in feet will result. (Yang cannot penetrate and this causes a headache.) A prolonged pulse indicates that there is an excess of Yin causing soreness in the feet.
6. routs and strikes upward, the shoulders and back ache.
7. is deep at the wrist, like a stone thrown in the water, and also vigorous, an illness within the body results.
8. superficial like a piece of wood floating on the water and abundant, an illness of the external body results.
9. slippery, superficial, and hasty, new disease results.
10. irritated and there is difficulty in breathing, pain is in the small intestine.
11. slippery and tardy, like a willow branch swaying to a light breeze, fever is raging in the body.
12. abundant but tense and hard and full, dropsical swellings result.

Readings of the Cubit Pulse

If the cubit pulse is

1. slippery and is not hot, then the eight motivating powers or eight winds are at work.
2. small and fine, numbness results.
3. slow, tardy, and small, the condition is said to be loosening, dissolving, and improving.
4. abundant and the person lies down quietly, the body is drained of blood.
5. small and slippery, there is excess of blood.
6. cold and slender, there is leakage of blood in the posterior.
7. coarse in particular and the pulse in general is coarse and rough and if there is constant heat, there are fevers within the body.
8. feverish and if person has one exhalation to three movements of the pulse and one inhalation to three movements of the pulse, one speaks of a warm sickness.

Pulses of the Five Viscera (Heart, Lungs, Liver, Spleen, Kidney) and the Stomach

The Heart

If the heart pulse

1. beats vigorously and the strokes are markedly prolonged, the corresponding illness makes the tongue curl up and the patient unable to speak.
2. is hasty or rapid, the sickness is angina pectoris and it is in the small intestines where the disease becomes visible.

The Lungs

If the pulse of the lungs

1. beats vigorously and long, the corresponding illness produces blood in the sputum.
2. is completely exhausted, the lo vessels rebel and emit blood, which is secreted with the sputum.

The Liver

If the pulse from the liver

1. beats vigorously and long and the complexion is not greyish green, the corresponding illness produces a sinking sensation as though one were fatally stricken; the blood within the ribs and the flanks descends presently, leaving the patient panting and exhausted.
2. is soft and scattered and the complexion shining and glossy, the corresponding illness requires abundant drinking. The thirst is violent and requires more drinking and changes befall the flesh and the skin and are transmitted to the outside through the stomach and bowels (jaundice and hepatitis and diabetes).
3. moves fully and is long, slightly tense, and felt on both light and heavy pressure and also is slippery, the liver is sick.

The Spleen

If the pulse from the spleen is

1. vigorous and long and the complexion turns yellow, the corresponding illness produces a shortness of breath and reduces the force of life.
2. soft and scattered and the complexion is not glossy and shining, the corresponding illness produces swelling of the coccyx and of the feet, which assume the appearance of containing water (edema).
3. healthy and softly flowing, the life-giving force of the stomach, which is at its height in summer, is functioning properly.

The Kidney

If the pulse from the kidneys is

1. vigorous and long and the complexion is yellow and red, the corresponding illness produces a bowed posture.
2. soft and scattered, the resulting illness causes a reduction of blood feet, which assume the appearance of containing water [edema].
which is then unable to circulate (anemia, hypertension). In winter, the life-giving force of the stomach is considered the origin of life.
3. flowing like the sound made by touching the stretched fibers of a bean and its strength is increased (the shape of the kidney is likened to the stretched fibre of a bean), the kidney is sick.

The Stomach

If the pulse from the stomach is

1. vigorous and long and the complexion turns red, the corresponding illness causes bent or broken thighs.
2. soft and scattered, the resulting illness causes great pain when one is eating food.
3. full and slightly tense, it indicates dropsical swelling.
4. empty, slow and compressible, it indicates a leakage in the stomach.

Generalization: In the spring, the pulse of the stomach should be fine and delicate, like the strings of a musical instrument. If the strings are touched too frequently, the stomach functions intermittently and the resulting illness affects the liver. If the strings give only one tone, the stomach ceases to function and death results. When the stomach has a defect, an illness will make its appearance in harvest time. When the defect is great, the illness will strike at once. (Compare with Ayurvedic medicine.) When it is stone-like but also like the beating of a hammer, a disease will make its appearance in summer. When the sound that is comparable to the beating of a hammer is too strong, disease will develop at once.

The great arteries (the **lo** or hollow vessels) of the stomach are described as "hollow lanes" creating a connection with the vessels of the lungs which descend along the left breast. The motion of these vessels corresponds to that of the pulse in support of the life force.

Fever Pulse

1. If the pulse is heavy, scattered, and irregular, chills and fever are indicated.
3. If the pulse beats are soft and scattered, the corresponding illness produces torrents of sweat to overcome fever and toxins in the body.
3. If the inch pulse is tardy and slippery, fever is in the body.
4. If the cubit pulse is coarse and rough, fever is present.
5. Even when there are disease and fever, the pulse can nevertheless be quiet and still; and even when there are leakage and much loss of blood, the pulse can nevertheless be full and large.
6. If the pulse is dense and coarse and large, its content of the Yin elements is insufficient and there is a surplus of Yang elements which cause fever within the body.
7. If the pulse beats are light, floating, but not hasty and stem from the region of the Yang, fever will result.
8. If the pulse is deep and feeble, chills and fever and even rupture of the bowels and pains in the small intestines result.
9. If the pulse is deep and is accompanied by shortness of breath, chills and fever will result.
10. If one feels at the outside the pulse which indicates the inside and if it does not indicate the inside, the body is hot and feverish.

Pregnancy

The Oriental physician has his own pregnancy test—the Pulse. When the motion of a woman's pulse is great, she is with child. If there is cessation of menstruation with no apparent disease and if threee pulses are slippery, it indicates pregnancy. If in addition the three pulses are rapid and scattered, it denotes three months' conception; if rapid and unscattered, five months'.

Diagnosis of Sex of Child by Pulse

Western medicine at present has no way of determining the sex[3] of the child. According to the Chinese: if the pulse on the left wrist is rapid, a son may be expected; however, if the pulse in the right wrist is rapid, the blessed event will be a daughter. On the left hand, a super-

---

3 A pediatrician friend of the authors is always correct in predicting the sex of the child. He uses the following method: he informs the mother that the child will be a boy and in his appointment book for that day he records that he informed the mother the child will be a girl. If it is a boy, he says nothing; if it is a girl, he shows the proud parents his appointment book.

ficial and overflowing cubit pulse or a large inch pulse denotes a male offspring; on the right hand, a deep full cubit pulse or a deep and slender inch pulse denotes a female.

Diagnosis of Multiple Births by the Pulse

To the Oriental physician, if the cubit pulses on both wrists are overflowing, it means twin boys; if deep and full, twin girls. Triplets, all girls, may be expected if the pulses of both wrists are smooth and equal; but if the pulses of both wrists are rough and unequal, the triplets will be boys.

The Celestial Stems and the Pulse

"Celestial Stems" is the term used to express the relationship between the points of the compass and the seasons. They were based not only upon the five element theory but also upon the ancient devices that measured time and denoted the heavenly directions. Most frequently they are correlated with the eight trigrams or Kua of the **I Ching** to symbolize the various stages of the movements of the sun and moon; hence the supposed fluctuations, the waxing and waning of the Yin and Yang elements. Alchemists considered this phase important for the choice of the precise times to conduct experiments. But what is of concern here is the matter of the time aspect as judged by the condition of the body reflected by the organs and their elements at the time of examination of the pulse. The Chinese doctor was aware not only of the energy flow of the organs but also of the rhythm of the body as a whole. Among other factors, these included the physical, emotional, and intellectual cycles as well as the auspicious time of the day for the health of the individual.[4]

Each of the five viscera has its own element as an inseparable relationship, and each organ functions in coordination with that particular element: e.g., the liver is associated with the element of wood. Should there be a shift to another element within any of the five viscera, the consequent imbalance would result in critical illness or death. Two examples will be cited so that this generalization about correlations is meaningful for the Western reader. The kidneys need water to function properly. Should the kidneys utilize air instead of water, grave damage or death would result. The lungs need air or oxygen to function. Should they absorb water, not air, drowning would take place. The Chinese view for such an inter-relationship applies therefore to the five elements and to the five viscera with respect to the "stems."

In the basic medical source book for these interpretations **Huang Ti Nei Ching Su Wên,** Wang Ping provides an explanation of the need for watching the relationship of organ to element. He warns that should the relationship between element and organ be violated, serious illness and death would result. His observations succinctly remark that

Death ensues when the celestial stem of

1. Metal becomes visible in the liver, for liver is the element wood.
2. Wood becomes visible in the spleen, for spleen is the element earth.

---

[4] The nearest discipline at present that approximates this type of reasoning is the bio-rhythm system popular in Europe today, especially in Switzerland.

3. Fire becomes visible in the lungs, for lungs are the element metal.
4. Earth becomes visible in the kidneys, for the kidneys are the element water.
5. Water becomes visible in the heart, for heart is the element fire.

Wang Ping then relates organ and element in this simple table:

1. Wood . . . liver
2. Earth . . . spleen
3. Metal . . . lungs
4. Water . . . kidneys
5. Fire . . . heart

Of Needham's four monumental volumes on **Science and Civilisation in China,** his second furnishes a table of correspondences[5] between the viscera and the five elements, a listing that differs from Wang Ping's correlations. Since the Su Wên is a basic medical source, the list is submitted with this explanation: there are many interpretations of these correspondences. The principle remains the same for medicine: a change in the relationship of the organs to the elements means illness and death. One must be aware of how the different purposes of the writers through the centuries dictated a great diversity of correlations and in some instances contradictory statements and discrepancies. Despite the more than a hundred correspondences listed by Eberhad, this interpretation of the celestial stems rests upon the most ancient surviving Chinese medical text — the **Huang Ti Nei Ching Su Wên** which was concerned with the physiological correlations. Though the date of this text is uncertain, the bulk of its observations, according to Needham, must be at least early Han (—202 to +9) and some of it may be from the Warring States period (—490 to —221).

The Death Pulse

The death pulse must be considered in relation to the organs of the five viscera and to the stomach before one can grasp the story being told through the pulse.

The Heart and the Death Pulse

When the normal heart pulse changes from its steady flow — like pearls joined together — to a rhythm where the beats become small and irregular, the patient is critically ill. Then, at the point of death, the pulse becomes irregular in the front of the finger and feeble at the back of the finger. The complexion turns red and black and loses its glossy appearance. When the pulse stands still, death ensues within a day.

The Lungs and the Death Pulse

When the normal pulse of the lungs stops its large and slow beat, when the pulse neither rises nor falls, and when the complexion of the skin turns ashen and red, the patient is in critical condition. At the point of death, the pulse becomes as light as a feather and death ensues within three days.

---

5 Joseph Needham, **op. cit.**, vol. 2, pp. 262-3, table 12.

The Liver and the Death Pulse

When the normal pulse of the liver changes its soft and weak beat to a large, long, slightly tense, and slippery rhythm upon one's applying either a light or a heavy pressure; when the complexion turns green and ashen and loses its glossy appearance, the condition of the patient is critical. At the point of death, the pulse of the liver increases in speed and strength and death ensues within a day. When the liver ceases to function, the pulse is like the string of a new bow or like the blunt edge of a sword; death will ensue within eight days.

The Spleen and the Death Pulse

When the normal pulse of the spleen changes from its wave—that softly flows to come together as well as gently to fall apart—to an arrhythm that is full, large, long. and slightly tense with extra beats and when the complexion turns yellow and green, the patient's condition is critical. At the point of death, the pulse of the spleen moves sharply and strongly and death ensues within a day. If the pulse resembles the pecking of a bird or of water dripping from a roof crack, or the upsetting of a cup, it means extinction of the spleenic pulse and death may be expected in four days.

The Kidney and the Death Pulse

When the normal pulse of the kidney changes from a flow as if it were weary and panting to that of a taut string with an increase in strength and when the complexion turns black and yellow, then the patient's condition is critical. At the point of death, the pulse changes like the tearing of a twisted cord or the snapping of fingers upon a stone, and death ensues within a day.

All these five pulse changes are visible signs of the changes in the five viscera. They cannot be cured, and all are followed by death. It must be noted that the **viscera cannot by themselves influence the pulse of the hand** and the region of the great Yin, as their source indicates. **They must influence the spleen** whose vital force then reaches the hand via what is described as the great Yin. But each of the five viscera has its own special period of time of the day when it can act by itself and thus influence the hand and the region of the great Yin.

Life is supported by the true pulse of the viscera. When the pulse of the liver is extremely uneven and hasty, death ensues after eighteen days; of the heart, nine days; of the lungs, twelve days.

The Stomach and the Death Pulse

The stomach cannot be considered together with the five vital organs, but must be discussed separately.

When the pulse of the stomach has only one tone and when the stomach itself ceases to function, death ensues within three days.

The Death Beats

When a person has one exhalation to four movements of the pulse, death is not far away.

When the pulse breaks off and does not extend, death is certain.

When the pulse gets abruptly disconnected or accelerates suddenly, it means death.

A pulse acting like a fish darting about in the water or like water oozing from a spring is a fatal symptom.

DISEASES AND THE PULSE—CHINESE VIEW

Alphabetical Arrangement

ABDOMINAL PAIN. A slender, slow p. denotes quick recovery; superficial and long p. denotes slow convalescence; p. always taut if rupture due to trouble in liver; if p. is wiry and rapid, all is well; if p. is feeble and rapid, it is fatal.

ABSCESS OF LUNGS. Inch p. is quick and full. In collapse of lungs, p. is quick and weak. In abscess of lungs and collapse, p. is short and small and complexion is white.

ACUTE DISEASES. P. is slippery, superficial, and quick.

APOPLEXY. P. should be superficial and slow. If p. is firm, rapid, large, there is danger.

ASTHMA. If p. is superficial and slippery, it is favorable; if p. deep and small and if especially hands and feet (extremities) are cold, it is unfavorable.

BRONCHIAL DISEASE. If p. is generally superficial and small and if deep, it is easy to cure; if hidden and tense, death is in the wings.

BURNS. P. is full and overflowing.

CANCER — INTESTINES. Quick and slippery p. is favorable; deep and slender p. means the undertaker.

CANCER — CARBUNCLES WITH. P. is full and overflowing. A large p. before suppuration is good, but large pulse after suppuration is critical.

CHILLS WITH PAIN. Tense p.

CHOLERA. Irregular p. should be no cause for alarm; but if there are curled tongue and shrivelled testicles, recovery is improbable.

CHRONIC CONDITIONS. P. is weak, small, very fine, slow, and short.

DEBILITY, GENERAL. Thready p.

DIABETES. P. is large and quick; if slender, thready, short, and small, prognosis is very poor.

DIARRHEA.. P. is deep, small, slippery, and feeble. If p. is strong, large, superficial, and quick, there is danger.

DIZZINESS. P. is light, floating, scattered, and irregular.

EPILEPSY. P. should be superficial and tardy; if deep, small, and quick, it is a sign of death.

EXCESSIVE PERSPIRATION. See perspiration, excessive.

EXHAUSTION. Extreme scattered p.

FEVER WITH PAIN. A tremulous quick p.

HEADACHE. Short, without volume, prolonged p.

HEART IRRITATION. P. is small and fine, slow and short; heart pains— p. is wiry.

HEMORRHAGE. A tremulous quick p.

HERNIA. P. is wiry.

HYPERTONIA. P. is strong and hard.

INSANITY. If p. is superficial and overflowing, prognosis is good; but if p. is deep and quick, prognosis is poor.

JAUNDICE. A full, overflowing, and quick p. is favorable, but if p. is superficial, large, thready, and small, prognosis is poor.

LOSS OF BLOOD. P. should be hollow, small and tardy; if p. is hollow, large, and quick, it indicates danger.

MALARIA. A taut p. is favorable. Taut and slow p. indicates fever; taut and quick p. indicates chills; case is serious if p. is large, scattered, and irregular.

NUMBNESS. P. is small, fine, and slow.

PAIN IN RIBS. P. is deep and violent.
— IN SHOULDERS AND BACK. P. strikes upward.
— IN FEET. Prolonged p.

PERSPIRATION, EXCESSIVE. P. is tremulous and quick.

PULMONARY CONGESTION. A wiry and large p. is favorable but prognosis is poor if it is deep and thready.

RETENTION OF URINE. If p. is full and large, the disease is curable; if slow and small, prognosis is poor.

RESPIRATORY MALFUNCTION. Pulses that are short, large, and small all denote derangement of the respiratory system.

SEMINAL FLUID LOSS. Is signified by a hard p.

SWELLINGS, DROPSICAL. The p. is superficial, large, full and strong; if deep, fine and thready, there is no hope.

TYPHOID FEVER. If p. is superficial, full and overflowing, prognosis is excellent but if p. is thready, small and soft, condition is grave.

UTERINE HEMORRHAGE. Is recognizable by a hard pulse.

VERTIGO. See dizziness.

VISION BLURRED. P. is scattered and irregular, light and floating.

VOMITTING AND REGURGITATION. P. should be superficial and slippery; when it is deep, quick, fine and small, it indicates intestinal bleeding and case is very serious.

WASTING DISEASES. P. should be weak and quick; if it is thin and small, death is around the corner.

Chapter X

DISEASES AND THE PULSE — WESTERN VIEW

Acute and chronic diseases will be alphabetically listed together with their characteristic pulse beats as viewed by the West. Further, the pulse associated with various mental derangements will be found under the listings for insanity.

Alphabetical Arrangement of Acute and Chronic Diseases
Acute Diseases

As a general rule, the pulse is full in acute diseases.

ALCOHOLISM. Full p.

APPENDICITIS. Proportional to temperature; serious if increasing rapidly.

ARTHRITIC DEFORMIS. P. disproportionately high.

ARTHRITIC (SUPPURATIVE) OSTEOMYELITIS OF HIP JOINT. Rapid p.

CHOLECYSTITIS. Rapid p.

CHOLERA. At first p. is weak, then imperceptible.

CHOREA—SYDENHAM'S CHOREA, ST. VITUS DANCE. Rapid p.

ENDOCARDITIS. Rapid p.

ENDOCARDITIS, SIMPLE. Rapid p., rate increases especially in febrile patients and p. may be altered in volume, tension, and rhythm.

HEMORRHAGE. Large, rapid, weak, frequent, easily compressible p.

INTESTINAL OBSTRUCTION. Rapid feeble p. Includes the following, all of which have the same rapid feeble pulse: **intussusception, volvus bands, hernia strangulated.**

MYOCARDITIS. Rapid low tension p.

NEPHRITIS. Hard p.

PANCREATITIS, HEMORRHAGIC. Weak, small, rapid p.

PERICARDITIS, FIBRINOUS. Feeble rapid p.

PERITONITIS, GENERAL. Small, hard, and rapid p., at first wiry; later thready.

PERITONITIS, PELVIC. Rapid wiry p.

PNEUMONIA, T.B., LOBAR FORM. Rapid p.

PNEUMOTHORAX. Rapid and small p.

RHEUMATIC FEVER. Soft, rapid p. 100-120.

TUBERCULOSIS, BRONCHO-PNEUMONIA. Rapid p.

TUBERCULOSIS, MILITARY. Rapid, feeble p.

YELLOW ATROPHY OF LIVER. Rapid p.

CHRONIC DISEASES

ABDOMINAL ORGANS (CHRONIC). Slower than usual.

ADDISON'S DISEASE. Accelerated p., feeble p.

ADENITIS, TRACHEOBRONCHIAL. Tachycardia p.

ADHESIONS. Pulse paradox.

ANEURYISM OF ARCH OF AORTA. See tachycardia p. Inequality of the pulses.

—OF THE AUXILIARY ARTERY. Diminished radial p., rapid and irregular in force and rhythm.

ANGER. Violent and frequent pulse. See psychological forces.

ANGINA PECTORIS. High tension p.

ANXIETY. P. feeble and of low tension. See psychological forces.

AORTIC INSUFFICIENCY. Bisferiens p.

—REGURGITATION—CORRIGAN'S. Large p., increased pressure, galloping radial p., visible capillary and arterial pulsation, high systole, low diastole. Water-hammer p., pistol shot p.

—STENOSIS. P. slow, small, hard, and prolonged. Bisferiens p., plateau p.

AMEBIC DYSENTERY. Rapid and small p.

ANEMIA. P. rapid.

APOPLEXY (CEREBRAL HEMORRHAGE). High tension, slow p., or bounding p., bradycardia p., also intermittent p.

ARRHYTHMIA. See cardiac arrhythmia.

ARTERIOSCLEROSIS. Tachycardia p.

ARTHRITIC DEFORMANS. Rapid pulse 90-110.

ASPHYXIA. Weak, rapid p.

ASYMETRICAL RADIAL P. May be due to aortic aneuryism, embolism, fracture causing compression on vessel, tumor, emotional states.

ATROPIN POISONING. Heart beats rapidly in proportion to the amount of atropin injected; due to the peripheral vagus paralysis.

AURICULAR FIBRILLATION. Rapid and irregular as to force, rate, intensity and rhythm. Jugulars are enlarged and beat is irregular.

AURICULAR FLUTTER. Rapid p., 120-160 (tachycardia) may slow down to 30-38, regular and constant. Ventricles beat at one ratio, auricles beat two, three, or four times as fast as the ventricles; uninfluenced by posture or exercise.

BACILLARY DYSENTERY. Rapid and small p.

BRADYCARDIA. A slow rate is normal with some indviduals. Any marked diminution below 50 or 60 should be regarded as pathological and the cause explained. The heart beat should be checked with the pulse to differentiate between failure of ventricular action which can stimulate bradycardia. It may be due to one of two causes: intracardiac disease involving the conduction bundle of His and pathologic or functional defects of the vagus nerve. If the former is the cause, atrophin has no effect on the rate nor is there a reaction to respiratory movements, exertion, posture or fever. When the vagus is at fault, with exertion, with respiration, with change of posture, and with fever, there is marked acceleration of the heart.

The following diseases are associated with bradycardia:

APOPLEXY. Heart rate is slow and p. is full and of increased tension.

CEREBRAL ABSCESS. Slowing of the cardiac rate, permanent or transient; is a corroborative sign of intracranial abscess; but p. rate may be accelerated in some cases.

CEREBRAL COMPRESSION. Heart rate is slow but becomes rapid and intermittent in the final stages.

CEREBRAL TUMOR. Especially in neighborhood of medulla oblongata. See cerebral abscess.

CEREBROSPINAL FEVER., EPIDEMIC. Rapid at first and is usually full and strong.

LEPTOMENINGITIS. Slow p.

DRUGS: DIGITALIS, HYDROCYANIC ACID, AND OPIUM POISONING. Slow p.

EMPHYSEMA, HYPERTROPHIC. Slow p., regular, low tension.

HEART ACTION. Slow. Generally found during post febrile stage of acute infections, especially typhoid fever and influenza.

HEART BLOCK (complete). Slow heart rate; usually permanent; may be lowered to 40-20-6 per minute.

HEMORRHAGIA PACHYMENINGITIS (cerebral form—hematoma of dura mater). Slow, irregular p.

MENINGITIS PNEUMOCOCCI. Slow cardiac rate in relation to temperature is basic characteristic of the disease.

MENINGITIS PYOGENIC. Slow cardiac rate in relation to temperature is basic characteristic.

MENINGITIS TUBERCULOSIS. Rapid at first and later irregular and slow.

MYXEDEMA (LARVAL MYXEDEMA, HYPOTHYROIDISM). P. 40 to 60, but regular; usually low tension.

PREGNANCY. During latter part and puerperium, p. may be slow, regular, usually low tension.

UREMIA. Heart rate may be slow.

BRONCHIAL ASTHMA. Small, rapid, irregular, intermittent p.

BRONCHO-PNEUMONIA (CAPILLARY BRONCHITIS, LOBAR PNEUMONIA). Rapid p.

CANCER. Slow p.

CARDIAC ARRHYTHMIC (PHYSIOLOGICAL). Seven are listed below:

AORTIC REGURGITATION. See aortic regurgitation.

AORTIC STENOSIS. Heart has a slow rate and the pulse is of moderate or small volume, of normal rhythm and of prolonged deliberate rise and fall; see aortic stenosis.

AURICULAR FIBRILLATION. See auricular fibrillation.

AURICULAR FLUTTER. See auricular flutter.

HEART BLOCK. See heart block.

PREMATURE CONTRACTIONS. Regular systole following an extra-systole; p. seems to be stronger than normal; disappears on exertions when due to functional causes; increases when accompanied by pathological changes.

SINUS ARRHYTHMIA. More rapid during inspiration, slower during expiration; p. is slow with irregularly long diastolic pauses.

CARDIAC CRISES. Tachycardia p.
CARDIAC DECOMPOSITION. Small weak p., often irregular; other times slow, depending on condition of the patient. Weak, but sharp on first sound; an enfeebled second sound is a sign of failing compensation. Tachycardia p.
CARDIAC DILATION. Small, rapid, irregular p.
CARDIAC HYPERTROPHY. High tension p.
CARDIAC LESION. Slow p.
CATARRH JAUNDICE. Slow p.
CEREBRAL ABSCESS. Slow p. and respiration.
CEREBRAL DISEASES. High tension p.
CEREBRAL HEMORRHAGE. Hard, slow p.
CEREBRAL THROMBOSIS. Relatively low blood pressure.
CEREBRAL TUMOR. Slow p.; intracranial pressure.
CEREBROSPINAL FEVER. Rapid at first, full and strong; later bradycardia p.
CHRONIC ANEMIA, PERNICIOUS. Rapid p.
   ANEMIA, SECONDARY. Soft, small and rapid p.
   COLITIS, ULCERATED. Rapid p.   ....
   MYOCARDITIS. Persistent high tension p; in cardiosclerosis, p. feeble and irregular, as for acute.
   NEPHRITIS. High tension p.
   PERICARDITIS, ADHESIVE. Systolic retraction, diastolic shock, pulsus paradoxus, diastolic collapse of the juguar vein.
   HYDROCEPHALUS, ACQUIRED. Slow p.
   PULMONARY TUBERCULOSIS. Accelerated p. is very frequent manifestation and may occur as an early symptom, even without fever. As the disease progresses, the rapidity of the p. becomes more marked. In the last stages of the disease, the p. rate is unusually high, going to 120 or more.
CIRCULATORY FAILURE, PERIPHERAL. Thready p.
CLOT. Tachycardia p.
COLLAGEN DISEASES. P. is rapid and feeble or imperceptible.
COLLAPSE. Rapid p. Low tension p.
CONCUSSION. Rapid p.
CORONARY THROMBOSIS. Rapid p.
DEBILITY. Small and hard p. Very rapid p. Low tension p.
DEGENERATION, FATTY. Infrequent p. Intermittent p.
DIGESTIVE DISORDERS. Slow p.
DIGITALIS. Intermittent p.
DILATION OF AORTA. P. of fair volume.
DIPHTHERIA. Slow p., small.
ECTOPIC PREGNANCY. Very rapid p.
EFFORT SYNDROME—NEUROCIRCULATORY ASTHENIA. Abnormally rapid p. on exertion or emotion; throbbing of carotid artery.
EMBOLISM — PULMONARY. Rapid, weak and irregular p.
EMPHYSEMA. Slow p.
ENCEPHALITIS. Rapid p.
ENDOCARDITIS, INFECTIOUS (MALIGNANT OR ULCERATIVE). Rapid irregular. p.
ENTERIC FEVER. Small and very rapid p. Severe case p. becomes weak.

EPILEPSY. Rapid p.

EPILEPTIC SEIZURE. High tension p.

ERYSIPELAS. Hard p., and slow.

EXOPHTHALMIC GOITRE—GRAVES DISEASE. High tension p., rapid p. 100-200.

FEAR. See psychological factors.

FEBRILE DISEASES. Bounding and collapsing p. Tachycardia p.

FEVERS. Full p. in hot stage; then rapid; after fever, pulse magnus.

FIBROID INDURATIONS. Infrequent p.

FRACTURE OF SKULL. Slow p., first stage feeble, then rapid.

GOITRE, TOXIC. Tachycardia p.

GOUT. Hard p., high tension p., intermittent p.

HAPPINESS. See psychological factors.

HEART BLOCK. Very slow p.

HEART DISEASE, ORGANIC. Rapid, infrequent p. See tachycardia.

HEAT COLLAPSE. P. is slow.

HEAT EXHAUSTION. Small, rapid p.

HEMORRHAGE. Heart action rapid and feeble, becoming progressively worse as hemorrhage increases. Tachycardia p. and running p.

HEPATIC DISEASES. Rapid p.

HIGH BLOOD PRESSURE. Celer p.

HYDROCYANIC ACID (PRUSSIC) POISONING. Slow p.

HYPERTENSION. Fast p.

HYPERTROPHY. Large p.

HYPOTENSION. Slow and small p.

INDIGESTION. In physiological disturbances, intermittent p. See psychological factors; p. hard, slow, and indistinct. Various pulses responsive to different organs affected as follows:

> **CONTRACTIONS OF BOWELS.** Curvilinear p.
>
> **EXCITEMENT.** P. faster and harder than the indigestion p. and depends for beat on location in digestive tract.
>
> **SMALL INTESTINES.** P. thin and slow.
>
> **STOMACH.** P. thick, heavy, slightly hard.
>
> **TUMOR.** P. restless and gyrating motion. May be psychological in origin.
>
> **ULCER.** P. restless and gyrating motion.

INFLAMMATION OR FEVER. Full hard p., strong p.

INFLUENZA. Slow p. as compared to fever p. Tachycardia in post-febrile stage. See bradycardia.

INSANITY. The pulse shows a marked increase: 7 over the physiological norm in the female and 9 for the male.

THE MANIACAL PULSE IN ACUTE ATTACKS:

> **OF PRECORDIAL PANIC IN MELANCHOLIA.** Has high frequency p., small volume, and intravascular pressure.
>
> **OF ALCOHOLISM** where the patient has cirrhosis of liver, kidney trouble, or sclerosed nervous center. Has high tension p.
>
> **OF SENILE DEMENTED.** High tension p.
>
> **OF SYPHILITIC DEMENTED.** High tension p.
>
> **OF PARESIS WITH CONTINUED DEPRESSION.** Low tension p.

THE MANIACAL PULSE

IN ALCOHOLISM, the state of the liver and the kidneys exerts a modifying influence as does the condition of the lungs.

IN DEPRESSION and IN MELANCHOLIA, shows muscular contractions and vascular spasms; the pulse is of high tension. In melancholia originating directly from cerebral exhaustion and in all forms of neural asthenia, p. is of low tension. In melancholia with hypochondriacal neurosis, the p. is of low tension.

where there is ACTIVE CUTANEOUS CIRCULATION, warmth, and color in the skin, there is a slight increase in frequency of p. beat. When excitement is very great, the p. becomes tricrotic.

Where there are PALLOR AND COOLNESS OF THE CUTANEOUS SURFACE, p. has high tension. Under very great excitement or under great exhaustion, p. becomes monocrotic.

WITH TOXINS, has a high p.

INTERMITTENT FEVER. Hard p.

IRRITATION. Small and very rapid p.

JAUNDICE. Full, slow, infrequent p., soft p.

LEPTOMENINGITIS, PURULENT (WITH CEREBRAL ABSCESS OR SINUS). Rapid or slow p.

LITHARGIA. Tachycardia p.

LITHEMIA. High tension p.

LOBAR PNEUMONIA. Full and bounding p.

LOCOMOTOR ATAXIA. Accelerated p.

MALARIA. Slow p.

MEASLES. Hard p. with rapid fever.

MENINGEAL HEMORRHAGE. P. at first slow and full, later rapid and feeble.

MENINGITIS, ALL. See bradycardia.

MENINGITIS, BEGINNING. High tension p., feeble, rapid, very irregular.

MENTAL DEPRESSION. Slow p.

MITRAL REGURGITATION. Irregular p.

—STENOSIS. Thready p., tachycardia p., small p.

MOUNTAIN SICKNESS; LUNG CANCER. Tachycardia p.

MYOCARDIAL FAILURE. Thready p.

MYOCARDITIS, ACUTE. Tachycardia p., irregular p.

NARCOTICS. Dicrotic p.

NEPHROLITHIASIS. RENAL COLIC. Rapid p.

NERVENES. Dicrotic p.

NERVOUS DERANGEMENTS. Changeable p.

NEURITIS. Rapid p.

NEUROSIS. Rapid p.

NEUROTHENIA. Low tension p.

OPIUM POISONING. Slow, feeble p.

PARALYSIS, ACUTE ASCENDING. Rapid p.

PAROXYSMAL TACHYARDIA. P. rate rapid and regular, as high as 200.

PERIARTHRITIS, NODA. Tachycardia p.

PERICARDITIS, CHRONIC ADHESIVE. Tachycardia p., pulse paradox.

—WITH EFFUSION. Rapid small p., heart beats rapid and small and sometimes irregular; pulsus paradoxus p., weak during each inspiration.

PERIPHERAL CIRCULATION FAILURE. Thready p.

PERITONITIS, ACUTE. Wiry p., small, rapid, tense p.

PNEUMONIA. Rapid p., infrequent p.

POLIOMYELITIS. Rapid p.

PREGNANCY. Pernicious vomitting has rapid p. See bradycardia.

PSYCHOLOGICAL FACTORS. Excitement of any kind accelerates the pulse. Every emotion has its own reaction and its own pulse rate as the result of secretions of the endocrine system, especially the adrenals, and the sympathetic system which affect the heart and which are then reflexed to the pulse. (The Easterners are trained to distinguish between physiological and psychological stimuli which affect the pulse.)

    ANGER. Violent and frequent p.

    ANXIETY. Feeble p. and of low tension.

    EXCITEMENT. Any kind of excitement accelerates p.

    FEAR. Feeble and frequent p.

    HAPPINESS. P. slow, of good tension at first; later quick and vigorous.

    INDIGESTION. If psychological in origin, p. hard, slow, and indistinct. Pulses vary in organ affected by the indigestion; six variations follow:

    INDIGESTION: CONTRACTIONS OF BOWELS: Curvilinear p.

    INDIGESTION: EXCITEMENT: P. faster and harder than indigestion p; depends on location in digestive tract.

    INDIGESTION: SMALL INTESTINES: P. thin and slow.

    INDIGESTION: STOMACH: P. thick, heavy, slightly hard.

    INDIGESTION: TUMOR: P. restless and gyrating motion. Tumors may be psychological in origin.

    INDIGESTION: ULCER: P. restless and gyrating.

    SORROW. Feeble and of low tension and very slow.

PUERPERAL FEVER. Quick p.

PULMONARY EDEMA. Feeble full p.

—INFARCTION. Abrupt rise of pulse rate.

—REGURGITATION. Small and frequent p.

REGURGITATION, TRICUSPID RELATIVE. Systolic, jugular and hepatic p., small, weak, and often irregular.

RENAL COMA. Hard full p.

RHEUMATISM. Hard hammer p., at joints; p. is rapid, full and soft.

RHEUMATOID ARTHRITIS. Tachycardia p.

SCARLATINA. Hard p.

SCARLET FEVER. Rapid p.

SEPSIS. Rapid p.

SHOCK AND COLLAPSE. Weak, thready, fast p. See Tachycardia.

SMALLPOX. Hard p.

SORROW. See psychological factors.

STENOSIS OF PULMONARY ARTERY. Small and rapid p.

STOKES ADAMS SYNDROME. Excessive slowness of p. 20-40; acceleration of pulse on recovery; otherwise death.

SUNSTROKE. Rapid full p.

SYNCOPE. Thready p.

TABES DORSALIS. Rapid p. See Tachycardia.

THROMBO ANGITIS OBLITERANS (BUERGER DISEASE). Absence of arterial pulsation in the feet.

TACHYCARDIA. The pulse rate is 90 or above. The heart action is increased in frequency after exertion with excitement or other emotional causes and following the ingestion of a meal. Pain often causes tachycardia. Shock and collapse are accompanied by a rapid feeble heart action. The commonly used stimulants — coffee, tea, alcohol, cigarettes — when taken in excess also produce rapid heart action. Febrile affections, except yellow fever and those accompanied by intracranial hypertension, are usually accompanied by frequent pulse, that generally increases 8 to 10 beats to each rise of one degree of temperature; exceptions are typhoid fever, influenza and pneumonia where the pulse is relatively slow; in sepsis, tuberculosis, scarlet fever, and acute military tuberculosis, the rate is disproportionately high. Violent coughing quickens the pulse.

The following diseases are accompanied by Tachycardia:

Adenitis, Tracheobronchial
Aneurism of Arch of Aorta
Arteriosclerosis
Arthritic Deformans (90 to 110)
Atropin Poisoning
Auricular Fibrillation
Auricular Flutter
Cardiac Crises
Cardiac Decomposition
Cholera, Acute
Collapse
Concussion, Cerebral
Coronary Thrombosis
Coughing, violent
Effort Syndrome
Encephalitis—simple, acute,
           malignant
Exophthalmic Goitre
Febrile Affections
Febrile Diseases
Goitre, Exophthalmic
Heat Exhaustion
Hemorrhage
Hypertension
Hypertension, Intracranial
Influenza, See bradycardia
Lithargica
Military Tuberculosis, chronic

Mitral Stenosis
Mountain Sickness—Lung Cancer
Myocarditis, Acute
Neuritis, Pneumogastric
Neurosis
Paralysis, Acute Ascending
    (120-130 per minute)
—Diphtheritic
Periarthritis Nodosa
Pericarditis, Chronic Adhesive
—with effusion
Pneumonia
Poliomyelitis, Acute Anterior
Pulmonary Tuberculosis
Scarlet Fever
Sepsis
Shock
Tabes Dorsalis
Tachycardia, Anterior Acute
—Paroxysmal
Thrombosis, Coronary
Thyroid Extracts
Tracheobronchial Adenitis
Tuberculosis, Chronic Pulmonary
—Military
Tumor, Mediastinal
Typhoid Fever
Yellow Fever

The Ayurvedic, Unani and Chinese Interpretation of Tachycardia:

To the Ayurvedic physician, typhoid fever, influenza, and pneumonia would be Kapha diseases. This accounts for the irregularity in the increase of 8 to 10 beats per one degree of fever. Sepsis, tuberculosis, scarlet fever, and acute military tuberculosis would be Vayu diseases where the pulse beats are exceptionally high. Here the Ayurvedic and Unani physicians are superior to the Western doctor since they can account for the fevers.

To the Chinese physician, who is aware of excess and depletion of the various organs affected by these diseases, no rules are necessary. He knows what goes on in the body as the disease progresses and thus is able to tell which organs are or are not responding to treatment, something the Westerner cannot do at the present time.

The Eastern physician is interested not in the break-down furnished in the above list, not in symptoms, but in the person and in the progress of the disease and the process of recovery since he has learned that symptoms change as the disease runs its course for better or for worse.

THROMBOSIS, CORONARY. Slow p.

—CEREBRAL. Tachycardia p.

—SINUS LATERAL. Unilateral jugular collapse which does not disappear immediately when the vein is compressed above the clavicle. Slow p.

THYROID EXTRACTS. Very rapid p.

TOBACCO HEART. Tachycardia p.

TRACHEOBRONCHIAL ADENITIS. Tachycardia p.

TRICUSPID INSUFFICIENCY. Bamberger and reverse paradox p.

—REGURGITATION. Venous p.

—STENOSIS. Pulsating jugular p.

TUBERCULOSIS MENINGITIS. Irregular p.

TUMOR. High tension, slow p. See tachycardia and psychological factors. Pulse paradox.

TYPHOID FEVER. P. slow compared with other febrile diseases; infrequent, slow p. during post-febrile stage.

ULCERATED COLITIS. Rapid p.

ULCER, GASTRIC. Slow p. See psychological factors.

—PERFORATED, PEPTIC (GASTRIC OR DUODENAL). Strong p. increasing steadily.

UREMIA. Slow p., high tension p.

VARIOLA. Rapid p.

YELLOW FEVER. Rapid p.

Chapter XI

EPITOME OF EASTERN AND WESTERN VIEWS
ON PULSE AND HEALING

THREE MONTAGES

Two montages interpret Ayurvedic and Chinese readings of the pulse and serve as graphic illustrations of how the physician scientist becomes the artist in understanding the body through his sensitive awareness of the various pulses. Perhaps it is desirable to quote Rilke's words about the artist Rodin's preoccupation with the study of the hand and the body, for they apply to the artist-physician:

> The farther he progressed on this remote road, the more chance remained behind, and one law led him to another . . . It was the surface, this differently great surface, variedly accentuated, accurately measured, out of which everything must rise, which was from this moment the subject matter of his art, the thing for which he laboured.

Montage 1

Chinese View of Influences on Pulse—Told in Terms of Western Equivalents
The Chinese Technique of Reading the Pulse

In this section the following will be tabulated:

    I. Components of Yin and Yang
    II. Application of Yin-Yang components to organs
    III. Five elements and eleven influences on the pulse
    IV. Eighteen variations on the pentarchy
    V. Five specifics with respect to taking the pulse: climate, viscera, taste-flavors, winds, and spiritual resources
    VI. Five key generalizations applicable to the pulse and seasons
    VII. The celestial stems, the seasons, the organs, and the pulse
    VIII. Five functional interrelationships of organs
    IX. Seasons as they affect the pulse
    X. Philosophic generalizations—the **Vade Mecum** of the Chinese physician.

The Components—Principles of Yin and Yang Fractured into three Components Each or a Total of Six

Note: Yang is active outwardly and acts as regulator of Yin; Yin is active inwardly and acts as regulator of Yang. Yang is light and Yin is darkness.

1. The Greater Yang	4. The Greater Yin
2. The Lesser Yang	5. The Lesser Yin
3. The Sunlight	6. The Absolute Yin

Modern Equivalents of Yin and Yang as Potential and Kinetic Energies

Yin is potential energy; Yang is kinetic energy; vibration consists of the interchange of the two from inception to climax: from kinetic to potential and then to kinetic, etc.

Kinetic energy characterizes the inception of the new vibration:

Positive kinetic energy is lesser Yang

Positive potential energy is lesser Yin

Negative kinetic energy is lesser Yang

Negative potential energy is greater Yin

Application of Yin-Yang Components to Organs

Note: As paired coordinate correlatives—these act together almost like Siamese twins: the force connects with an organ.

6. Absolute Yin . . . . liver

2. Lesser Yang . . . . gall bladder

5. Lesser Yin . . . . heart

1. Greater Yang . . . . small intestines

4. Greater Yin . . . . spleen

3. Sunlight . . . . stomach

4. Greater Yin . . . . lungs

3. Sunlight . . . . lower intestines

5. Lesser Yin . . . . kidneys

3. Sunlight . . . . bladder

The Five Elements, Yin and Yang, and Their Shifting Interrelationships
to Ten Important Influences on the Pulse

The Five Elements Yin and Yang	Wood	Fire	Earth	Metal	Water
	Yin in Lesser Yang	Yang or Greater Yang	Equal Balance	Yang in Yin or Lesser Yin	Yin or Greater Yin
Psycho-Physical Functions	Demeanor	Vision	Thought	Speech	Hearing
Sense Organs	Eyes	Tongue	Mouth	Nose	Ear
Parts of Body	Muscles	Pulse (Blood)	Flesh	Skin and Hair	Bones (Marrow)
Viscera	Spleen	Lungs	Heart	Kidney	Liver
Psychological States	Anger	Joy	Desire	Sorrow	Fear
Color	Green	Red	Yellow	White	Black
Seasons	Spring	Summer	Long Summer	Autumn	Winter
Taste	Sour	Bitter	Sweet	Acrid, Pungent	Salty
Planets	Jupiter	Mars	Saturn	Venus	Mercury
Weather	Wind	Heat	Thunder	Cold	Rain

Eighteen Variations on the Pentarchy: The Chinese Theme
of Five Manifestations

Affecting Yin-Yang and the Pulse—as Played by the Physician

	Yang	Yang	The Change in Relations	Yin	Yin
1. Season	spring	summer	late summer	fall	winter
2. Direction	east	south	center	west	north
3. Climate	wind	heat	humidity	dryness	cold
4. Viscera	liver	heart	spleen	lungs	kidney
5. Elements	wood	fire	earth	metal	water
6. Color	green	red	yellow	white	black
7. Music	chio	chih	kung	shang	yu
8. Number	eight	seven	five	nine	six
9. Flavor-Taste	sour	bitter	sweet	pungent	salt
10. Odor	rancid	scorched	fragrant	rotten	putrid
11. Sound	shouting	laughing	singing	weeping	groaning
12. Emotion	anger	joy	sympathy	grief	fear
13. Animal	fowl	sheep	ox	horse	pig
14. Planet	Jupiter	Mars	Saturn	Venus	Mercury
15. Grain	wheat	glutenous millet	millet	rice	beans (peas)
16. Bowels	gall bladder	small intestines	stomach	large intestines	tri-heater bladder
17. Tissues	ligament	arteries	muscles	skin and hair	bones
18. Orifices	eyes	ears	nose	mouth	lower orifices

Five Specifics with Respect to Taking the Pulse:
1. **Five Climates Affect the Viscera:**

Heat injures the		heart
Cold	" "	lungs
Wind	" "	liver
Humidity	" "	spleen
Dryness	" "	kidneys

2. **Five Controls Exerted by the Viscera**

Heart	controls	pulse
Lung	"	skin
Liver	"	muscles
Spleen	"	flesh
Kidney	"	bones

3. **Five Effects of Taste-Flavors upon the Body**

Excess of salty flavor-taste hardens pulse; salty taste has softening effect on body.

Excess of bitter flavor-taste withers skin; bitter taste has strengthening effect on the body.

Excess of pungent flavor-taste knots muscle; pungent taste has dispersing effect on body.

Excess of sour flavor-taste toughens flesh; sour taste has gathering (stringent) effect on body

Excess of sweet flavor-taste causes aches in bones; sweet taste has retarding effect on body.

4. **Effect of Winds on the Body**

East wind causes ailments of nose, throat, or neck.

South wind causes ailments of heart, chest, ribs.

West wind causes ailments of lungs, shoulder, back.

North wind causes ailments of kidneys, loins, thighs.

5. **Five Spiritual Resources Controlled by the Viscera**
(Buddhist Influence)

Liver	controls	soul
Heart	"	spirit
Spleen	"	ideas
Lung	"	inferior spirit or animal spirit
Kidney	"	will

Five Key Generalizations Applicable to the Pulse and the Seasons
The injuries caused by
1. The climate of one season become manifest in the following season.
2. The cold weather recur as illnesses in the spring.
3. The winds of spring make people unable to retain food in the summer.
4. The heat of summer cause intermittent fever in the fall.
5. The humidity of the fall cause a cough in winter.

N.B. The injuries incurred in one season affect the person in the following season. Let the reader imagine the havoc this generalization would cause in accident and compensation cases in the West where the framework of reference is different.

The Celestial Stems, the Seasons, the Organs, and the Pulse

The relationship between the points of the compass and the seasons was based not only upon the elements they had in common but also upon an ancient device, called the **Celestial Stems,** that measured time and denoted the heavenly directions. There are ten celestial stems whose eternal cycle represents the passage of time. In the **Nei Ching,** they appear in dual combinations and serve as alternate designations of the seasons although, strictly speaking, they are the two signs for the first ten days of a season of seventy-two days.

The Celestial Stems, the Seasons and the Elements

Season	Element
Fall	metal
Winter	water
Spring	wood
Summer	fire
Long Summer	fire
Late Summer	earth

The Visera and the Bowels as Influenced by the Celestial Stems

Note: The bowels here listed determine the function of all other parts of the body and also act to store products, not to eliminate.

Five Viscera	Six Bowels
Heart	gall bladder
Spleen	stomach
Lungs	large intestine
Liver	small intestine
Kidney	tri-heater, bladder

Five Functional Interrelationships of Organs

Heart is connected with the pulse and rules over kidneys.
Liver is connected with the muscles and rules over lungs.
Spleen is connected with the flesh and rules over lungs.
Kidney is connected with the bone and rules over spleen
Lung is connected with the skin and rules over heart.
Liver nourishes muscle; muscle strengthens heart.
Heart nourishes blood; blood strengthens spleen.
Spleen nourishes flesh and flesh strengthens lungs.
Lungs nourish skin and hair; skin and hair strengthen kidney.
Kidney nourishes bone and marrow; bone and marrow strengthen liver.

Seasons as They Affect the Pulse

In the spring, the pulse is dominated by the liver.
In the summer, the pulse is dominated by the heart.
In the fall, the pulse is dominated by the lungs.
In the winter, the pulse is dominated by the kidney.
The pulse of the spleen, however, is not related to any season, but to the earth, for the "spleen is a solitary organ; it irrigates the four others."

Philosophic Generalization—the Vade Mecum of the Chinese Physician
1. Perfect harmony between the two primary forces signifies health. Disharmony or undue preponderance of one element brings disease or death.
2. The process of aging is attributed to the waning of the Yin element within the body. Man is not at the whim of Yin and Yang; by means of the doctrine of the Tao, man has a means of maintaining perfect balance and thus can secure for himself health and long life.
   Nei Ching: "Those who have the true wisdom remain strong while those who have no wisdom grow old and feeble."
3. When Yin and Yang are in balance, Tao or The Way is observed.

Preface to Montage 2

The Life Force—a Concept of Immortality—and the Three Elements Common to the Eastern Cultures: Fire, Water, and Earth

The theory of an indestructible or immortal life force—Chi Hua or Prana—is basic to Ayurvedic, Unani, and Chinese medicine. Their medical practices are also based upon an acceptance of the five elements, but there is agreement among them on only the three: fire, water, and earth. Why did the Chinese omit air? Why did the Indians ascribing the term Prana to the life force also assign the same term to one of the five divisions characterizing Vayu or air and exclude metal?

It is the authors' opinion that when the Chinese explained Chi Hua as the moving power of the universe and as indestructible, they did not use air because to them, Chi Hua and not air affects all the other energies—nervous, thermal, chemical, etc. The Meridians or channels that carry Chi Hua are different from the pathways of the nervous system, state the Chinese; they also affirm that the lungs are the first organs mentioned in describing the Meridians, but they associate the lungs with the element metal, not with air. (Calcium and copper are needed to repair lung tissue.) The Ayurvedists regard Vayu or air as the moving power of all the other elements; they too maintain that Prana is an indestructible life force and is distributed through the Chakras, which are not the neural pathways. In describing the flow of energies through the Chakras, the Ayurvedists set up the philosophical and theoretical bases for endocrinology and neurology. Later, their practitioners—by intuition, experimentation, and clinical evidence—supplied the needed physiological data. To this day, the Chakras are used because they are power batteries in the body for the distribution of nervous (electric) and endocrine (chemical) energy. The medical beliefs of all three cultures maintain that the channels for the life force must be accommodated to in disease and in health: the Meridians and the Chakras.

The Chinese selected metal because as one of the five elements, it was related to their theory of evolution, not creation, of the universe, with their belief in Yin and Yang; their knowledge of the smelting process may also have influenced them. Did they surmise that there was no air in outer space, that there could be life on this planet or on other planets without air? Is it possible that their philosopher sages did not want to confuse air with the life force and that they therefore used metals as one of the basics not only for the individual, but for all life? In this application of Chi Hua to the body, their medical theoreticians emphasized the importance of metals as well as of the other elements for life since all worked together. The Chinese in their medical practices never deviated from using the five elements in their shifting hierachy of relations. This organismic theory kept them away from the cause-effect mentality leading to the generalization that air or Prana was more essential to life than the other elements as some Ayurvedists affirmed.

The absence of the life force immediately causes death to the organism, so the Chinese affirm and practice. The Indians state that life ends when Prana vanishes, but they do not always apply this in practice because some of their medical practitioners confuse Prana with air; further, in their medicine, though they state all five elements are important for life, they tend to concentrate on the three elements in derangement: Vayu, Kapha, and Pitha. The reader is here referred to the section on Ayurvedic medicine dealing with the Tridhatus and with the individual properties of the Tridoshas. There too fire is explained, as it will be in the Montage following, as an element appearing both in healing and in mythology where examples are cited of Tantrism, Shiva, Shakti, and Prajapati.

Montage 2

The Pulse and the Soul or the Life Force: Relationship to Mythology and the Element Fire in the West

The Ayurvedists believe that the pulse throbbing at the base of the thumb is a manifestation of the soul: a principle of vibration. Sceptics East and West should understand the wisdom of the body that lies buried in the beliefs that philosophy, religion, and mythology portray. Associated with the readings of the pulse are two categories for interpreting the soul: the macro and the microcosmic. The soul may be contained within the body and thus relate to disease or it may be outside the body, but be inseparably intertwined with it. The validity of these beliefs is not pertinent to this study, but their total impact on medical theory and practice constitutes a part of pulse history and also explains psychosomatic medicine.

A brief recounting of the varied explanations of the sites of the soul and the forces of the elements fire, water and air constitutes a note of medical continuity to man's awareness of the vibrations in the body and the significance of death, the permanent absence of the soul or of vibration from the body. Here is a neglected and forgotten language, but the keys for opening its door are available. If the reader substitutes for the force of air, the Western term "nervous energy"; for fire, "metabolism"; for water, "circulation"; and for soul, "vibration, life-force", he will comprehend how much wisdom about illness and health is buried in the corpus of world mythology and how numerous are the treasures therein to be explored. Air as force and motion controls the other two elements;

in medicine, air is thus the coordinator of motion, a force which becomes the nervous system. Fire destroys or builds up, but requiring air or oxidation, its heat gives the necessary energies to carry on chemical reactions; thus the anabolic and catabolic processes are equated with fire. Water is the carrying medium and as a mode of transportation uses the blood for its circulation.

There is no denying that different cultures dictate different interpretations of the soul, but all agree that when the soul is present, there is life or, in technical language, vibration. The ancient Egyptians believed that every man had a soul, termed Ka, which was his exact counterpart. So exact was the resemblance of the manniken to the man, of the soul to the body, that descriptions appear in their literature of fat and thin souls, heavy and light souls, long and short souls to correspond with the different body forms. The Sumatrans believe that every man before he is born is asked how long or how heavy a soul he would like, and the desired weight or length is measured out to him. The length of his life is proportional to the length of his soul, and children who died had requested short souls. The Punjabi believe that the tattoos on their bodies would also adorn the mannikens when at death the souls would ascend to heaven.

Compare these beliefs of the manniken with the description of the homunculus: the little man or the dwarf, the size of the thumb, who is located in the brain and who standing on his head, controls every part of the body. Here is a reality in neurology. Further, this aspect could be related to the varied insights of Indian indigenous medicine about the ways in which the Chakras work on the body. In Western terminology, the Chakras are the endocrine glands. The Indians interpreted these centers as dynamos of energy—physical, psychic, and spiritual—and associated each center with colors vital to the health and well-being of the total man. Western science has subjected these glands to scientific study since 1910, but in India, this study is thousands of years old. Both in China and in India, indigenous medicine stresses the life force: for the Chinese, the Meridians and for the Indians, the Chakras conduct the energy or the life force.

The explanation that the manniken's soul casts its shadow has as one counterpart the belief that the soul of the sleeper is supposed to wander away from the body and actually to visit the places, to see the persons, and to perform the acts of which he dreams. Thus the dream becomes the reality and the tales recited about the events transpiring during the dream are accepted as gospel truth. Reference is made to the beliefs maintained by the Indians of Brazil, Guiana, Macusi, the Gran Chaco, of the natives of Dyak, Fiji, Sumatra, and Korea. The issue raised by the Tibethans is a moral dilemma that rests fully upon this assumption about the validity of dreams. They maintain that if a man dreams of committing a murder, he is a murderer even if he has not actually killed the person. Another variant to the belief that the manniken casts its shadow is that the soul may quit the man's body in his waking hours, but then sickness, insanity, or death ensues: this is maintained by the Kenyahs of Sarawak, the Ilocanes of Luzon, some of the

Congo tribes, the Bataks of Sumatra, the Tobungkus of the Central Celebes and the Lolos. The Greeks told how the soul of Hermotimos used to quit his body and roam about to bring back news of what he had seen until his enemies seized his deserted body and committed it to fire. All folklore is rich in such tales.

Apply the Indian and Tibetan accounts of teleportation as well as the modern interpretation of the psychology of dreams, especially of the Jungian school, to this phase of belief. Further, the investigations of extrasensory perception complement these generalizations. All world literature deals with this phase of the soul and dreams; this is a fruitful field for further inquiry by psychology, psychiatry, psychosomatic medicine, forensic medicine, and religion as well as literature.

The belief that the departure of the soul is not always voluntary since it could be extracted from the body by ghosts, demons, and sorcerers has led to the whole corpus of material on ghosts, demons, magic, and witchcraft which the twentieth century is reassessing for its determination of the force of the mind upon matter and upon disease. This belief which has walked consistently with man down the corridors of time relates to thought-body vibrations or disease-health. The mind-cures and hypnotism of modern therapy together with hypnoanalysis and powers of suggestion, all betoken this interest in the effect of man's beliefs upon his health and physical well-being. Oriental philosophy projects the effect of man's thought upon his well-being; Buddha's message, not yet a religion to his contemporaries, traced the ills of man to his desires; his was a lesson in psychological behaviour long before the techniques of psychology were publicized. Today one studies the devices used by various persuaders, some not "hidden", on television, in the motion pictures, and by the newspapers for the invasion of man's mind and its effect on the body. "Watch out for Cancer" or "Guard against B.O." are slogans that show how the demons and witches have assumed different forms, but they operate on the same principles of affecting the vibrations that spell health or disease.

Another interpretation of the soul as a shadow or reflection gives it a pragmatic relation to health. Some people believe that if a shadow is trampled upon, struck, or stabbed, the person will die. This belief prevails among the Wetars, the Babar Islander, the Tolindoos of the Central Celebes, the Ottawa Indians and the Bagandas of Central Africa. It is amusing to report that among the Bavilii of West Africa if the man allows his mother-in-law's shadow to fall upon him, a divorce ensues and the wife is returned to her parents. The loss of the man's shadow has also been interpreted as a precursor of death as one sees in the customs prevailing in Southeastern Europe, in modern Greece, or among the Roumanians of Transylvania. Thus any threat to the well being of the body must be exorcised, and here folk customs have their accretions of body wisdom wherein the taboo plays a significant role. To this day, the germ or virus must be exorcised from the body to restore health. The technique varies, but the principle is the same.

Some people believe a man's soul is in his shadow and others maintain it is found in his reflection whether in water, in a mirror, or in a portrait. Thus one can understand why it became a maxim in ancient India and in ancient Greece not to look at one's reflection in water and why the Greeks regarded it as an omen of death if a man dreamed of seeing himself thus reflected. This too explains the widespread custom of covering up mirrors or turning them to the wall when a death has taken place in the house. It is feared that the soul, projected out of the person in the shape of his reflection in the mirror, may be carried off by the ghost of the departed which is thought to linger about the house until the burial.

The soul is commonly supposed to escape by the natural orifices of the body, especially the mouth and the nostrils. The belief even extends to the custom of saying "God bless you" to the one who has sneezed so that the soul which had escaped from the body will return to it. The natural expressions "His heart is in his mouth" or "He wears his soul on his lips" show how widespread is the belief of the relationship of the soul to the mouth, the lips, or the nostrils. In India, the authors noted how the prism, used in diagnosis of the ills of the body, always projected the color green about the nostrils when life was present, but when life vanished, the green color immediately left the nostrils. It is unnecessary to remind the reader that color and sound are vibrations, but he must remember that they are interchangeable, as mass and energy are interchangeable. The inter-relationship and the interchangeableness of these vibrations on the various levels are frequently lost sight of in Western medicine, but not in Eastern practice, for there the physician is taught to recognize the death points, to note even the hour when the life force will depart from the body as Chi Hua leaves the Meridians or as Prana leaves the Chakras. This belief in the soul's power to escape by the natural orifices of the body is found to prevail among the Sumatrans, the Eskimos, the Southern Celibes, the Australian Wakelbura, the Itonamas in South America, the Marquesans, the New Calendonians, the Calchaquis Indians near Paraguay, and the Dyaks.

The hyphenation between body and soul in its vibratory responsiveness to sound will be briefly mentioned since this study has elsewhere related how the Indian Aum principle opens man to all levels of awareness. The West is familiar with variants of this principle, but does not always know the identity between the teachings of the East and the West. Most people are familiar with how the magical phrase "Open, O Sesame" was used by Ali Baba, but do not see its modern technological equivalent in the electronic eye which opens doors in railroad stations or in supermarkets. Those scientists familiar with sonar are now charting the sounds of the sea in marine acoustics while those familiar with radar are monitoring the skies as part of the program for national defense. Music therapy has been more efficacious than drugs in alleviating emotional illnesses; the electrical encephalogram and the cardiogram are standard operating procedures; the x-ray and radium are used in the treatment of cancer. These reinterpretations of the Aum principle show how the West has rediscovered an aspect of vibration which was a commonplace in India for centuries and which now does not appear to be utilized by Indians of today except for its recognition in indigenous medicine. The Chinese had a variant of the principle, but began with this different assumption: each organ has its own vibration and its own rising and ebbing energy tide with its own pulse beat. The cultures traveled different courses, but the principle is the same: vibration. (The reader, however, is cautioned against seeking a very close point by point analogy or correspondence among the theories prevailing in the different cultures.)

The life force is present everywhere and comes into the body through the Chakras according to the Indians and through the Meridians according to the Chinese. When this life force leaves the body, death ensues, but the life force itself cannot be destroyed. This concept of immortality was carried over into mythology, religion, philosophy, sociology, and political science, but emphasis here is limited to the medical aspects of the doctrine. The Indians are at least consistent when they state as one of their diagnostic approaches that the life force cannot be destroyed and then project this into their philosophy of Reincarnation. (The political use of the belief is not discussed here.) The West fused the concept of immortality into its religious matrix, but its relationship to healing was gradually lost. The life force as a vibratory principle remained an inherent part of Chinese and Ayurvedic pulse lore, but not of Western lore.

As soon as man began to look about him for an understanding of the life force, the macrocosmic interpretations of the soul appeared to explain the vibrations that spelled out life; this shift of emphasis accounts for the rise of various schools of indigenous medicine. As has been stated, the life force is present everywhere and comes into the body through the Chakras or through the Meridians and it functions on many levels with different vibrations or wave lengths. Therefore the herbs, vegetables, fruits, and plants of the particular vicinity where the people lived became more efficacious than those elsewhere and were necessary to the life of men and animals: to prevent or to cure disease. This concept led to the founding of indigenous medicine. Four macrocosmic aspects of the soul will be briefly discussed for their relation to the life force and to the elements of fire, water, and air as they affect the body rhythm and vibrations: interpreting the soul as a bird that takes flight and identifying the soul with man's hair, with a plant or with a tree. Reference will be made to the golden bough or the mistletoe and how it became a symbol of fire and energy in order to explicate the differences between the Western and the Eastern interpretation of these elements.

There is no need to give examples of the belief that the soul is a bird ready to take flight, for this conception is found in the literature of all cultures. What is of consequence to the study of the pulse is the application of the soul taking to air, which as force and as motion controls the other two elements.

The belief that a man's soul is bound up with his hair is another commonplace which need not be recounted. The story of Samson reminds one of the belief that when a man's hair is cut off, he grows weak or dies. The corollary — disposing of his cut hair, his cut finger-nails, or his spittle so that no evil would befall the body — has its reflection today in radionic healing. The De La Warr Camera as a diagnostic instrument, the Burr Northrup findings, and the Reiser experiments all show that light, sound, heat, magnetism, color, and electrical energies are different forms of one source of energy and they differ only in frequency of vibration and medium of conduction. These six forms are interchangeable, an approach to diagnostic vibrations. (See authors' **Color Therapy**.)

The more inclusive view is to associate the life and soul of the person with a plant or with a tree. If he is identified with a plant, its withering will be followed by the death of the person. It is said that there are families in Europe who are accustomed to this day to plant a tree at the birth of a child in hope that it will grow with the child. But perhaps the basic differences between West and East with regard to the life force can be pinpointed by using Frazer's **The Golden Bough** for its explanation of the macrocosmic view of the soul and then showing how the East differs from the West in its utilization of vibrations to spell health or disease. Here is an unexpected use of Frazer's classic on folklore, religion, and society as it applies to the pulse and to the vibrations within and without man.

Readers of this classic will recall that the golden bough refers to the mistletoe as the symbol of the external soul where the Priest of Nemi, also known as the King of the Wood, personified the oak tree on which grew the bough. Before the priest could be slain, it was necessary to break the golden bough. His life was concealed in the mistletoe growing on the oak. As long as the mistletoe remained intact, the priest could not die. He, like Balder, could be destroyed only by the mistletoe.

To determine the significance of the priest's being an oak spirit to this study of the pulse, one must review certain facts and customs of the fire festivals and the statistical frequency with which oak trees were struck by lightning.

It was believed that the King of the Wood was formerly burned at the midsummer fire festival annually celebrated in the Arician Grove. The perpetual fire there could be likened to the perpetual fire which burned in the Temple of Vesta at Rome and under the oak at Romove, to the sacredness of fire among the Iraneans, to the regard for fire as an element by the Indians and the Chinese, and even to the modern use of the perpetual light burning at John F. Kennedy's grave. Thus the priest could escape the fire of immolation only to fall by the sword of the hero who could cut the bough, a symbol also of fire. His was a choice between two fires. In this belief that mythology recounts is the thread that identifies the Roman with the Celt of Gaul, the Dane with the Aryan of India: all projected the ancient Aryan worship of the oak tree. (But the Chinese must be excluded from their company. Their myths recount how the lords of the birds' nest learned from the sages who had stumbled on a way to make fire how to cook their foods so that no illness to the stomach would result. These lords then became the lords of the fire drillers. Thus fire, removed from magical ceremonies, was never given an esoteric interpretation by the Chinese. Further, they proceeded to explain in their doctrine of Yin and Yang, the meaning of Chhi, Tao, and Li. Here can be found the theoretical beginning of atomic physics; these terms could not be interpreted as body and as soul, but as the arrangements of parts of bodies in space and in time with all interaction and as invisible organizing fields or forces existing at all levels within the natural world. There was no conception of a god head and no supreme being.)

The mistletoe gathered at Midsummer or at Christmas — the summer and winter solstices — was supposed to possess powers of revealing treasures in the earth and to be an emanation of the sun's fire. The old Aryans kindled the solstice fire as a sun charm aimed to supply the sun with fresh fire. Since these fires were usually made by the consumption of oak wood, it may have appeared to them that the sun was periodically recruited from the fire which resided in the sacred oak because the oak seemed the original storehouse of fire. But because the life of the oak was found in the mistletoe, the mistletoe contained the seed or germ of the fire; the sun fire was then also regarded as an emanation of the mistletoe. A third interpretation of the mistletoe may have grown out of the mistaken notion that the plant was dropped on the oak by a flash of lightning. This belief is common among those people who associated the cutting of the mistletoe with mystical rites whereby they secured all the magical qualities of a thunderbolt. Thus the Priest of Nemi in the Arician Grove, like Balder, could be killed only by the mistletoe, the emanation of the fire from the sun, or the thunderbolt. In medical language, the priest could be killed only by a fever.

Another theory related to fire must be recounted here before the relationship to disease and fever and the hidden wisdom of myths can be clarified.

Many people maintain that a tree which has been struck by lightning is charged with a double or triple portion of fire, an attitude which may account for the reverence which the ancients of Europe paid to the oak. It is also derived from the fact that the oak trees appear to be struck by lightning more frequently than any other tree of the European forests. Statistics cited by W. Warde Fowler report that the number of stricken oaks exceeds the number of beeches by sixty to one. Similar results have been obtained from observations made of French and Bavarian forests. In short, statistics compiled by scientific observers who have no interest in the soul reveal that the oak suffers from the stroke of lightning far more often than any other forest tree in Europe.

A very brief account of the function of the sky gods in comparative mythology will show how all peoples have been aware of the mystery the sky represents — something they could see, but could not hope to touch. The Tower of Babel and the ziggurat reflected man's effort to climb upward to reach the sky. The rains that came pouring down on the people, the lightning, and the thunder were all associated with the sky gods' qualities in both Occidental and Oriental mythology, but then the cultures went along different paths: the way of the lotus, the cross, and the Yin-Yang symbol. The Indians interpreted the fire as a force which could heal or destroy and it became an integral part of their indigenous medical interpretation of the tridoshas. In their symbology, the trident, bident and thunderbolt of the sky gods were transformed into the lotus flower. Their image is of the fire emerging as cosmic energy out of Vishnu's navel and being transformed into the lotus. The Yin and Yang or the positive and negative forces were arranged by the Chinese in hexagrams as mathematical reflections of the life force — abstractions capable of endless transformations of the five elements that manifest themselves in a hierarchy of shifting relationships, where fire is only one element especially in indigenous medicine. In the West, the sky god Zeus with his trident and the thunderbolt was replaced by an omnipotent deity, and his symbols then became Satan's pitchfork and the cross. (See Cook's two volumes on Zeus as a sky god for an account of how the symbols evolved.) But the powers of fire, thunder, lightning that the sky gods represented were not retained in the corpus of Western allopathic healing or in its philosophy. Instead, the West now has evolved an account of how life began on this planet with two schools of biology relating that lightning or the ultra-violet ray is the force that initiated life. Both, however, project a vibratory principle. Mythology, indigenous medicine, religion, philosophy, although taking different roads seem to arrive at the same destination: vibration and the response to the elements fire, water, and air both within and without the surroundings where the life force (or the soul) is immortal and cannot be destroyed.

The West without a life principle devised a way to generate electricity. The East with a life principle did not discover electricity although the Chinese had used the magnetic compass long before the West. Only in their readings of the pulse did the Orientals put to practical and pragmatic use their readings of the body's life force. The Occident without a knowledge of the life principle but with a theory of the immortality of the soul leaped over the barriers of belief in other areas, but remained tradition-bound in medicine and failed to apply to the knowledge of the body in its pulse readings the vibration principles that open up the various organs and the life force. Here is a manifestation of the curious way by which knowledge of the universe evolves. It remains now for both cultures to look at their methodology once anew: to rephrase the total concept of man in terms of field forces of energy and levels of vibration where force and matter are all interchangeable; and to treat man on a different plane of reference. But that becomes another study for another day!

Montage 3
Ayurvedic and Unani Doshas and Their Functions — Told in Terms
of Western Physical Properties

Dosha Five Divisions	Location of Dosha		Function of Dosha	Functions of the Dosha's Five Divisions
Vayu: Controls other two doshas and is prime mover				
1. Prana	brain	dryness coolness roughness subtleness levity vivacity	controls respiration; movement; excretion enthusiasm.	1. controls mental functions; special senses; circulatory system; mind; sense-organs; aids respiration, deglutition, spitting, sneezing
2. Udana	vagus and spinal accessory hypoglossal and trigemenal nerves			2. controls speech, articulation activity, enthusiasm, strength complexion, and memory; maintains the erect posture of the body.
3. Samana	solar plexus, semilunar, superior mesenteric ganglia			3. controls metabolism and excretion
4. Vyana	vasomotor, pilomotor, sensory and motor nerves			4. controls vasomotor and pilomotor functions; sensations; locomotion
5. Apana	intermessentric ganglia; pelvic region			5. controls and ejects excretio and birth of child
Pitha: Large Intestines				
1. Pachaka	stomach and large intestines	hot fluid liquid sharp oily keen	controls digestion; produces heat; affects sight, appetite, thirst, taste,	1. helps digestion; separates food from waste; supports other subdivisions of Pitha; secretes enzymes and juices for digestion
2. Ranjaka	liver and spleen	fishy odor	complexion	2. manufactures blood
3. Bhrajaka	skin			3. gives complexion to skin
4. Sadhaka	heart			4. controls endocrines
5. Alochaka	eyes			5. is responsible for vision— rhodopsin
Kapha: Chest				
1. Avalambaka	chest	cool slimy smooth heavy	controls growth, weight, size and watery	1. is responsible for virility, sexual powers; strength; builds tissues; supports other four subdivisions of Kapha
2. Kledaka	stomach	fixed dull	elements and oiliness of	2. lubricates stomach; liquifie food
3. Bodhaka	throat		body; smooth-	3. is responsible for taste
4. Tarpaka	head		ness and strength to joints; softness of skin;	4. nourishes sense organs; is responsible for knowledge or ignorance, understanding or stupidity
5. Sleshaka (Sleshmaka)	joints		intelligence, wisdom, courage.	5. keeps joints limber; is responsible for their lubrication and functioning

Equivalents

Variations Relating to Age, Time of Day and Food	Results When Dosha Is Increased	Results When Dosha Is Decreased	Results When Dosha Is Vitiated
Increases in old age, ; in afternoon and at daybreak ; after meals	Vayu leads to emaciation ; dark complexion ; darkness of skin ; desire for warm things ; tremor ; flatulence ; constipation ; weakness ; insomnia ; delirium ; giddiness ; and impairment of the special senses	incapacity to work ; scanty speech ; depression ; loss of consciousness ; presence of symptoms of Kapha	dislocation ; expansion and contraction of tissues, causing cracks, roughness, dryness ; convulsions ; paralysis ; twisting type of pain ; astringent taste in mouth ; incoherent speech
Increases in middle age ; at noon and midnight ; in middle of meal	Pitha is the metabolic principle having two aspects: gross and subtle. Too much results in yellow complexion, jaundice, as reflected in eyes and in yellow urine ; thirst, burning sensation, loss of strength, weakness, insomnia, loss of consciousness, desire for cool contacts or liquids	loss of appetite ; loss of lustre ; diminution of body heat	burning sensation ; heat ; excessive thirst ; hunger ; giddiness ; sweating ; unconsciousness ; redness ; congestion, exudation ; suppuration ; gangrene ; increase of pungent and sour taste
Increases in infancy ; at sundown ; and at the beginning of a meal	Kapha is the preservation principle of the body ; has two aspects: gross, and subtle ; and excess leads to indigestion ; cough, dyspnea ; excessive sleep ; heaviness ; pallor with looseness of the various structures of the body	dryness ; insomnia ; giddiness ; thirst ; burning sensation ; general weakness ; feeling of emptiness	excessive oiliness ; hardness, coldness, heaviness ; dullness ; sense of fullness ; laziness ; excessive sleep ; indigestion ; pallor ; numbness ; immobility of parts ; desire for sweet and saline foods

Index